MIGHTY MIDGETS & SPECIAL SPRITES

John Baggott

The Crowood Press

First published in 1998 by
The Crowood Press Ltd
Ramsbury, Marlborough
Wiltshire SN8 2HR

© John Baggott 1998

All rights reserved. No part of this publication may be reproduced or transmitted in any form or by any means, electronic or mechanical, including photocopy, recording, or any information storage and retrieval system, without permission in writing from the publishers.

British Library Cataloguing in Publication Data

A catalogue record for this book is available from the British Library.

ISBN 1 86126 106 3

Typeset by Annette Findlay
Printed and bound in Great Britain by Bookcraft, Bath

Contents

	Foreword by John Watson	4
	Introduction and Acknowledgements	5
1	The Warwick Connection	8
2	Alternative Racing Sprites	38
3	Early Days of Club Racing	50
4	The Dick Jacobs Coupés	71
5	'A' Series Engine, 948cc to 1496cc	84
6	Supercharging	94
7	The Abingdon Connection	102
8	Made in Britten	116
9	Sounds of the Seventies	129
10	Round Shiny Things and Sticky Black Things	147
11	Development of Chassis and Body	152
12	Ark Racing Twin-Cam Sprite	161
13	The MG Midget Championship	168
14	Half-Way House	182
15	Purely Personal	185
16	Steve Everitt	193
	Bibliography	207
	Index	207

Foreword

by John Watson

In 1963 I acquired a Frogeye which was to be my everyday transport until the end of 1963, when I decided that I wanted to go motor racing. As I already had the Sprite and enjoyed driving it, it was the natural choice as my competition car. After suitable modifications, I campaigned it in my maiden season of circuit racing in 1964.

Mighty Midgets and Special Sprites tells the story of many drivers who also set out in motorsport behind the wheel of a Spridget, and whilst not everyone went on to become a professional racing driver, I am sure that like me they thoroughly enjoyed the experience and found they were tremendous cars on the track. Thirty-five years on the models have attained classic status, but I am pleased to learn there are still several championships in which they are eligible to race, including the MG Car Club Sprite and Midget Challenge, run specifically for them.

John Baggott is perhaps uniquely placed to tell this story. As a Midget racer himself, he has first hand knowledge of the cars and the trials and tribulations of racing them. He also knows many people who are stalwarts of the class and has managed to gather together a number of fascinating accounts and anecdotes that make lively reading. He not only describes the special spirit and atmosphere that was evident at the track in the heyday of the racing but talks of the camaraderie that existed and of friendships that were forged. *Mighty Midgets and Special Sprites* is a fine tribute to those people and those remarkable cars.

1964: John Watson in his Sprite at Kirkistown, where he won his first ever motor race. Apparently the beard was grown to make him look a little older.

Introduction and Acknowledgements

From 1977 to 1992 I took part regularly in Modsports and Modified Midget races, as well as sprints and a few hill climbs, in my own Midget. I found my fellow competitors a friendly bunch and, by talking to those who had been racing for longer than I had, I began to learn a little of what it was like in the early days. During 1992, the idea began to form in my mind that to chronicle the development of the Modsports Sprites and Midgets would be a fitting way to put something back into a sport I had enjoyed so much.

An Austin Healey Sprite or MG Midget has been the first sports car for many a driver since the Mark I Sprite, which became known as the 'Frogeye', was introduced in 1958. This cheap and cheerful little vehicle brought true open motoring within the budget of the man in the street. It was inevitable that the Sprite and the later Midget would, like their larger stable-mates the Healey 3000 and the MGB, find their way on to the race track. Many who thought they did not have enough money to compete in motor sport found that they could just about afford to in a Spridget. In the early days, owners would simply drive their car to the circuit, remove the windscreen, empty the boot, pump up the tyres, don a helmet and go out and race.

This book traces the competition history of the cars, from those basic beginnings, to the 130 brake horsepower machines that contest the MG Car Club Halfords Midget Challenge today. Thanks to a large number of fellow competitors and enthusiasts, I have been able to include a wide range of information, much previously unpublished.

There was a terrific atmosphere in the heyday of British club racing, during the 1960s and 1970s. This text re-lives the early races of such notable drivers as Andrew Hedges, Alec Poole, Gabriel Konig and the late Steve Everitt, surely the most successful Midget racer ever. Did you know that former Formula 1 drivers John Watson and Jonathan Palmer had their first races in a Sprite, or that the great Stirling Moss drove one for the Healey works team? International rallycross driver Rob Gibson moved from autocross to rallycross in a Midget. Win Percy, arguably the most successful touring car driver of all time, got fed up with rallycross and bought a Midget as his first circuit racer.

In common with many British manufacturers, when the motor industry was at its height, BMC (later BL) used technology tested on the circuits to develop their cars. In 1965, the prototype 1275 Midget was raced by Roger Enever, using the engine block from a Mini Cooper S, turned round the other way. Have you ever seen an MG Midget pick-up truck? At least two of these unusual vehicles were built by 1960s Midget ace John Britten, to tow his racers.

The governing body of motor sport in Britain is the RAC Motor Sports Association. Over the years, the regulations which govern the modifications allowed to racing Sprites and Midgets have varied considerably. The

Introduction and Acknowledgements

official names of the categories under which they have raced – Sports Cars, GT Cars, Production Sports Cars, Special Sports Cars, Marque Sports and Modified Sports Cars – have also changed from time to time. In more recent years, the Austin Healey and MG Car Clubs have introduced their own series for Sprites and Midgets, with separate regulations. However, no matter what the name or the rules, Spridget drivers have always been at the forefront of having fun when it comes to competing in their cars.

When they conceived the Frogeye, upon which all subsequent Sprites and Midgets were based, Donald Healey and his body designer Gerry Coker can hardly have expected them still to be racing 40 years later. The Sprite ceased production in June 1971, and the last Midget rolled off the line in November 1979. Because they were built in such numbers, they are now among the most affordable of classic British sports cars, and remain one of the cheapest ways of getting into motor sport today.

I hope you derive as much pleasure from reading my account as I have from taking part in motor sport. Who knows? It may even encourage you to have a go yourself!

During the three years it has taken to research and write this book, many past and present Spridget drivers, enthusiasts, mechanics, officials and preparation specialists have provided me with information, for which I am most grateful. Without them there would be no book.

My thanks go to: Graeme Adams, Wally Agus, Chris Alford, Arthur Appleby, Brian Archer, Keith Ashby, Steve and Jill Ashby, Roy Ashford, John Baglow, Andy Bailey, Clive Baker, John Banks, Ian Barrowman, Bob Beaumont, Peter Beech, Syd Beer, Tony Bending, Paul Bernal-Ryan, John Boness, Julian Booty, Richard Borthwick, John Bradburn, Bill Bradley, John Brigden, John Britten, David Brooker-Carey, Tony Broom, Peter Browning, Robert Buckingham, Richard Budd, Paul Burch, Peter Burn, Paul Butler, Alan Capell, Robin Carlisle, Jim Cashmore, Mike Chalk, Colin Charman, Barry Coghlan, Peter Cope, Peter Cox, Lawrence Cutler, Brian Cutting, Rae Davis, Peter Denham, Richard Dobson, Mike Donovan, Peter Dron, Malcolm Ellis, Ray English, Jim Evans, Doreen Everitt, Roger Everson, Roy Eyers, Brian Fisher, Alan Foster, Ernie Foster, Richard Gamble, Mike Garton, Rob Gibson, Alan Goodwin, Keith Greene, Martin Hadwen, Mark Hales, Ian Hall, John Harris, John Hawley, Andrew Hedges, Jeff Hinde, David Hipperson, David Hirans, Paddy Hopkirk, Gordon Howie, Roger Hurst, Richard Ibrahim, Martin Ingall, Charles Ivey, Peter Jackson, Lynn Jeffrey, Richard Jenvey, Bob Kemp, Brian Kenyon, Robin Knight, Gabriel Konig, Roy Lane, Bunny Lees-Smith, Richard Lemmer, Colin Light, Ron Livingstone, Don Loughlin, Dudley Lucas, Stephen Luscombe, Roger Mac, Graham Marchant, Art Marcus, Chris Martyn, Derek Matthews, Chris and Peter May, Roger Menadue, Richard Miles, Steve Millard, Alan Minshaw, Chris Montague, John Moore, John Morris, Stirling Moss, Jon Mowatt, Gerry Neligan, Robert Nettleton, Bob Neville, David Newland, Roger Newman, Knobby Nield, Garo Nigogosian, Peter Nott, Mike Oldfield, Terry Osbourne, David Paige, Robert Parker, Tony Pay, Win Percy, John Phillips, Mike Pigneguy, Ian Polley, Alec Poole, David Pratley, Peter Preston, Geoff Price, John Pugsley, Larry Quinn, Nick Ramus, Ted Reeve, John Rhodes, Mike Ridley, Barry Rogers, Nigel Roscoe, Derek Ross, Mike Scott, Chris Seamans, Dave Sheppard, Barry Sidery-Smith, Roger L. Sieling, Barry Simons, Dick Skinner, Barry Smith, Chris Smith, Enid Smith, Roger Sparling, Roy Stanley, Howard Steel, David Strange, Pat Strawford, James Thacker, Lynden Thorne, Julius Thurgood, Frank Tiedeman, Chris Tolchard, Willy Tuckett, Stuart Turner, John Wallinger,

Introduction and Acknowledgements

Richard Ward, Russ Ward, Steve Watkins, John Watson, Geoff Weekes, Denis Welch, Vivian West, Chris Westell, Steve Westwood, Jack Wheeler, Jonathan Whitehouse-Bird, Sir John Whitmore, Robin Widdows, Geoff Williams, Roger Williams, Paddy Wilmer, John Wilmshurst, Douglas Wilson-Spratt, Barry Wood, Bill Wood, Alan Woode and John Woods. Their information and reminiscences have greatly assisted in the compilation of my text, and now I realize why I get such large 'phone bills!

Fellow authors Tom Coulthard and Trevor Pyman have willingly assisted me by providing information plus telephone numbers that I had been unable to locate elsewhere. They, too, know what a daunting task it can be to track someone down, especially if you are not even sure if they are still living in the UK.

My long-time friend Lawrence Heasman has acted as my honorary computer consultant, lending me his spare machine and then taking it so calmly every time I rang up with a problem, even when it became apparent the hard disc had failed and he no longer had a spare computer. Following this, Trudi Martin stepped into the breech and put the lost data back into the new system.

After the 1992 Steve Everitt Memorial Race, I approached his former race mechanic Dave Woodgate to ask if he could assist me in trying to work out just how many race wins Steve had scored. During our conversation it came to light that Dave has an enormous selection of motoring periodicals in his loft. This was the beginning of Dave spending many hours under the eaves with a torch, searching for any printed word about Sprites or Midgets. Once a fortnight, a familiar envelope would drop through my letter box containing Dave's 'latest offerings from the loft'. It is largely through his painstaking research that I have been able to go into such detail as to how drivers fared in their respective events.

Back numbers of *Autosport*, *Cars and Car Conversions*, *Classic Cars*, *MG Enthusiast*, *Motoring News*, *Motorsport*, *Motor Trend*, *Road and Track* and *Safety Fast* have all provided invaluable information from contemporary reports and articles. To their editors and staff, both past and present, thank you.

Without my race mechanics Steve Gardiner and Geoff Wright I would not have been able to compete in my own Midgets. Thanks, lads, for all those late nights in my garage and early-morning starts on the motorway.

My wife Jane virtually knows the contents of the book off by heart, having proof-read every page, re-write and subsequent up-date.

Many photographers have been responsible for the illustrations that have been used. Not all the prints I have borrowed bore the name of the person behind the lens, but they include: Chris Alford, Clive Baker, Harold Barker, Paul Bernal-Ryan, John Bichmill, Jeff Bloxham, John Britten, Sue Brooker-Casey, James Brymer, Peter Chowne, T.C. Collins, Peter Cope, Gavin Davies, Patrick Dempsey, Richard Budd, Richard Ellis-Dobson, Mike Donovan, Mrs Gibson, Chris Harvey, Jim Evans, Roy Eyers, Ernie Foster, D. Fulluck, John Gaisford, Dave Headford, Piers Hubbard, Richard Ibrahim, Martin Ingall, Charles Jaggard, Evan Jones, Steve Jones, B. S. Kreisky, Roger Mac, John March, Lynton Money, David Pratley, Mike Rushton, Evan Selwyn Smith, Brian Shaw, John Stanley, Vivien West, Jack Wheeler, John Whitmore, Tim Whittington, Willow Studios, Douglas Wilson-Pratt and Dave Woodgate. I apologise to those who are not in this list because I have been unable to trace them.

Aldon Automotive, *BARC*, *Cars and Car Conversions*, Pat Horsley, *Safety Fast* and the *Sevenoaks Chronicle* have also provided photographs from their archives. Jo Bradbury assisted with the restoration of some of the old black and white prints.

1 The Warwick Connection

WORKS SPRITES AT THE RACES

The registrations of the works Sprites that competed in the various International events are based on information available from photographs, surviving vehicle registration records, drivers' recollections and various publications. However, it has been said that only Geoff Healey himself had a true record of which car raced where. This information was contained in what one insider referred to as 'Geoff's little black book', apparently an exercise book in which he kept details of each competition vehicle built.

Le Mans in France, the Targa Florio in Sicily and Sebring in the USA were the three major outings for the works Sprites, but they also appeared regularly at three other International races: Nassau, Nurburgring and Mugello.

MARK I SPRITE

Collaboration between BMC and the Donald Healey Motor Company saw the Mark I Sprite launched in May 1958. It was, in the best of BMC traditions, based on the running gear of other cars already in production, mainly the Austin A35, although it did use the rack and pinion steering from the Morris 1000. The 948cc engine produced a meagre 43bhp at 5,500rpm and the 'power' was transmitted to the road via a set of skinny wheels only 3.5in wide. Despite its shortcomings, the car had a low centre of gravity and handled fairly well, except, perhaps, for a tendency to be a little 'tail happy' under certain circumstances.

Within weeks of it being announced, the Sprite had scored its first major race success. At Dunboyne, in County Neath, Ireland, John Anstice-Brown won the Leinster Trophy Race outright, after covering thirty-six laps of the famous 4-mile (6.5-km) Irish road circuit. On 18 July 1959, the 12th British Grand Prix was held at Aintree. Before the main event, each of the twenty-four drivers was chauffeured around the circuit in a brand-new, unregistered, LHD Old English White Frogeye. Drivers taking part included Jack Brabham and Stirling Moss, who went on to come 1st and 2nd in the Grand Prix itself.

Stirling Moss describes the Sprites as 'great fun to drive and very forgiving'. In recent years he has driven the Chuck Shields Sprite at Monterey in California, both for Chuck and for the car's new owner, Peter McLaughlin. The 998cc engine produces about 100bhp and, whereas in the works days Moss got valve bounce at 7,000rpm, he can rev to 8,000 or, if really pushed, 8,400rpm. He finds the Sprite is still a competitive motor car, 'miles faster than they were in the sixties', obviously as the result of improved engine technology. The 2-mile (3-km) Californian circuit is particularly suited to the Sprite, and it regularly finishes ahead of more powerful Alfas and Porsches.

The Mark I car was endearing because of its cheeky grin and its 'Frogeye' nickname, but contemporary owners found the heavy bonnet and the inaccessible boot difficult to live with. It was almost a foregone conclusion that its replacement would be of a more orthodox design. The Mark II Sprite was introduced in May 1961, followed by the Mark I Midget in June. Subsequent versions of the models would keep the same basic body design until the end of production in 1979.

ON TO THE TRACK

Given the Healey family's previous racing successes with their other models, it seemed inevitable that a works Sprite would find its way on to the track. Donald Healey and his son Geoffrey decided that the works would only get involved in International events and leave the UK club races to amateur drivers, many of whom were their private customers anyway.

The first appearance of a Donald Healey Motor Company racing Sprite was at the Sebring 12 Hours in March 1959, when four cars were shipped out for a team of eight up-and-coming American and Canadian drivers, who scored a class 1-2-3. In May of the same year, a Sprite was entered for the Targa Florio. The car had a fairly standard body, at least compared to subsequent versions, was fitted with a mildly tuned engine, and was driven by Tommy Wisdom and French journalist Bernard Cahier. Despite a broken throttle cable, it managed 17th overall, 6th in class.

THE FALCON SPRITE

In 1960, many companies were making glass fibre bodies for specials, which were usually based on Ford 10 running gear. An advertisement for such a body caught the eye of Geoff Healey. The next morning, during his usual mid-morning tea with Roger Menadue, head of the Experimental and Racing Department, he showed him the advert in *Exchange and Mart*. He suggested that they buy the £60 body, made by Falcon Shells from Essex, 'for a bit of fun, and graft it on to a Sprite floor pan'. The body was 12in (30cm) longer than the Sprite, so Menadue cut the required length out of the middle, then bonded it back together again. The Healey involvement with boats meant

Nick Ramus driving his ex-works Sprite, 5435 WD

that they were used to working with fibreglass and had all the materials on site.

Roger Menadue and his assistant Jock Reid then built up the car in about three weeks. Menadue believed that the nearside of a racer should be softer sprung than the offside, which carried the driver, so he removed two of the leaves from the nearside quarter-elliptics. The rear shock absorbers were up-rated but the front suspension remained standard except for the addition of an anti-roll bar. When the car was up and running, various people drove it and all said they were impressed with the handling. Geoffrey Healey entered the Falcon Sprite, 5983 AC, for the 1960 Sebring 12 Hours. It was to be driven by John Sprinzel, who was running the Healey Speed Equipment Division at the time, and had already established the reputation of being a very fast man behind the wheel of a Speedwell Sprite. His co-driver was John Lumkin.

Stirling Moss, who was driving for another team in the 12 Hours, agreed to represent the Healeys in the four-hour event. He knew Donald Healey, both from the motor sport scene, and because each of them had a property in the Bahamas. He was to drive a new Sprite, modified by the Canadian distributors with parts flown out from Warwick. Towards the end of practice, he asked if he might drive the Falcon; he threw it round the circuit with great verve, and the organizers let him stay out an extra two laps for the benefit of the crowd. Moss later made a couple of suggestions to Sprinzel that might save him a second or two a lap. Both cars had successful races. The two Johns, after a pit stop to change a blown head gasket, went on to take the class. The Fiat Abarth of Paul Richards just beat Stirling, who finished 2nd in class in his event.

The Falcon Sprite, now with a mandatory windscreen and amended bodywork, incorporating a head restraint to the rear of the cockpit, went to Le Mans in June 1960. The engine was a 996cc unit, built under the direction of Eddie Maher, the wizard from Morris engines at Coventry. For this event, it was fitted with wire wheels and Dunlop disc brakes all round. The car was used to great effect by John Colgate, a member of the famous toothpaste family, partnered by English club racer John Dalton, to take a class win. The mechanics dubbed it 'the Toothpaste Special'. A great deal of interest was created by the Falcon and, having been offered open cheques by people who wanted to buy it, Roger Menadue suggested that the company do a limited production run. He offered to oversee the project, but the Healeys were not interested.

SEBRING 1961

For Sebring in 1961, the Healeys arrived at the American airfield circuit with no less than seven examples, although two of these were in fact Sprinzel Sebring Sprites. The Warwick Frogeyes had lightweight glass fibre bodywork in standard shape. In the four-hour race, Walt Hansgen came 3rd, Bruce McLaren 4th, Ed Leavens 6th and Briggs Cunningham 8th. Stirling Moss was 6th in one of the Sprinzel cars, whilst his sister Pat and co-driver Paul Hawkins were 7th in the other. The twelve-hour race saw the American pair Joe Buzetta and Glen Carson come home 15th overall and score a class 2nd, with John Colgate and Ed Leavens 25th overall, an excellent showing considering the traumas the duo endured.

John Colgate took the start. The first part of the race was uneventful and he came in to hand over to Leavens, who tangled with another car toward the end of his stint. He struggled into the pits with one wheel fouling on the badly deranged bodywork. Pushing the bumper off the wheel, Geoff Healey looked at Colgate as if to ask him if he would like to volunteer, which he duly did. Three laps later, he braked for a hairpin and found himself spinning down the escape road. As he slowed, the whole headlamp fell out, landing in front of a wheel which immediately locked up. He cut the wires and continued on his way.

Colgate continued the race and the next problem to beset him was lack of any drive, so he pushed the Sprite one and a half miles back to the pits. Fortunately, Sebring is a fairly flat track. On arrival, he jumped out of the car and, assuming it was gearbox failure, thought he could go home. In a few minutes the Healey crew had replaced the broken half shaft and called him back to the cockpit. As he got to the end of the pit lane, an official stopped him to say that it was getting dark and he could not allow him out on the circuit with just one headlight. Reversing was prohibited, so he pushed the car back to his pit, and sat down for a rest while the lamp was fixed. In a matter of seconds he was on his way again, alarmed at the lack of light at each left-hand bend. At the end of the race, he discovered why the headlight had been fixed so quickly – the mechanics had simply taped a torch in the hole!

THE MARK II AT SEBRING

The year 1962 saw the first appearance of the Mark II shape at Sebring, with four light alloy panelled cars being prepared for Stirling Moss, Pedro Rodriguez, Innes Ireland and Steve McQueen, a fine array of drivers. In addition to the works entries, there were six other Sprites, and these little cars made up over one-third of the grid of the race, now three hours. The wet conditions in the early stages suited the Moss/Sprite (9254 WD) combination, particularly as Moss was running on Dunlop SP Tyres, and he was able to pull out a nine-second lead, which he held for the first forty laps. However, during the closing stages, after a late pit stop for fuel, he had to give best to the Abarth coupés on the drying track. He crossed the line third, thus preventing an Abarth 1-2-3-4, with Rodriguez 6th, Ireland 7th and McQueen 9th.

For the 1962 Sebring 12 Hours, John Colgate and Steve McQueen drove a special alloy-bodied 1098cc coupé. The pair built up a lead of one lap during the early part of the race, but after nearly five hours the car had to retire with a rough engine; this was later discovered to be a broken centre main cap. A Sprite 1098 coupé took the class for the 12 Hours in 1963, in the hands of John Colgate and Clive Baker. The car weighed 10cwt (500kg) and had a stated power output of 95bhp. In 1963 the three-hour GT race was run for the last time. The special limited slip diff broke, causing the Sprite to retire.

CLIVE BAKER AND SEBRING

To help keep costs to an acceptable level, Donald and Geoff Healey would go to Sebring to oversee the cars, accompanied by Roger Menadue. The remainder of the service crew were provided by Ed Bussey, who owned Shore Motors, the Fort Lauderdale BMC dealer. Geoff Healey used several drivers in International events, but Clive Baker drove for the team more than anyone else. Including races when he borrowed a car to compete as a private entrant, or was 'lent' to another team to drive for them, Baker made over thirty International appearances in Sprites.

It was no surprise that Clive Baker became involved with motor sport, as his father ran a supercharged Sprite and had been a works rider for Sunbeam motorcycles. Baker went to Australia in 1960, and, on signing his first contract with BP Australia, drove for Jack Barber. In 1961, he had a Sebring Sprite sent out from England and competed at Longford (where he did particularly well), Hobart, and Sumar

Plains. To make the Sprite go faster, the team re-worked the head and installed some larger, Hillman valves. Baker, then 19, was one of the youngest drivers to be racing in Australia with a full international licence. At the end of the season, a local journalist asked if he might road-test the Sprite, and wrapped it round a telegraph pole. The car was later rebuilt and, apparently, is still in Australia in the hands of Don Biggar.

Clive Baker decided he wanted to make his living driving racing cars, so he wrote to BMC in the UK saying he would like to be considered for a works drive. On his return, he was invited by newly appointed Competition Manager Stuart Turner to one of his test days at Silverstone. This led to a contract with Abingdon, who assigned him to drive for the Austin Healey team. During 1962, Baker competed at most of the British circuits, driving an ex-works Sprite, 5435 WD, rarely finishing outside the top three in his class. He also raced the Sprite at the 1962 Nurburgring 500km with co-driver Peter Jackson, but this outing ended in retirement.

Jackson knew the Ring well, having spent many a Sunday there during his days as a British Army officer, when anyone could turn up, pay a small fee and drive round. He had learnt the intricacies of the track from his friend, German ace Hans Geert Jaeger, so it was decided that Jackson would start. He was lying third overall half-way round the first lap, when the car spun on the approach to Adenau, clipped the bank and rolled. Having got the car back on its wheels, he returned to the pits where the mechanics hastily repaired the car.

The hardtop was so badly damaged they had to commandeer a spare from Barry Shawzin, who had called in to watch the race on his way back from competing in the Liège Rally with his own Sprite. The engine was topped up with oil and the car sent on its way, with Baker at the wheel. He only got as far as the end of the pit lane, before being sent back because the car was spewing out oil. Closer inspection revealed that the engine had thrown a rod, the damage initially concealed by the dynamo. It then became apparent that the accident had been caused by Jackson spinning on his own oil.

At Sebring on 22 March 1964, works drivers Clive Baker and John Colgate once again took the class, despite a broken oil pump. The engine was kept going by overfilling the sump, so the crank was always immersed in oil. They drove 770 KNX, a coupé fitted with a 4.2 diff, with an engine that produced 110bhp. The pair were 25th overall out of thirty-five finishers; sixty-six had started the race.

Clive Baker was joined by Rauno Aaltonen for the 1965 Sebring race, in a new aerodynamic coupé. DAC 952C was first registered on 17 February 1965, fitted with a 1293cc engine (XSP 2426-2), four-speed close ratio box and 3.9 diff. Stopping power came

Clive Baker with co-driver Mike Wood at the start of a rare rally appearance, the 1967 Tour de Corse. The pair retired while lying 6th.

from 7in Lockheed disc brakes with Mintex pads. The pair took the class and came home 15th overall, three places ahead of the other works Sprite, 770 KNX, driven by Paddy Hopkirk and Timo Makinen, who were 2nd in class. The team was able to adhere to its original strategy of pit stops for driver change and fuel every three hours, with a tyre change at half distance, and both cars ran at a steady 82mph (132km/h) for most of the event.

After seven and a half hours of racing, the heavens opened and parts of the circuit were ankle-deep in rainwater. The Sprites' performance appeared to be the least affected by the adverse conditions and, during the downpour, they were the third and fourth fastest cars on the circuit, making up two full laps on the leaders. Much to the amusement of the crowd, Timo Makinen passed the race-leading Chaparral right in front of the pits.

Makinen described the race as 'fantastic fun'. He recounted that there was four inches of water in his cockpit; when he accelerated, it splashed round his shoulders and when he braked it ran down to his toes. To clear the water, he accelerated into a corner and opened the door at the right moment! The storm eventually eased and things slowly got back to normal. The race finished at 10pm, when the two Sprites and the Healey 3000 of Warwick Banks/Paul Hawkins crossed the line in formation, the highest-placed British cars.

Chief mechanic Roger Menadue recalls that the team was realistic about not having the budget for outright victory in the endurance events, and that class honours were the object of the exercise. They certainly achieved this in style during the following two years. For the 1966 event, to improve axle location, the day-glo orange Sprites were fitted with angled telescopic dampers with single anti-tramp bar. They also had five-speed close ratio versions of the MGB gearbox. With the 1293cc engine producing 110bhp, this enabled them to reach a top speed of 136mph (219km/h) down the Sebring straights. Timo Makinen and Paul Hawkins won the class, followed by another successful pairing of Aaltonen and Baker for 2nd in class, despite a three-hour pit stop to repair the damage after the oil filter blew off!

In 1967 the Sebring class win went to Aaltonen and Baker. The pair had been running 9th overall during the early stages of the race but, after losing six laps in the pits to sort out oil pump problems, they eventually crossed the line 13th overall. Roger Enever, Alec Poole and Carson Baird were due to drive a virtually standard Mark IV Sprite in the Group III Sports Car class. Unfortunately, the newly announced Mark IV was not homologated in time, so the trio raced their standard looking car, fitted with a 1293cc engine, in the Prototype class with the other Sprite. They gave it a fine maiden outing, taking a class 3rd.

LAST OUTING AT SEBRING

A new petrol-injected Sprite was unveiled for the team's last visit to Sebring, in 1968, race stalwart Clive Baker being joined by Mike Garton for the race. The car came in for its first refuelling stop and, following this, Baker was quickly on his way. A few minutes later he reappeared at the back of the pits, telling Roger Menadue that he had terrible problems – the car had only gone a short distance round the first bend before spluttering to a halt. Menadue ran with him back to the car, checked it over, and saw water in the fuel injection trumpets. They managed to bleed off some of the water and then Baker had to struggle back round to the pits for the best part of a lap, as it was not permitted to push the car backwards for even a short distance on the track.

When the car returned to the Healey pit, Roger checked the refuelling rig and confirmed his suspicions that the petrol had been contaminated with water while being tested the day before the race. He got Geoff Healey to keep the other team cars out for a couple more laps whilst they got hold of some five-gallon drums and filled them from a nearby bowser. It took two hours to drain and clean the Sprite's fuel system through. Despite this delay, Baker and Garton continued to take a class win. Had the car been running carburettors and not injection, Baker would not have been able to manage that one lap to get the car back to the pits. Roger Menadue's attention meant that the team could bow out of the sunny American classic on a high note.

THE LE MANS COUPÉ (1411 WD)

Following the Falcon Sprite's 1960 class win at Le Mans, the 24-hour classic was set to become another regular event on the Healey itinerary. The next year, the team entered a sleek aluminium-topped coupé, 1411 WD, the first in a series of very special prototypes for International events over the next seven years. John Colgate was joined by Paul Hawkins as co-driver; despite their efforts they were forced to retire after eight hours with a holed piston. This Sprite was later raced by Mike Garton.

A former motorcycle scrambler, Mike Garton had got into circuit racing by accident, when he was persuaded to run his sprint/driving test Frogeye, XOC 322, as a member of a relay team at Mallory in April 1961. He enjoyed himself in the rain and his enthusiasm for circuit racing began. He entered a number of events, driving his car to and from the circuits, but, after braking a crank at Snetterton, he decided he needed a purpose-built racer for the 1962 season. He enlisted the help of his friends Mike Treutlein and Peter Knipe to put one together.

The car was based on a slightly damaged body shell utilizing the running gear from a written-off 1959 Frogeye. When it was complete, Garton managed to get the registration number MEG 199, matching his initials. This Sprite was noted for its smart appearance, with hardtop, an Ashley bonnet and gleaming Tartan Red paintwork. During that first season, it competed at thirty-eight meetings and was later developed with help from Geoff Healey, gaining a glass fibre rear end, Konis dampers, ZF diff and Girling discs.

In 1963, Mike Garton got an entry for the 500km race at the Ring, a fact that did not escape Geoff Healey's notice. In July, he asked Mike to come to Warwick 'and bring the flyer'. Healey had the Le Mans coupé, 1411 WD, parked outside on its trailer and asked Garton if he would like to buy it. Garton replied that, much as he would like to, he could not afford it. After several puffs on his pipe, Healey told him to hitch it up anyway. The outcome was that MEG stayed at Warwick and Mike Garton came away £100 lighter, towing 1411 WD behind his VW Caravette.

The following weekend, Garton raced the coupé for the first time at Snetterton, taking two class wins and a 3rd overall. Seven days later, he returned to the same circuit for the Archie Scott Brown 100-Mile GT Race, where he was up against the Jacobs Midgets. Keen to impress, he overcooked it in practice, on new and untried tyres, and badly bent the rear end against the bank. He was overwhelmed by the help he received to straighten out the car for the race, complete strangers lending a hand to get it ready in time. From a lowly grid position, the determined Garton worked his way through the field, passing Christabel Carlisle and the two Jacobs cars. As Garton crossed the line, Dick Jacobs held out his own team's pit signalling board with '£' signs chalked all over it.

Since the rear end needed proper repair after the accident, Garton had it modified with what was to become its famous 'bobtail', a flat panel bolted direct to the chassis and continuing up to a small lip spoiler just below the rear window. In 1963, the Nurburgring 500km was run for the last time for cars up to 1000cc, so Geoff Healey lent him a 998cc engine to replace the 1098cc unit that was in the car.

Sadly, the outcome of Garton's trip to Germany was a retirement. A half shaft broke while he was lying 3rd in class, 12th overall from ninety-eight starters. He did have better luck the following year, when he got a class 2nd in the August GT race at the famous German track. In 1965 he scored a class 4th in the same GT race and a class 2nd, 10th overall, in the September 500km race.

Among his many UK successes was 2nd overall in the Brands Hatch 1,000-mile race that year. Early on in the event, while Garton was driving, the gear knob snapped off, making gear changes difficult and somewhat painful. To let his crew know what the problem was, he dropped the offending detached piece out of the window as he passed his pit, forgetting that he was travelling at over 80mph. The knob travelled down the pit lane at great speed and it took the team a while to find it. They eventually got the message and were ready to tape up the lever when Garton came in to hand over to co-driver Paul Hughes after one hour.

Following this race, Garton was continually pestered by Spitfire driver David Corderoy to sell him the car. He eventually agreed, replacing the Sprite with a Lotus 23B. In 1966, David Corderoy raced 1411 WD in club events. On 9 July, he and Mike Garton shared the driving at the Ilford Films 500-mile race at Brands Hatch and were leading the 1150cc class until they had to pull into the pit to change a defective differential. Despite the long stop, Garton put in a determined drive, taking the car from last to 2nd in class by the time the chequered flag fell.

1413 WD

At Le Mans in 1961 the other works Sprite was 1413 WD. The factory built up the car for the Scottish racing team, Ecurie Ecosse, basing it on the 1961 Hansgen Sebring car. It was driven by one-time race-winner Ninian Sanderson, partnered by Bill MacKay, who rolled the car at White House early during the fifth hour, while running 45th. The factory later sold the damaged car to Roy Lane, an acquaintance of the Healeys who worked near by.

Roy Lane, a former cyclist who fancied a go at motor sport, repaired the Sprite, straightening the chassis and buying a second-hand steel Frogeye bonnet and glass fibre hardtop. He then used it to compete in about half a dozen circuit races during the following season, including events at Oulton Park and Silverstone. Lane then bought a Lotus 11, in which he started his prolific hill climb career. In September 1963, he sold the Sprite to Richard Groves who lived down the road and ran an engineering firm in Tipton that specialized in making factory equipment.

Richard Groves had been a builder of specials and knew fellow special exponent John Moore, who started his racing in 1955 in a 750 Formula car. Groves entered Moore in three sprints at the end of the season prior to a substantial winter rebuild for a full season of circuit racing in 1964. John Moore had twenty outings in the Sprite, now fitted with an ex-works 1098cc engine, and won eighteen top three class positions, including eight 1sts. He worked in the competitions department at Automotive Products in Leamington Spa and became well connected

The Warwick Connection

with the Healey works team, through his brake and clutch development on their cars.

Arthur Appleby was the next owner of 1413 WD. He worked in the aircraft industry and raced Mike Garton's old Sprite, MEG 199, which he acquired from Nick Hobbs early in 1964. After racing another Frogeye for a while, Appleby had gone to see Geoff Price at Healeys to ask how he could tune it up a bit. Price showed him MEG, which was in for some work and said he knew Nick Hobbs had to sell. It was his only form of transport and he had received an ultimatum from his wife who was fed up with the bumpy ride and bruises from the spartan interior. The two owners got together and in the end arranged to swap Sprites; Appleby was a bachelor...

Having done eighteen races in the season, securing an outright win at Mallory in July 1964 plus a number of class places at other events, Appleby felt MEG would need significant improvements, including comprehensive lightening, to make it competitive the following year. Not wanting to spoil the car, he sold it and bought, from Richard Groves, the ex-Ecurie Ecosse Sprite, which he felt was quicker. He raced and developed it from 1965 to 1967, picking up a number of class placings, including three 1sts, from about twenty outings. It came with a 998cc engine, but Appleby soon bought from Geoff Healey the 1293cc (XSP 2173-4) unit that had been used at Sebring in 770 KNX, although Healey told him he would be better off with a 1098. After a blow-up at Mallory, Appleby, who was disappointed in the power, rebuilt it to his own specification utilizing some specially cast magnesium alloy pistons. The 1098 engine was later sold to Appleby's pal Dave Crook, who proved Geoff Healey right by enjoying a most successful season with it in his own Sprite.

Appleby found 1413 WD 'very twitchy, particularly in the wet', and crashed the car into the lake during the BARC meeting at Oulton Park, on 24 April 1965. Following an off at Silverstone, the Groves special alloy

Arthur Appleby driving the ex-Ecurie Ecosse Le Mans Sprite at the Castle Combe Guards Trophy Race, May 1966

bonnet was replaced with an Ashley front, like the one fitted to MEG. During that first season with 1413 WD, Arthur took two 1st s, a 2nd and a 3rd. He had occasional outings during the next two years, and was a member of the overall winning Austin Healey team in the Birkett 6-Hour Relay Race at Silverstone on 5 August 1967. BMC always took this event very seriously, paying the entry fees for the Austin Healey teams and supplying the drivers with free petrol and oil.

When it became apparent that the new standard-silhouette Modsports regulations

MEG 199, another of the ex-works Sprites, later raced by Mike Garton and Arthur Appleby, pictured in the Silverstone paddock in 1964

Arthur Appleby on his way to a win in the Austin Healey/MG race at Castle Combe driving his ex-Ecurie Ecosse Le Mans Sprite

would limit the races he could enter with the Sprite, Appleby decided to retire the car and began sharing the ex-1965 Targa Sprite with its owner Dudley Lucas, who campaigned it mainly in International Prototype races. The original bare shell of 1413 WD was sold for autocross, while the running gear provided spares for Dudley's car.

THE CAPE, WARWICK CINEMA AND TREBAH FARM

The early works racing Sprites were designed and built in the experimental shop at the back of the Donald Healey Motor Company, 'Cape Works'. Donald Healey bought this former Belmont aircraft hangar from the Ministry just after the war and had it erected on a plot of land he had bought at Millers Road, in a part of Warwick known as 'The Cape'. Roger Menadue recalls that the experimental shop, which never had a work force of more than nine, was constantly being moved round the building.

Based on a standard floor pan, the competition cars had as many panels as possible replaced with aluminium. A tubular frame was grafted on and this carried the aluminium body, hand built by resident panel-basher Bob Buckingham and his apprentice Terry Westwood. Roger Menadue, having been in the aircraft industry during the war, was a great alloy and Perspex man and had no time for heavy sports cars with weighty, wind-up, glass windows.

Cornishman Donald Healey had gone into the motor business in the Midlands during 1933. Roger Menadue, who also came from the West Country, joined him in 1936 and was to become the longest-serving employee. By 1960, Menadue and his wife, who was born in Devonport, were feeling homesick and decided to return to Cornwall, but Donald Healey persuaded them to stay to complete the current project. Healey had decided to buy a house in his native county and establish an experimental shop 'to do all of those things we have never got round to'.

Healey bought Trebah Farm, Mawnan Smith, in 1963 and set up workshops in the coach house a short distance from the house. Menadue and his wife moved to a bungalow on the outskirts of the village at about the same time. Many of the subsequent Le Mans and Sebring competition cars were built at Warwick and taken on the firm's Bedford lorry to Cornwall for Menadue to set up and tune. As he had no sophisticated testing equipment, Menadue would time up the cars with the aid of a stopwatch. He would take the car to a fairly quiet, level piece of road, at Goonhilly, and measure the time it took to accelerate from 30 to 60mph over exactly the same section of road, then adjust the timing and clock the run again, repeating the process till the optimum setting was found. Despite the fact he was no longer working at Warwick, Menadue continued to go to Le Mans and Sebring as chief mechanic.

At about this time, the company decided that it needed more central premises for its increased activity in retailing cars. In July 1963, it transferred from The Cape to the redundant 'Warwick Cinema', formerly the 'New Cinema', in Coten End, Warwick, a much better position for their expanding Austin dealership. Jim Cashmore, who had joined the company in 1954 and was previously Roger Menadue's assistant, now headed the Development Department, his team working on the former stage of the cinema. This sloped slightly forward, so that jigs set up on the floor looked somewhat strange until they were levelled with wedges. Any tools left on the floor tended to roll towards the partition that had been built to divide off the department from the main workshop, which was in the original auditorium.

LE MANS 1963-65

For Le Mans 1963 another works coupé, 58 FAC, was built; this one had the 'sawn-off' back end treatment. Sir John Whitmore and Bob Olthoff were the drivers and things looked good after a practice lap in excess of 100mph (160km/h), the first time this threshold had been broken. John Whitmore found that when driving the Sprite, comparatively one of the slower cars, it was often difficult to stay awake. The outing was to end in disaster when Olthoff crashed out at White House at 2.30am and was hospitalized as a result. The following year, Olthoff and Whitmore set the British Saloon Car Championship alight in their Lotus Cortinas.

770 KNX was the registration number of the Le Mans coupé for 1964. Similar in construction to its predecessors, it was to be driven by Bill Bradley and Clive Baker. Bradley, a former Formula Junior and rally competitor, was the Lola F2 and F3 works driver at the time. During one lap of practice, he got a good tow down the Mulsanne Straight and, encouraged by this, drove the rest of the lap at eleven-tenths, posting a time of less than five minutes.

Bill Bradley recalls that they broke a valve during Sunday morning and to enable them to continue the race, the relevant push rod was removed; the car then ran the rest of the event on three cylinders, the drivers coasting whenever possible, to save the engine. On what was to be his penultimate lap, he entered the main straight and glancing at the clock, noticed it was getting towards 3.55pm. Not wanting to do two more laps, he slowed right down for the final tour. Coming out of White House, he looked in his mirror and saw a long queue of cars behind him, all doing the same thing. As he passed the tower, the clock clicked over to 4pm and the chequered flag was waved, to signify the end of the race, as he crossed the line. Despite 'taking the flag' they were, of course, classified in their actual position, 24th overall, from fifty-six starters.

Following wind tunnel testing at Austin's facility at Longbridge by John Ebrey, an all-new design was evolved for 1965, the sleek coupé body utilizing a cut-down Mini windscreen. Two cars were taken out to France for the 24-hour event. These Sprites featured a four-speed gearbox with Laycock overdrive, which gave a 28 per cent change in ratio. The box was basically a specially built XSP casing fitted with MGB internals. The transmission was completed by a 4.2 diff with a ZF limited slip. Power came from a 1300cc engine, which gave the 13cwt (660kg) cars a top speed of 148mph (237km/h) down the Mulsanne Straight.

To complete his team of drivers for the event, Geoff Healey organized a test session in the 1965 Targa Florio car, EAC 90C. As each person's turn came, Healey stepped forward and told him to set a time, not exceeding 6,000 revs. John Rhodes, who was to prove one of the successful candidates, was intrigued that at the end of each driver's stint, Healey would open the bonnet and make a big thing of checking the oil. He worked out that the engine bay housed another rev counter with a tell tale and that the real purpose of lifting the bonnet was to check the maximum revs each person had actually used and then re-set it. No one used fewer than 7,800!

In 1965 the Le Mans scrutineer took objection to the fluorescent green the works Sprites had been sprayed. This had been done to make the Sprites more visible to the other cars as they lapped them, often at speeds more than 50mph faster than their own. The team hastily repainted both cars British Racing Green in a chicken coop at the back of their hotel the night before. The Clive Baker/Rauno Aaltonen car, ENX 416C, retired two hours before the end as a result of a seized engine. Clive was sitting in the pits counting up the prize money in his mind

The Warwick Connection

John Cooper officially opens 'John Rhodes Motoring' in 1966. Cooper (left) shakes hands with the proprietor, pictured between Rhode's racing Mini Cooper S and one of the works Le Mans Sprites

– so much for a class win, so much for the Thermal Efficiency Index (which paid almost as much as an outright win) – when there was an enormous bang as, placed 8th, Rauno drove past. Baker learnt not to count his chickens before the car crossed the finishing line.

Under the regulations, teams were allowed to change the drivers around within the pairings and Geoff Healey took advantage of this provision in 1965. Early on in the race Paul Hawkins called unexpectedly at the pits, rushed out of the car and disappeared out the back of the team pit. He had eaten something that had disagreed with him and had to get it out of his system. Having done this, he rushed back into the car and continued on his way, Geoff covering the offending evidence with a shovelful of sand. Not surprisingly, Hawkins was a little off the pace so it was decided to give Clive Baker a stint in the car. When he came in for the hand-over he jumped out, wearing a rather messy pair of overalls and Baker had to sit in an equally messy seat! He spent quite a while thinking about how he could get his own back.

John Rhodes and Paul Hawkins, in ENX 415C, went on to win the class, coming home 12th overall and 3rd in the Thermal Efficiency Index. Rhodes considers one contributory factor was the fact that Hawkins insisted they spent the whole day before the race sleeping, something Rhodes had never done before. He admits that he did feel the benefit of the extra rest when he was driving at 3am. When he came into the pits for the last driver change, he hurriedly told the team that the car had no brakes. Donald Healey looked at Paul Hawkins and said, 'You can drive a car with no brakes, can't you Paul? There's a tenner in it for you if you're still running at 4 o'clock.' Hawkins did his final two and a half hour stint without problems. This was not the only pit lane drama. During an earlier stop, Rhodes had arrived at the Healey pit only to receive instructions to go out and do another lap as Hawkins was still in the loo!

John Rhodes remembers the cars as being very skittish, particularly when flat out down the Mulsanne Straight. When being lapped, it was necessary to steer into the slipstream of the overtaking car, in order to keep the Sprite stable. The smaller cars were quicker through the corners, so judicious use had to be made of the mirrors, in order not to baulk the faster drivers. When asked if there was anything he would have changed on the Sprite, he replied that he would have fitted a panhard rod and changed the steering wheel for a smaller one, two things the team was adamant its cars did not need. He remembers the late Paul Hawkins as very droll and a terrific person to have as a team-mate.

RICHARD GROVES' TEAM

Richard Groves bought ENX 416C for £700 at the end of the season and acquired the sister vehicle, ENX 415C, after it had been displayed on the Austin Healey Club stand at the Racing Car Show, in January 1966. It was his intention to contest all suitable long-distance races during the year. John Moore, Groves's long-standing driver, recalls they used to test on the old airfield at Wellesbourne, which had by then reverted to a local farmer. Here it was possible to set up a track almost identical to the Silverstone Club Circuit, and the venue was also used for the occasional sprint. Both Automotive Products and the Donald Healey Motor Company had come to a financial arrangement with the farmer to use the Wellesbourne facility and Moore did some early spoiler development there on the works Le Mans Sprites. He found the addition of a spoiler took about 200/300 revs off the top end, but made the car much easier to drive.

The Groves team had no official agreement to use Wellesbourne, so if they wanted to test they had to drive the car up there, and make sure there was no one about before taking it round for a quick blast.

John Moore enjoyed racing for Richard Groves. They worked together well, Richard an excellent engineer and John always wanting to make the car go faster. He feels very privileged to have been part of the racing scene at the time.

In May 1966, John Harris/John Moore and Mike Garton/Alec Poole appeared under the Groves banner at the first-ever 1,000km at Belgium's Spa circuit in the Ardennes. The two-day practice session, held on the Friday and Saturday before the race, was overcast but dry and the two Sprites performed fairly well. However, the engine on the Garton/Poole car failed, the pair having to make do with a 1098cc unit, the only spare available, for the race. On the day, the two Johns finished 11th overall, 6th in class, with Alec and Mike coming home two places behind, 13th overall. The little cars were reaching 145mph (235km/h) on the downhill section of the Stavelot. At the Ring 1,000km in June, the Groves cars had another good outing, with Mike Garton/John Moore (415) and Alec Poole/Clive Baker (416) coming 2nd and 3rd in class.

The Groves team's next outing was the Mugello Grand Prix in July. One car (415) was entered for Clive Baker and John Moore. During practice, Baker suffered a broken half shaft, probably as a result of the rather harsh road circuit. The wheel, brake drum and broken section of the shaft were recovered from the undergrowth by a young Italian spectator. Baker managed to force the remains of the shaft in the end of the axle tube and struggled back into the pits on three wheels, with the other hanging off the fourth corner.

The axle was bent and obviously the thread for the hub nut was badly distorted,

The Warwick Connection

but the team needed somehow to start the race in order to receive their start money; they were relying on this to buy petrol to get home. A visit to a local blacksmith in the mountains offered some hope. The car was jacked up on the immaculate stone floor and the proprietor, a man in his eighties gave directions to his giant of a son-in-law, who straightened the axle in situ with a very large sledgehammer. They then reassembled the hub as best they could, welding the nut on the end to prevent it coming off again.

The team, not impressed with the repair, decided that Moore would just do part of the first lap, the bare minimum to qualify for their start money. Once he got going, Moore forgot this plan and, as the 'red haze descended', he drove increasingly competitively, eventually coming in for a pit stop to cure a misfire and handing over to Baker. Baker returned to the pits later, for further attention to the carb, Moore took over again and went on to finish the race 2nd in class, in a car they considered could become a three-wheeler at any moment! Baker then drove the car back to England from Italy and did a test session at Silverstone before returning the car to the works for a new axle to be fitted. Geoff Healey was amazed it had lasted so long.

In August, the organizers of the inaugural race at the newly rebuilt Hockenheim circuit invited Groves to enter his Sprites in the 500km, 2-litre Sports Car event. Driven by John Moore (415) and Peter de Klerk, who deputized for Clive Baker (416), they put up a good performance but did not feature in the results as their 1293cc engines were outclassed by the larger capacity cars. The 500km race at the Ring in September saw Moore come home 4th overall, 2nd in class in '415', while Alec Poole finished 6th in class, despite an engine problem. The next outing, at Montlhéry, resulted in a rare retirement, when John Moore and Steve Neale had to pull out during the 1,000km race when a cylinder liner moved. This marked the end of the season. ENX 416C was sold to Mike Pigneguy, with '415' being retained.

The team planned a much more limited programme of events for drivers John Moore and Steve Neale during 1967 and, sadly, on the two occasions the car raced, success evaded them. At the Nurburgring 1,000km race, the car broke a half shaft at about half distance while leading the class. Moore changed it at the side of the track, for the spare that was always carried on board, and got back up to 2nd in class. Not long after Steve Neale took over, he was surprised to see spectators and marshals waving at him as he came down through the Foxhole. 'What a friendly lot,' he thought. Alas, the waves were to attract his attention to the fact that one of his rear wheels was hanging out of the side of the car on the remains of yet another broken half shaft. His race was over.

Steve Neale, perhaps better known for his exploits behind the wheel of a Jim Whitehouse Mini, remembers his first test drive in a Groves Sprite. He was shown round the car and could not believe it when the team pointed out under the passenger seat a spare half shaft, with jack and spanners to change it with. He thought they were joking, but how wrong he was! He is still involved in motor sport, running cars in the British Touring Car Championship.

The final outing for the Groves Sprite was the 1967 Mugello Grand Prix. This was notable in that the starter, who flagged the cars off in pairs, got his clothing caught in the bodywork of one of the cars, and ended up in a heap on the road minus his trousers. He still managed to get up in time to flag the next pair off. On the last lap, while the Sprite was running second, it got away from Steve Neale and retired. Groves now moved on to campaign a Ginetta, which he ran for the rest of 1967 and 1968, and he sold ENX 415C to Howard Fawsitt, who subsequently raced it in the Nurburgring 500km race.

MIKE PIGNEGUY AND WILLY TUCKETT

Mike Pigneguy, who purchased ENX 416C (the former Aaltonen/Baker 1965 Le Mans car), worked for Richard Miles Downton, in Elsmore Mews, London, where he prepared competition cars for other drivers. Pigneguy campaigned the Sprite in the 1967 European Sports Car Championship. Partnered by well-known Austin A40 exponent Mick Cave, he took a class 3rd in the 1,000km at Nurburgring. One spectator at that event was Willy Tuckett, who raced an MGB GT in the UK and knew Pigneguy, as Downtons prepared the B. Pigneguy wanted to persuade him that the thing to do was to race in Europe and had invited him along to see what it was all about.

Willy Tuckett, who had acquired enough signatures to qualify for an International licence, bought ENX 416C and raced it in Europe for the 1968 season. He towed with a Humber Hawk estate, in the back of which were a spare (998cc) engine, tools and a tent, for those times when he could not afford to stay in a hotel. Mike Pigneguy prepared the car and also shared the driving on long-distance races. From March to September, the pair travelled around Europe, living off the start money from the various events. As well as races, Tuckett did a number of hill climbs, for which he brought the car down a class by utilizing the smaller engine. Such events also paid start money.

The first race was in Germany, where the pair failed to complete the 1,000km. A week later they were in Belgium for the Spa Grand Prix 1,000km of Francorchamps, won, Tuckett remembers, by Jacky Ickx who drove brilliantly in the appalling, wet conditions. Visibility was so bad that Tuckett spent the first five laps just following the spray of the car in front, Number 47, a

Willy Tuckett competing in his ex-works Sprite at the Austrian Tauplitzlem hill climb, toward the end of the 1967 season; the adjustable air intake flap below the race number is barely open

Willy Tuckett (left) and Mike Pigneguy (right) receive awards for winning their class in the Nurburgring 500km race, September 1967; they finished 15th overall.

Chevron-BMW GT, driven by Roy Johnson. He admits that if the Chevron had gone off, he would have followed him. The Sprite did finish, coming home 22nd overall, and Tuckett and Johnson had a good laugh about the race conditions afterwards. July saw Tuckett and Pigneguy at Mugello where they scored a 3rd in class.

In September, they came 18th overall and won the class in the Nurburgring 500km. Only eighteen, Tuckett was the youngest driver to score an International race win at the circuit. Later that month, the pair had another class 3rd at Enna. Tuckett considers his success in endurance races to be due to his photographic memory, which enabled him to remember where all the bends were. He also likens racing on European street circuits to driving round the lanes of his home county of Devon! The 1968 season proved to be a memorable one, and Tuckett's accounts show that it cost him £38; manufacturers' bonuses, and start and prize money, combined with the proceeds of the sale of the car at the end of the year, covered nearly all his costs, including living expenses.

ENX 416C AND ENX 415C MOVE ON

When Willy Tuckett began driving Chevrons, he sold ENX 416C to a Scot by the name of Boswell, who only drove it once, at Silverstone. In 1988 it was discovered in Scotland by Healey expert Denis Welch. Out of the blue, he received a telephone call from a man asking the value of an ex-works Sprite. He recalls that he really was rather offhand, telling the caller that 'all Sprites came out of the works at some time'.

When he was told that the car in question had alloy body panels and the remains of Perspex windows, and a brass plaque under the bonnet bearing the inscription 'Donald Healey Motor Company', he started to take notice. He discovered that the caller had acquired the car from the late Lord Kildaire, on the understanding he restored it. It had been standing in a field on his lordship's estate for over twenty years. Amongst other damage, the alloy panels were peppered with holes where the local lads had used the car as a target for their air guns.

Obtaining a twelve-hour option on the Sprite, Denis Welch drove up to Scotland with a trailer and bought the car. Two years of painstaking research and restoration enabled him to put the car on the start line at Le Mans for the 1990 pre-race parade of previous competitors, twenty-five years after it had actually raced. During the rebuild, a small area of the original bright green paint was found behind one of the headlights; Welch re-sprayed the car in this colour and thus cocked a snook at those race organizers who had banned it in 1965.

The sister car, ENX 415C, passed from Howard Fawsitt's ownership and a couple of years later resurfaced, after being bought by Peter Bloor, who sold it to Charles Dawkins and Bob Neville. They restored it and later put it up for auction. The car found a home in the Patrick Collection from 1982 to 1995 when, following the dispersal of the museum, it was sold to John Clarke. Denis Welch did the restoration for him.

Both 415 and 416 appeared in the Healey Memorial Race, at the Coys International Historic Festival at Silverstone in July 1995. Denis Welch was driving his big Healey, in which he took overall victory, and asked Alec Poole to take charge of his Sprite for the day. Despite not having raced at all that year, Poole took a class victory and fastest lap,

The 1966 works Austin Healey Sprite Team at Le Mans: from left to right, Andrew Hedges and Paddy Hopkirk (drivers), Geoff Healey, unknown, trade support representative, Clive Hendry (mechanic), Jim Cashmore (chief mechanic), Basil Wales (BL Special Tuning), Tommy Wellman (BL Competition Dept), Mrs Val Wellman (catering), unknown, Derek Ross (refueller), Clive Baker and John Rhodes (drivers), trade support representative

The Warwick Connection

with John Clarke coming home second in his first-ever outing with his car. The Sprites will surely now appear in historic races on a regular basis.

HNX 455D AND HNX 456D

For Le Mans 1966, HNX 455D and HNX 456D were two works Sprites very similar to the previous year's cars. The only modification was Laycock overdrive, the one and only time this was used. John Rhodes experienced some problem with the overdrive causing the engine to over-rev when it was engaged. He returned to the pits at the end of the lap, where topping up the oil cured the problem. After handing over to Clive Baker for the early morning shift, Rhodes went to the competitors' bedrooms for a couple of hours' sleep, asking to be called at 4am. He woke at 7am, got up in alarm, and ran all the way to the Healey pit only to discover that both his car and the sister car, driven by Andrew Hedges and Paddy Hopkirk, had retired during the night with broken con rods. HNX 455D was later sold to someone in the USA and is believed still to be out there.

Clive Baker was joined by Andrew Hedges to pilot the 1293cc, five-speed HNX 456D for the 1967 Le Mans event. Despite a pit stop to rectify rear end body damage, the pair came home 15th overall and, being the first British car home, scooped the prestigious Motor Trophy. The car also averaged in excess of 100mph (160km/h) for the twenty-four hours, the first Sprite to do so. Fuel consumption throughout the race averaged 19mpg.

The Healey refuelling at Le Mans was carried out by Derek Ross who, while he only worked for the company from 1961 to 1962, subsequently took a holiday from his new job to go to the race. The cars were only allowed to take on petrol, oil and water every twenty-eight laps and, to make sure the teams did not deviate from this regulation, all three fillers were sealed by a race official at the start. When the refueller knew one of his cars was due in for a designated fuel stop, he would find one of the official *plombeurs*, who would remove the seals and replace them with new ones once the neces-

The award-winning 1967 works Sprite pictured in the Donald Healey Motor Company Showroom in Warwick after the race, complete with damaged bodywork

The 1966 Le Mans Sprite driven by Clive Baker and John Rhodes

sary liquids had been added. Ross fuelled the car with a 3in (76.2mm) diameter pipe from the gantry via a special quick-release, wide-neck filler on the Sprites. Both he and the *plombeur* checked the meter readings to ensure the correct volume was recorded on the forms for the indexes of performance and thermal efficiency.

Each vehicle could only be worked on by two designated mechanics, identified by official armbands. In their early days of competing at Le Mans, the Healey team would have Roger Menadue as number one mechanic with the second driver as the other. This helped keep costs down; a fitter sent out from the works for the weekend would have to be paid overtime. Being staff, Menadue regarded weekend attendance at the circuit as part of his everyday job.

The mechanic was only allowed to use spares and tools that were actually carried in the car. One year, the exhaust mountings broke and there was no suitable wire to lash it up with on board. Menadue whispered to Geoff Healey, 'Go and find me a piece of stout wire.' Healey duly returned with some wire, which he had literally torn off a fence, rolled into a ball and stuck down the top of his trousers. Menadue unravelled it, while they stood side by side looking under the bonnet, without being seen by the officials, and soon the car was on its way with the exhaust wired in place.

During Le Mans practice sessions drivers, particularly those new to the team, would ask if they ought to scrub in a new set of tyres. Geoff Healey would always reply that this was not necessary as the Sprites would easily run the full twenty-four hours plus the practice session on one set of Dunlop Green Spot R6 tyres and there would still be tread left at the end. During the successful Le Mans entries the cars required very little by way of routine maintenance – perhaps a set of pads and the odd quart of engine oil. Other than that, they ran like clockwork. To make changing the hot pads easier, a self-tapping screw was fitted to the lug on the end of the pad backing; this could then be pulled on with pliers or a piece of rag.

In 1968 the Le Mans 24-hour race was run for the last time on 28-29 September. This year also marked the last appearance of a works Sprite at an International event. After the race, BMC announced they could no longer continue to back the entry. Alec Poole and Roger Enever, who cut their teeth in Sprite and Midget club racing, enjoyed a good outing in HNX 456D, the 1966–67 1293cc Sprite, now updated with Lucas petrol injection and an eight-port head. From fifty-four starters, Poole and Enever were 33rd after six hours and 19th after seventeen, finishing the race 15th.

Again, the Sprite was the first British car home and collected the Motor Trophy. As a result, Poole and Enever also won the Rudge Whitworth Bi-annual Trophy, presented to the car that collected the same award two years running. This was the proudest moment for Roger Menadue in his long association with Sprites. The car achieved a maximum speed of 154mph (248km/h) down the Mulsanne Straight, thanks to its 3.9 diff.

Having been re-sprayed and displayed at the 1968 Motor Show, HNX 456D was offered to Arthur Appleby, but he could not afford it. In November 1969, Healeys advertized it in *Motoring News*, and on 3 March 1970 the name of the new owners, magazine publishers Speed Sport Publications, was entered in the log book. It was never raced during their ownership, but it did do some demonstration runs and was displayed at a number of shows. It then ended up in John Sprinzel's garage. In June 1972 Charles Dawkins bought it, put it into club racing spec and then prepared the Sprite for himself and Bob Neville to run in the 1971 Targa Florio, converting it back from fuel injection

Ian Polley leaving the Goodwood chicane in July 1978, driving his ex-works Sprite

The Warwick Connection

to a 45 DCOE Weber carburettor. In the end, Dawkins did not take part in the Targa, and in December 1975 the Sprite was sold to Ian Polley.

Intending to race the car within three months, Ian spent three years stripping it down and rebuilding it as near as possible to its ex-works spec, before racing it in club and historic events until 1984. He took the HSCC end of year class award on two occasions. Shortly after buying the Sprite, he was lucky to be able to buy some spares, including an extra set of wheels, which originally went with the car, through an advertisement in *Motorsport*. All the prototype racing Sprites ran on special 5-in wide alloy wheels. Aeroplane & Motor Aluminium Castings of Birmingham cast 140 of them for the Healeys, and each wheel represented a saving of about 4lb (nearly 2kg) on the unsprung weight of the car. Nowadays, these original wheels are very rare.

693 LAC

In 1964, the Targa Florio was to become the third regular International outing for the Healey Motor Company. Tommy Wisdom made his maiden outing with a Sprite in 1959, and again led the assault in 1964, sharing the driving with Paddy Hopkirk. 693 LAC, a sleek open two-seater with an alloy body, emerged from Warwick and was driven down to Sicily by Geoff and Margot Healey. In the race, Hopkirk was really flying, but after four laps a half shaft cried 'enough', as a result of the bumpy 44-mile (70km) road circuit, forcing the car into retirement.

Subsequently, Warwick fitted the car with a short hardtop and Clive Baker had a class win with it in this form at the Nassau races in December 1964. The top was extended to a fast back by Richard Groves, when he bought the car for the 1965 season. His dri-

Targa Florio Sprite, 693 LAC, originally built as an open car for Paddy Hopkirk and Tommy Wisdom to drive in the 1964 Targa. In 1965 it went to Richard Groves, who added the hardtop and altered the rear end. Subsequent owner Alan Goodwin added the rear quarter windows

ver John Moore did fifteen club races, netting two 1sts and eight 2nds. In May, Geoff Healey had persuaded Richard to enter the Nurburgring 1,000km race. Clive Baker and John Moore drove the car and took a class 1st. It was Moore's first visit to the famous German circuit and he admits that initially the track terrified him; in the race he drove the middle stint with Baker doing the start and finish.

Later that year, 693 LAC made two return visits to the Ring. In the support race to the German Grand Prix on 1 August, Moore drove it to a 3rd in class. For the 500km on 5 September, John Moore and John Harris shared the driving, and the car ran well up the field during the first half of the race in Moore's hands. Harris then took over and held place until the last lap, when he ran into a cloudburst out at the back of the circuit, which resulted in an off. He managed to get going again but dropped to 10th and thought that would be the last time Groves would ask him to drive for the team.

Looking back on 1965, some years later, Richard Groves reflected that 'it was not a bad season for a team of two people working part-time in a garage on the side of a house'. This season gave the Groves team an appetite for more International racing in 1966 and 1967.

693 LAC was further modified with the addition of windows in the side of the fast back when later raced by Alan Goodwin, of Aldon Automotive, who acquired it at the end of 1965. It was subsequently sold as a rolling shell to John Priestley, who, having got another engine and box, did some events in the Sprite as well as using it on the road. The next owner was Charles 'Chick' Barrett, a Bedfordshire builder and Sprite enthusiast. After a comprehensive 500-hour rebuild it was out in the hands of his driver Martin Field, competing in the Rochas Classic Car Championships, and scoring a number of class places.

In 1969 Mike Ridley took 693 LAC on. He sprinted it for a while and even thought of taxing it as a runabout, but the somewhat spartan interior made him change his mind. In the end it went to John Bradburn, a garage owner who dealt in a few historic cars, for an ex-works Targa Florio Nash. Bradburn sold the Sprite to a Japanese buyer and there are rumours that the car may have been destroyed in a race out there.

EAC 90C

The 1965 works Targa car, EAC 90C, was built with a lower centre of gravity in an attempt to alleviate the understeer experienced by Hopkirk and Wisdom the previous year. Practice proved it to be ideal for the punishing circuit, and it produced one of the top ten lap times in the hands of Rauno Aaltonen and Clive Baker. During the race, the Sprite was the victim of a sticking caliper; the necessary pit stop meant that it came home 15th overall, 2nd in class. The car returned to the UK after the Targa and was used by Geoff Healey as a road car until it was converted to a coupé for the 1966 event. By this time, many people had driven it and their comments about handling were used in the preparation of the 'new' model.

Aaltonen and Baker again shared the driving for the fiftieth running of the Targa Florio, which turned out to be one of the wettest in the event's history. The pair had a troubled race, first losing time for a pit stop to change a wheel following a slight off. Baker later had to stop on the circuit and replace a half shaft, which he later admitted he had done with the help of two British spectators. Despite all this, they ended up with a class 3rd, coming home 16th from twenty-nine finishers.

From 1967 to 1969, EAC 90C was seen at club events in the hands of Austin Healey Club member Dudley Lucas, who had started racing in 1962 in a Mark II Sprite, 470 CUE. Geoff Price, the service manager at Healeys, maintained the car for him, so, early in 1964, Lucas was able to get hold of one of the spare Sebring 997cc dry sump engines to drop into the car and gain a few more horsepower. He got to know the Healey crew quite well, mainly through spending many Friday evenings talking cars and supping M & B Brew, at a shilling a pint, in the Millwright Arms in Warwick. When the ex-Targa car came up for sale at the end of the 1966 season, he was able to buy it at a competitive price.

Dudley Lucas remembers that the car was great fun to drive on the road, except in the wet, when water had a habit of getting into the cockpit. The car was really a little heavy for ten-lappers, but came into its own in relay races. To take advantage of the car's original design, Lucas decided to have a go at endurance racing himself. Having ruled out the Targa as a bit too far to travel, he opted for the 500km event at Mugello, the 125 lire start money helping to make the whole operation viable.

In 1968 and 1969 Arthur Appleby and Dudley Lucas raced the car in the Italian Classic, coming 6th in the 2-litre Prototype class at their first attempt; in those days there was no 1300cc class. On the last lap Appleby had had to change a wheel on the side of one of the narrowest parts of the circuit. Apparently, the Sprite felt skittish; he inspected the rear end and discovered that the nuts had pulled right through the hub. Although they beat more powerful Porsches and Alfas, the pair were a little disappointed in their position, as the organizers only paid prize money down to fifth place! But for the wheel problem, they would surely have been in the money.

On the long journey home, they got to the Mont Blanc tunnel in the early hours of the morning. Appleby joked that the Italian customs would be too pie-eyed to give them any hassle. Sure enough, the man on duty shuffled out of his little hut, pointed at the Sprite and in broken English asked what sort of car it was. Knowing the Italians did not like British cars, Appleby said it was a Ferrari. 'Ah, Ferrari,' muttered the customs man, as

Dudley Lucas at the wheel of his ex-Targa Florio Sprite during a 1968 race meeting at Silverstone

The sad remains of EAC 90C after colliding with a bridge parapet at Mugello in 1970; the car was broken up

Arthur Appleby in the damaged Sprite, arm in a sling. The ferocity of the impact threw him into the rear of the car with the spare wheel

he stamped all their papers and waved them through. The Swiss check at the other end was the complete opposite, with the uniformed official verifying the chassis and engine number on the car against those on the documents before allowing them on their way.

The following year, during practice, Lucas bounced the car off the side of a mountain, deranging the front suspension, which collapsed when the fulcrum pin dropped out as he was cruising back to the pits. The Sprite went straight on at the next right-hander, and the driver spent the rest of the session watching proceedings from a field. The pair trailered the Sprite to Zanratti's garage in Florence, the local BMC agents. They were always prepared to help out BMC drivers, Zanratti having competed himself in his younger days.

The dents were beaten out and the suspension rebuilt in time for the race, but to no avail; the organizers refused to let the Sprite start as the pair had covered insufficient laps during official practice. Despite pleading that they had both done more than the required number during unofficial practice and had raced there the previous year, they were unable to change the officials' minds.

They begrudgingly packed up and came home.

Arthur Appleby did Mugello alone in 1970, full of confidence after the introduction that year of a 1300cc Prototype class. On lap 4, going through a fast right-hander on the approach to Giogo, an Abarth moved over on Appleby, catapulting the Sprite into a bridge parapet, putting the driver in hospital with a broken elbow and completely destroying the car. Appleby ended up in the back of the Sprite with the spare wheel. On his return from hospital, Appleby discussed with Lucas what to do with the car, and they eventually decided that repair was beyond them financially, even if Geoff Healey's crew had time to straighten it. Reluctantly, they agreed the car should be broken up.

LWD 959E

For the 1967 Targa, an all-new coupé, LWD 959E, emerged from Warwick. It had a lower roof-line and sported Girling discs with lightweight calipers all round. Aaltonen and Baker returned to Sicily for another crack at a class win, but their efforts were thwarted by a spectator who ran across the track and

The Warwick Connection

LWD 959E. the 1967 Targa Sprite, as raced by David Pratley in the 1981 Willhire HSCC Special GT series

was collected by Baker, causing the car to career into the barriers and to be retired on the spot. Luck was to evade the team again the following year, when a production-bodied Sprite, LNX 629E, boiled while being driven by Clive Baker, destroying the engine.

Geoff Healey and Barry Bilbie designed the last of the Targa Sprites. Bill Buckingham hand beat the sleek open body from 20-gauge half-hard Birmabright and the car was powered by one of the team's special Le Mans spec 1293cc engines. This Sprite did not appear at the 1968 race owing to withdrawal of BMC backing. It was sold to Florida BMC distributor Ed Bussey, is still in the USA and is known to have competed in SCCA events in the mid-1970s.

The 1967 Targa/1968 class-winning Sebring Sprite, LWD 959E, enjoyed a competition history after it was sold by the Healeys to Jim Baker in the USA in 1968. The buyer ran it as part of a two-car team of orange and blue Sprites in the 1969 Sebring event. LWD was driven by an all-girl team, including Donna Mae Mims, who came to fame when she became the 1963 SCCA National Champion, in her pink Sprite. She was well known for her pink race suit and unusual matching hair. The Baker cars came home 1st and 2nd in class.

Dudley Cunningham, who acquired LWD 959E, fared over the headlights and used it for USAC long-distance events. While working in the USA in 1979, English Sprite racer David Pratley saw the car advertized in the *New York Times*. He persuaded his wife they should take a holiday in Vermont, went to look at the car and bought it. The seller was running it on the road but, despite this, the car was in fairly original condition.

Pratley shipped the car back to England at the end of the year and rebuilt it for the HSCC Willhire Special GT series in 1981. He ran the car all season with its old Sebring number – 73 – coming second to Ian Polley's Le Mans Sprite in the championship. The following year, when he returned to work in the States, David Pratley put the car in the Midland Motor Museum, where it remained until 1994, when he sold it to finance the restoration of the Lola which he now races. The Sprite is now owned by Japanese enthusiast Tayuka Hata, who competes in historic events in his home country.

The Warwick Connection

THE 1966 PRODUCTION PROTOTYPE

The technical and design features of the Le Mans Sprite were used to build a prototype production road version in 1966. Its shape bore a striking resemblance to the racers, although the body was heavier, to cut costs. The car was first displayed on the Austin Healey Club stand at the January 1967 Racing Car Show and registered 4 HAC on 1 March that year. The proposal was that these very special vehicles would only be made at Warwick, to special order. It was anticipated that production would be at the rate of one a month, and the initial price quoted was £1,240 plus purchase tax.

Eventually, it was decided it would be too expensive to put the car into production, so no other versions of this very special Sprite were ever made. On 28 February 1968, the prototype was sold to David Parker, a local industrialist. He and members of his family drove it for about a month before it reappeared back at the Healey Motor Company showroom. Richard Budd, a long-time MGB racer, saw the car on his way to work and bought it in April 1968, so he could get involved in Spridget racing. Within a week, he drove it to its first event, the Austin Healey meeting at Castle Combe. In June, he took it to Silverstone and came home with the Vice President's Trophy for winning the Sprite and Midget race. He was also a member of the winning Austin Healey team in the 1969 Six-Hour Relay at Silverstone. Richard continued to race his unique car until 1974.

BAHAMAS SPEED WEEK

The Bahamas Speed Week, an International event, was held in December, on an airfield circuit of just over 4 miles (6.5km), in the private grounds of Sir Sydney Oakes' Nassau estate. Donald Healey often spent Christmas out there, as he had a house on the island, next door to that of Ian Fleming, the creator of James Bond. Healey was invited to enter cars in the various races, which included a special one for wives and girlfriends. Despite its status, the event was unique; Roger Menadue always regarded it as 'an intimate little affair', while for Stirling Moss it was 'a week of having fun in cars and partying'.

4 HAC, the only production road-going version of a racing GT Sprite ever built by the Donald Healey Motor Company, displayed at the 1967 Racing Car Show with a price tag of £1,240. The intended limited run was never manufactured. Richard Budd bought this prototype from Healey's showroom in 1968.

In 1959, the Falcon-bodied Sprite, subsequently run at Sebring and Le Mans in 1960, was shipped out to Nassau for what was to be its first-ever competitive outing. Roger Menadue, who had supervized the building of the car, flew out just before the race to look after it. Canadian Ed Leavens was the designated driver for the week and during practice got down to a lap time of 3:50, finding the handling very much to his liking. In the first five-lap race for GT cars up to 2000cc, he finished 9th overall. The best was yet to come – an amazing 6th overall in the 25-lapper, beating most of the Big Healeys, much to Donald Healey's embarrassment!

Following this, the 4.2 diff was changed to a 4.5, in order, some suggested, to prevent the Sprite eclipsing the 3000s in subsequent races. Certainly, only one other driver bettered Ed's time and this was only on one lap, when the Falcon was on the very ragged edge of adhesion. Leavens had to fly home unexpectedly, as his father had died, so Healey arranged for other local drivers to pilot the car for the rest of the week. Motoring writer John Christy was behind the wheel for one race and even managed to get in a road test beforehand; Augie Pabst, who recorded the 3:45 lap, drove in another; Phil Stiles, a regular team member, competed in the main race.

The Falcon returned to Nassau in 1960, when it was entered for John Colgate to drive in the 100-mile Governor's Trophy Race on Friday 2 December, and the 250-mile International Nassau Trophy Race on Sunday 4th. After the event, the car was sold to American Leo Picard who asked John Colgate to drive it for him at the Thompson Race Track; he did not finish on this occasion, as the result of a broken half shaft. Later, Picard ran the car again at Thompson with Colgate and Fred Darling sharing the driving. It is also believed that both John Sprinzel and Steve McQueen drove the car for him at Nassau. Other Sprite outings at Nassau saw Clive Baker score a class win in 1962 and again in 1964, in the three-hour race, driving 693 LAC.

NURBURGRING

In 1963, BMC Competitions Department persuaded the Healey team to enter a Sprite in the Nurburgring 1,000km and proposed that Christabel Carlisle, who was doing very well in Minis at the time, should be one of the drivers. She was paired with Clive Baker and they finished 2nd in class, 17th overall, driving the 1962 Sebring car 9254 WD. The next year, a works Sprite was back, this time with Bill Bradley sharing the driving with Clive Baker. The result was a 3rd in the prototype 1300cc class, behind the two Jacobs Midgets, 29th overall. The Midgets did have the advantage of running the new 1275cc-based engines, as opposed to the 1100cc unit the Sprite used. Bradley found the lack of torque most noticeable on the long uphill pull out of Adenau.

Clive Baker was joined by Keith Greene, something of a Ring specialist, for the 500km in September 1965. Not only did the pair take the class, but they were also the first British car home. This, as with other 500km races in which Baker competed, was a private entry arranged by him. Healeys prepared and lent him the car, and he towed it out to Germany with his own crew, having previously negotiated travelling expenses and start money with the race organizers.

For the 1968 1,000km, Clive Baker was again in the cockpit, this time sharing with John Handley. They finished 29th from seventy-six starters and were classified as 2nd in the up to 1600cc, Group 6 class, behind the Chevron of Killenberg/Bialas, with whom they had enjoyed a race-long duel. However, the organizers later found a mistake had been made and the Sprite was awarded the class by 16.8 seconds.

MUGELLO AND OTHER EVENTS

While several British Sprites had already ventured to Mugello as private entries, it was not until 1967 that Geoff Healey sent a factory-prepared car to the event. This lightweight, standard-shape Mark IV Sprite was entered for Clive Baker and Andrew Hedges to drive, and the pair scored a win in the class for Sports Cars of 1000–1300cc. The two drivers repeated the feat the following year in the former Sebring car LNX 629E, leading the class from the second lap.

LNX 629E, which had raced in both Sprite and Midget guise, was later sold, at an advantageous price, to works test driver John Harris. He used it mostly as his road car, but he did race it in a Silverstone six-hour relay. Jean Denton then bought it and, having had it converted, rallied it, as did next owner Don Griffiths, who, after competing in the 1972 Welsh Rally, sold it to John Baglow, who added to the car's rally history.

In 1967, Clive Baker had an outing in the Tour of Corsica driving a former Sebring car, partnered by top navigator Mike Wood. Although the event was classified as a rally, Baker says it was basically an out and out road race around the island. The pair were running 6th overall, when an electrical fault caused them to retire.

The American Daytona 24-Hour race in February 1969 saw a Jim Baker Sprite compete. Jim Baker, an Atlanta BMC dealer, entered his ex-works car, painted in the orange and blue team livery of its sponsors, the Ring Free Oil Company of New York. Jim shared the driving with Paul Richards and Clive Baker; Clive had on previous occasions been 'lent' to Jim as a driver, taking the class in the July 1968 Watkins Glen 6-Hour race. The fact that there were two Bakers in the team was considered good PR for the garage, which bore the same surname. At Daytona, the car ran well, finishing a creditable 17th from sixty-two starters, and won the class, having covered 2,008 miles (over 3,200km) in the 24 hours, representing an average of nearly 84mph (almost 135km/h).

THE HEALEYS AND CLUB RACING

When each successive works Sprite became surplus to the Healeys' requirements, it was sold, but Geoff Healey would only let the cars go to other enthusiasts who would continue to do the Healey name proud in competition circles. Saturday morning was the time for club racers to go to Warwick to get spares or parts to upgrade their cars. Provided an owner had got some reasonable results and kept his or her Sprite in pristine condition, these were usually made available without cost.

It seems that over the years a sort of pecking order was established. Competitors initially dealt with Geoff Price, the service manager, but eventually they would get to see Geoff Healey himself. John Harris remembers that when he ran a 3000, he made his own manifolds. During one of his Saturday-morning visits, Price called Healey over to admire the work. The boss was duly impressed, invited young Harris over to supper that evening, and thus began a thirty-year friendship. During this time, Harris, who was a full-time Rootes test driver, did a great deal of testing in the works Sprites.

The Sprites were shaken down at Gaydon and Silverstone as well as the MIRA test track at Nuneaton, to which, as a registered motor manufacturer, the Healey Motor Company had access. Harris recalls testing one of the Sprites, which had just been fitted with a pair of angled telescopic rear shock absorbers, to augment the Armstrong lever arms; this modification, he considers, 'trans-

The Warwick Connection

```
                    DONALD HEALEY MOTOR CO. LTD
D. M. HEALEY                                              TELEGRAMS
G. C. HEALEY              WARWICK                         HEALEYCARS
J. COOPER                                                  WARWICK
G. R. L. PRICE            ENGLAND                         TELEPHONE
B. S. C. HEALEY                                          WARWICK 41235
H. J. HEALEY
K. J. HODGES


GCH/PJB                                       9th October, 1968.


Mr. W. H. Tuckett,
9 Queensbury Mews West,
London S.W.7.




Dear Sir,

     We have decided to concentrate on the S.R. type competition
vehicle. We will therefore be dispensing of all the Sprite racing cars
and spares. We probably have material of use to you.

     It is suggested that you could view this after the Motor Show.


               Yours faithfully,
         for DONALD HEALEY CO. LTD.,




                         G. C. Healey
                          Director
```

When the Donald Healey Motor Company gave up racing Sprites, at the end of the 1968 season, a letter was written to all known owners of the ex-works cars, offering to sell them the remaining spares

formed the car'. During his long association with the Healeys, Moore purchased 9253 WD, an ex-Sebring car, which he ran in club events during 1964, regularly dicing with much more powerful machinery.

Keen to help Sprite club racers as much as possible, Geoff Healey was determined that, once the company had stopped racing the cars, all the remaining spares should be put to good use. On 9 October 1968, he wrote to all known competitors and owners of ex-works Sprites, advising them that as the factory was now concentrating on the SR type of competition vehicle, it was dispensing with all Sprite racing cars and spares, which could well be of use. It was suggested that cars and parts could be viewed after the Motor Show. The continued Healey interest in their former works Sprites must have contributed to the cars having such a long and successful competition history in private hands.

2 Alternative Racing Sprites

JOHN SPRINZEL

It was not only the Healey works that produced special-bodied Sprites for racing, and John Sprinzel's Sebring Sprites were probably the best known of the alternatives. Sprinzel, a former partner in Speedwell Conversions and subsequently a Healey employee, set up in his own right in 1960 when, in partnership with Paul Hawkins, he took over the Healey Speed Equipment Division premises in London. The high rent soon found the pair moving to Lancaster Mews where John Sprinzel Ltd rose to fame.

The early Sebring Sprites were standard-shape cars modified to customers' requirements. Sprinzel then asked well-known Edmonton coach-builders Williams and Pritchard to make a new one-piece front; the alloy prototype, run on Sprinzel's 1960 RAC Rally car, was used to make a mould for the subsequent glass fibre versions. The pretty alloy coupé hardtop soon followed and a Sprinzel Sebring Sprite appeared on the firm's stand at the January 1961 Racing Car Show.

Sprinzel himself was better known as a rally driver, but he did have occasional race outings in Sebrings, all bearing PMO 200, the personal registration which appeared on his own competition cars. On 12 August 1961 he was a member of Team Sebring which won the 750 MC Six-Hour Relay race, and he finished the season with a class 3rd in the Boxing Day meeting at a snow-covered Brands Hatch. Andrew Hedges (410 EAO),

The Peter Jackson Sebring Sprite in open-topped form taking part in the 1960 Six-Hour Relay Race

Gabriel Konig (E 700), David Seigle-Morris (D 20), Cyril Simpson (S 221) and Ian Walker (WJB 707) were among other well-known drivers who raced Sprinzel Sebring Sprites.

DOUGLAS WILSON-SPRATT AND THE WSM

Douglas Wilson-Spratt was another name that became well known for alternative Sprites. He was the proprietor of Delta Garage in Hockcliffe Street, Leighton Buzzard, which held an Austin agency. On 14 May 1958, two weeks before the Sprite was officially announced, he took delivery of one of the first cars to come off the production line – VBM 7. He used his previous competition record, in a TR2, to persuade the factory to let him have one early, to enable him to ready it for competition use prior to the launch date. In order to maintain secrecy he ran it in after dark on trade plates. On 24 May 1958, driving this car, Wilson-Spratt and navigator John Bayliss recorded the first-ever Sprite rally win, taking overall victory in the Sporting Owner Drivers Club Rally.

During the year, Wilson-Spratt competed in all manner of events, clocking up some 35,000 miles (55,000km) in VBM 7. His first race was the AMOC meeting at Silverstone on 12 July, the car in absolutely standard form to enable comparison after subsequent modifications. He claimed a 1st class award in the half-hour high-speed trial, *Autosport* describing the dice between Wilson-Spratt and fellow Sprite driver Geoff Dear as 'one of the features of the meeting'. After a driving test and a hill climb, the car was readied for the Seven Fifty Motor Club's Six-Hour Relay race at Silverstone, on 16 August.

Modifications for this event included installing a 4.5 diff, filched from Mrs Wilson-Spratt's A35. The head was ported, skimmed and polished and the centre port of the exhaust manifold was opened out. Now running with a 9.5:1 compression ratio, but still with the standard small carbs, the previous

Douglas Wilson-Spratt driving VBM 7 in the 1958 Six-Hour Relay at Silverstone in August 1958

month's Silverstone cruising speed was improved by 10mph (16km/h). Unfortunately, the work was to no avail as all the cars in the team experienced problems, the Sprite breaking an exhaust pipe, although the team did record a finish. After a number of other rallies, including the Monte Carlo, the Sprite was sold at the end of the year and replaced by another.

Even in those very early days, Douglas Wilson-Spratt was already sketching designs for a lightweight fast-back hardtop. Given he had previously run a Fiat Coupé and a TR2, he was also keen to get away from the raised headlights that were common to the Mark I Sprite. He was so busy enjoying himself in the Sprite, his ideas stayed on paper. When he found his car up against John Sprinzel's lightweight Sprites, however, Wilson-Spratt began to think more seriously of building his own special version.

His first project, a personal version of a Sprinzel Sebring, was based on a standard Sprite chassis platform, with an alloy rear end, which incorporated a hinged boot lid and Rolls Royce rear lights – only because he got them at a good price from his local branch of Lucas. The car had lightweight doors and an aluminium roof with a curved screen, a large rear window and a pair of deep side screens. Above the rear window was a duct to allow the air out of the cockpit, to help keep the temperature down. A Sebring bonnet was used to complete the body. Wilson-Spratt continued to enjoy good results in this one-off, taking in a good number of sprints and hill climbs, as well as rallies and a few races. Driving this car, bearing his personal plate DWS 97, he was a member of Team Sebring that won the 1961 Six-Hour Relay race. John Sprinzel, David Seigle-Morris and Peter Jackson were the other members of the team.

Early in 1962, in conjunction with Jim McManus, Wilson-Spratt set up the London Healey Centre at 17 Winchester Mews, Swiss Cottage, and was appointed the City distributor for Healey Speed Equipment. McManus, a founder member of the Healey Drivers' Club (later the Austin Healey Club), had great experience with the marque, having been Donald Healey's London sales manager. The business moved to the Leighton Buzzard garage, where it continued to trade as the Healey Centre. The time was now right for the plans of Douglas Wilson-Spratt's ultimate Sprite to come to fruition.

The car that became known as the 'prototype' was built in summer 1962, based on the plans Wilson-Spratt had drawn up in 1959. It took three months to complete. The object was to create a body suitable for competition and also for the designer's own use on the road as a grand touring car. He tailored it to fit his 15-stone, 6-foot frame. Again based on a standard floor pan, at the rear the car had a tubular space frame, incorporating outriggers, a perimeter rail and a roll cage. The new aluminium body was then fixed to this framework; the front end was also fabricated in aluminium.

The aluminium panel work was done by Peel Coachworks at Kingston on Thames, a business run by two skilled men: Alec Goldie and Fred Faulkner. Fred Faulkner had been the panel foreman at AC Cars before the war, and the pair had a reputation for doing a good job at a very reasonable price. They always had plenty of work, but, no matter how busy they were, they worked a strictly five-day week and refused to go in at the weekends, regardless of how important the customer was. Fred Faulkner was still working until well into his eighties.

Wilson-Spratt's preparation strategy was to build his cars as light as possible and then tune the engine. He considers that many of his rivals lost reliability by over-tuning an engine to propel a vehicle that was too heavy in the first place. He used such tweaks as an alloy gear lever, remote control cover and earless wire wheel spinners, to optimize the weight reduction. His car was painted in the team livery, a Ford light blue which Wilson-Spratt named Chiron Blue, after the French racing driver Louis Chiron. The Chiron Blue Sprite made its debut at the Austin Healey Club Silverstone practice day in October 1962, where it caused considerable interest. A month later, it was doing well on the RAC Rally, until sustaining suspension damage 400 miles (650km) from the finish.

Soon after the car first appeared, a number of Sprite enthusiasts began to ask how much the production version was going to be. Until then, Wilson-Spratt had not seriously intended to build more than one but, realizing there could be a market, he began to plan a limited run. Among the first interested parties were George Snivley and his colleague, two visiting American doctors who were carrying out research on vehicle safety at the University of Sacramento. Needing a name for homologation purposes in the USA, Wilson-Spratt decided to call the new model a WSM (pronounced 'Wuzzum'), short for Wilson-Spratt McManus. The production models were built to order only, with aluminium bodies and slightly longer glass fibre bonnets than the prototype car, without louvres, but having separate sidelights. The first two production models were soon put together and on the way to the two doctors in the USA, who were going to race the cars.

The WSM was available in either Sprint or GT form. The Sprint was designed for the club competitor and incorporated additional lightweight aluminium chassis sections, offering very little by way of interior trim. The GT was a fully trimmed car for road use. Customers providing their own cars for con-

Peter Jackson on the line in his prototype WSM

Alternative Racing Sprites

version paid £375 for the GT and £450 for the lightweight Sprint version. To avoid purchase tax, the original car had to be over six months old.

Mechanically, the car had softer rear springs and adjustable shock absorbers, whilst at the front the anti-roll bar and shockers were up-rated. Engines were available in various standards of tune, to customers' requirements; most were based on a 948 block, but the last GT had a 1300cc unit. The average WSM Sprite Sprint tipped the scales at around 11cwt (560kg), a saving of 1cwt (50kg) over a standard Frogeye. Wilson-Spratt always favoured wire wheels since they gave some warning – by the spokes 'clicking' – if they were going to give out on you. The question of keeping them clean was never a problem – 'It was a job for the apprentice!'

In all, about a dozen Spridget-based WSMs were manufactured, half of which went for export to the USA. All but two had alloy coupé top and rear body sections. Mike White had one of just two all-fibreglass cars, Wilson-Spratt later building the other up for himself. This was probably the ultimate light version, weighing just over 10cwt (500kg), powered by an Abingdon-built 997cc Formula Junior engine, which produced about 80bhp. The company, which ceased production in 1967, also built about twelve further WSMs using other chassis, including a one-off based on an MG 1100.

Wilson-Spratt did a great deal of preparation work on rally cars and, along with others in this field, such as John Sprinzel, Paddy Hopkirk and Peter Harper, was a member of The International Rally Traders Association. This group met once a month for lunch at a Knightsbridge restaurant to discuss matters of mutual interest. To take cars to race meetings, the Healey Centre purchased an AEC coach, registration GEA

Mike Lewis about to get into his WSM in the Silverstone pits

Alternative Racing Sprites

100, which was converted to carry two Sprites. Wilson-Spratt used his previous skills as a caravan manufacturer to provide sumptuous living accommodation at the front.

Mike White (MW 3) and Mike Lewis, Wilson-Spratt's son-in-law (793 XPP), became two other leading exponents of the marque, and Wilson-Spratt's wife Lorette and daughter Laura drove Sprites in the occasional club event. By 1966, Wilson-Spratt was using a Cooper S for rallying and his faithful WSM for hill climbs and the occasional race. Maybe he would have been more successful as a driver if he had specialized in just one discipline of the sport, but on reflection he considers that it would, perhaps, not have been such fun.

During the GT and Sports race at the West Essex Car Club meeting, at Snetterton on 18 August 1963, Mike White and Mike Lewis hotly disputed the class lead. White eventually used his more powerful 1139cc engine to take victory, after Lewis had a couple of excursions in his 997cc version. Lewis was a tenacious driver. Once, he arrived late for practice at Silverstone and was put on the back of the grid. When the flag dropped, he took to the grass, was first into Copse and took the laurels. Wilson-Spratt often said of his son-in-law, 'If Mike kept the car on the track, he was very likely to win.'

While most of the WSMs were Sprite-based, Lewis, an avid MG enthusiast, had his car built on a Midget chassis. When back trouble forced Wilson-Spratt to give up competing at the end of 1966, Lewis sold his own car and took over DWS 97, but still insisted on entering the car as a Midget. Lewis' original Midget survives in Scotland, the subject of a long-term restoration project. He went on to compete successfully in a WSM-bodied MGB.

Laura Wilson-Spratt on the hill at Firle in the Mike Lewis MG WSM, with the original MkI and II front end

Alternative Racing Sprites

During 1961 Peter Jackson, the service manager at the London Healey Centre, had regularly competed in Britain driving his lightweight, ex-Jamaican Sprite, now registered 46 BXN. He had won his class in the December 1960 Nassau TT Race. The car's alloy rear end was burnt out on that year's Welsh Rally so Jackson decided to rebuild it as a coupé. He asked Peel's, who had already worked on his Sprite, to build the 'new' car using one of Wilson-Spratt's early designs. The whole of the rear was cut off in line with the quarter-elliptic spring hangers and a space frame and panels were grafted on. At the front a one-piece aluminium Speedwell Monza bonnet was utilized.

The roof-line was much lower than that of the subsequent WSMs, if only because Jackson was not as tall as Wilson-Spratt. Having been built before any of Wilson-Spratt's WSMs, Jackson's car never took the name and was entered as a 'Sebring Sprite'. Peter Jackson continued to race his Sprite until 1966, when he sold it to a dealer by the name of Frank Williams. He saw it some years later, 'chopped about', racing in Modsports. The car survives, authentically restored to its original coupé specification, in a private collection and still appears on the race tracks from time to time.

Throughout the 1964 and 1965 seasons, Peter Jackson often raced a WSM, both in the UK and elsewhere in Europe. In 1964, Wilson-Spratt worked out an itinerary which took in a slalom event in Belgium, travelling down to Trier on the Rhine the next weekend for a hill climb on the Saturday and the International Airport Races on Sunday, in which Jackson came 4th overall. The same year he scored a class 4th in the 1,000-mile race at Brands.

Jackson was racing Wilson-Spratt's lightweight WSM at the Brands Hatch August Bank Holiday weekend meeting in 1965, and damaged a rear corner against a concrete marshal's post during a brief off at Hawthornes during the Saturday practice session. The car was transported back to Leighton Buzzard on Saturday evening. On the way to the garage they collected Ray

Peter Jackson competing in his Sebring Sprite 46 BXN in 1965

Halsall, the man who did their fibreglass. He considered that to repair the damage would be too time-consuming, so he cut the corner out of the team's spare body and bonded it on to the car.

On Sunday afternoon, while they were finishing the job off, Peter Jackson heard the sound of an altercation coming from outside the premises. Opening the door, he saw two louts kicking the local vicar who was lying on the ground in a pool of blood. Despite being black and blue from the previous day's accident, he set to and rescued the clergyman while the police were called. It seems that, having been told off for relieving themselves in the chapel garden, the lads had decided to take it out on the poor vicar. Some months later, Jackson got a letter from the Chief Constable thanking him for his help and advising him that the culprits, who were 'known to the police', had both been sent to prison. After the excitement, the damaged section of the WSM was re-sprayed and Peter took up his grid place on Monday. Despite having gained a few more bruises for his trouble, he came 4th in class.

The Healey Centre had the original prototype rebuilt on to a new platform as a GT WSM. Following a major shunt in the hands of one of its owners, it was later acquired by Peter Jackson, who used it as a road car as well as entering it in a few events. Having calculated that the start money for a two-car team made the journey financially viable, Jackson and Wilson-Spratt each took cars to Nurburgring, in the transporter, for the 1965 German Grand Prix support race on 1 August. Jackson came home 3rd in class, and the following month he raced Wilson-Spratt's lightweight car in the Nurburgring 500km, again scoring a class 3rd.

Douglas Wilson-Spratt still has most of the one remaining glass fibre body, together with the damaged corner cut off DWS 97, following Jackson's Brands shunt. He is now talking of building himself another WSM Sprite, using this body on a new Wheeler and Davis floor pan. As he says, given that the body was built in the 1960s, such a car

Peter Jackson in his Sebring Sprite (89) during a Sportscar race in 1962

would not really be a replica. Although he no longer competes in a car, Douglas Wilson-Spratt is still actively involved in aviation.

JACK WHEELER

Jack Wheeler raced probably the most radically developed non-works Sprite coupé, the car ultimately ending up with Lotus suspension. 7080 AC was an ex-Donald Healey Motor Company car that Tommy Wisdom probably used on the Alpine Rally. In response to an *Autosport* advertisement, Jack Wheeler purchased it, for £695, from Healey's London showroom in Grosvenor Street, on 4 October 1960. Wheeler competed in a couple of British club races, but found that the car's supercharged 1000cc engine made it uncompetitive, once the 40 per cent loading had been applied. Following its conversion to a Sebring coupé in 1962, the car was entered into further competitive events, including a few rallies, then put away; it did not see the light of day for three years.

Wheeler shared a London flat with a number of other enthusiasts, including Grahame White and rally exponent John Brown. One night late in 1965, the trio sat in a pub, lamenting the passing of the Mille Miglia and discussing whether the Targa Florio or Nurburgring 1,000km races equalled it as events. By the end of the evening, Wheeler had decided to enter the Sprite for the Targa.

Over the next four years of long-distance racing, the car was continually developed. It was converted from quarter-elliptic to half-elliptic rear springs in 1967. These were later replaced with the rear suspension from an Elan. In 1968, an Elan front cross member was grafted in, the little Sprite ending up with Lotus suspension all round. The body remained a Sebring coupé until 1969, when the top was removed to enable the car to run open, in accordance with the new Group 6 rules.

The engine and transmission also underwent a metamorphosis. The original Sprite engine first made way for a Cooper S blocked 1340cc unit. This was later mated with an MGB overdrive gearbox, then replaced by an ex-works Le Mans engine and five-speed box from Geoffrey Healey. This finally ended up with a cross flow head from Eddie Maher, having special manifold and Weber 40 DCOE courtesy of Paul Ivey.

Wheeler's first European outing was the half-centenary Targa Florio race in May 1966, the car running its original Sebring bodywork. This was one of the wettest races in the history of the event, continuous rain the day before making track conditions treacherous. The Sprite, co-driven by Harry Martin, had been entered by Coburn Improvements, of which Jack Wheeler was a director. The pair failed to make the start. As a result of locking up a wheel in practice, the Sprite turned over and it was considered unwise to try and carry out a quick repair.

This did not put the intrepid Wheeler off the Targa, and he entered it for the following three years. In 1967, he again shared the driving with Harry Martin. The Sprite was towed to Sicily on the back of Wheeler's 1500 Cortina Estate and they qualified without problem, recording a lap time of 44 minutes. It was generally felt by regular competitors that the track surface got progressively worse each year, and it certainly took its toll on the Sprite's suspension. Harry took the first three-lap stint at the wheel and found that the rear end seemed to have a mind of its own. He eventually succumbed to a spin toward the end of lap 1, but then managed to keep it on the island for the remaining two tours.

Wheeler then took over and found that the rear shockers were completely shot, with the suspension bottoming out at every opportunity. However, he managed an uneventful three laps before returning to the pits and handing over to his co-driver for the last turn at the wheel. He averaged a spin a lap, deciding it was safer to let the car have its way, rather than try and fight it. The chequered flag was shown after six hours of racing by which time the little Sprite had covered nine laps of the circuit, as opposed to the ten put in by the race-winning Porsche of Paul Hawkins and Rolf Stommelen.

The fact that there were only seventeen finishers proves what a tough race the Targa was. The Sprite, now virtually devoid of any rear suspension, was 10th over the line. Despite their bumpy ride, the two drivers were elated at finishing at all, let alone coming home just over half-way down the field and 5th in class. Unfortunately, the regulations of the event stated that, to qualify as an overall finisher, each car must complete the race within ten per cent of its class winner's time. As they had failed to do this, they were not eligible for overall classification. The total cost of the outing came to about £500.

July saw the car on its way to Mugello. It was one of two Sebring Sprites and a Spitfire being taken to Italy in the ex-Dick Jacobs transporter, two inside and one towed behind on a trailer. Just outside Calais, the transporter broke down. Grahame White and Terry Hunter, who had entered the other Sebring, decided that the only solution was to abandon the transporter and drive the cars down. Wheeler's car was the only one with any documentation, so on the strength of his registration number and Green Card, they and Harry Martin drove the three cars in convoy through France, into Switzerland and over the Alps into Italy, arriving in time for practice.

In the closing stages of the race, Wheeler was leading the up to 2-litre class, but on the

A change of plugs for the Jack Wheeler special Sprite just outside Campo Felici en route to the Targa Florio, 2 May 1968

last lap the stub axle snapped forcing his retirement. The next day he borrowed a car and drove down to Florence to buy an A40 stub axle off the shelf from the local Innocenti dealers – the two cars shared the same front suspension. The new part was fitted and the car returned to the cross-Channel ferry the way it had come, this time with Wheeler at the wheel.

Like many Spridget racers, Wheeler found the half shafts were a weak link, so he always had a spare in the car. However, when the stronger competition shafts (BTA 940) were introduced, he fitted a pair and ceased to carry a spare, considering it was unnecessary weight. Unfortunately, one of the new shafts let him down at Nurburgring in 1967. He jacked up the car, removed the broken shaft and stood on the side of the circuit waving it at the driver of any passing car who might know what it was. Roger Enever recognized his problem and, on his next visit to the pits, passed a message to Wheeler's crew. Half an hour later, co-driver Peter Jackson emerged from the woods with a spare shaft inside his jacket (strictly speaking, competitors were only allowed to utilize spares carried on board). Wheeler fitted the offending item, went on his way again and the pair recorded a finish. At the same race, in 1969, Jack Wheeler and Martin Davidson came home 4th in the class for Group 6 cars.

Mike Franey shared the driving at Mugello on 29 July 1968, where the pair led the class until a pit stop to fix a loose steering rack lost them any chance of a class win. On 20 July 1969, Franey again went to Mugello. He slid wide on some loose stones on one of the mountain sections, bending a rear wishbone, forcing retirement.

The coupé's last appearance was at the Nurburgring 500km in September 1969. Lying 2nd in class, Wheeler had a big spin at the Karussel, destroying the shell. He later scrapped the shell, putting the undamaged running gear to one side and used the engine in a Ginetta G12, which he re-bodied himself and called a 'Jeroba' (a Desert Rat). In 1994 he ordered two new Frogeye shells from Wheeler and Davis (no relation) and intends to use the bits he has left to rebuild the car in two forms: the original Sebring style closed car, and the 1969 version with Lotus suspension. It seems Brian Wheeler is not too sure about grafting in the Elan front cross member, but he is sure to succeed. Jack Wheeler summed up his time running the car in Europe by saying, 'It was one long list of stories, but, above all, tremendous, tremendous fun.'

LENHAM

The Vintage and Sports Car Garage at Harrietsham, Kent, used the name of the nearby village of Lenham, the place where they first set up shop (in a building behind the Dog and Bear Hotel), to brand their special GT-style bodywork. The conversion, conceived in 1962, turned a Spridget into an attractive coupé. Later, when the big car manufacturers abused the term 'GT', by using it to brand any up-rated tin top, Julian Booty, one of the directors, changed the name to 'Lenham Le Mans Coupé'. This name was applied to all cars based on wind-up window Spridgets built after 1964. The company, which had now moved to a former bakery in Harrietsham, never raced a Lenham Sprite itself, although many lightweight bodies were sold to club competitors.

Peter Denham, who had started racing Formula Fords in 1968, was one driver who raced a Lenham. He enjoyed the seasons when he ran the car, but not all of his races were problem-free. Denham recalls his first trip to Oulton Park in 1973, towing his racer on the back of his everyday car, a Midget. As it was a Saturday meeting, he left work early on the Friday and drove alone to Cheshire. Arriving on a dark and foggy evening, he got completely lost. Eventually, he saw the lights of a bus station and the inspector, who Peter had asked for directions, invited him into the waiting room for a cup of tea and then suggested that he spent the night on one of the benches. In the morning the friendly official sent him on his way with directions.

During practice, Denham had a big off, which very effectively ended his day's motor sport. On the way home, he hit fog again, so decided to spend the night in a convenient lay by. He finally got to sleep in the front of his Midget – not an easy feat – only to be woken at dawn by a member of the local constabulary. The officer, seeing the damaged Lenham on the trailer, was concerned for its occupant's welfare.

Some argued that the Lenham's slippery shape did not overcome the additional weight of the body with its large rear windows. Garo Nigogosian certainly proved that it did. At Brands Hatch on 20 November 1967, his Lenham dared to overtake Warren Pearce's considerably more powerful E-Type Jaguar on lap 2 and manage to stay in front till a blown head gasket forced Nigogosian to retire on lap 7, much to the disappointment of the crowd.

Over the years, a number of other well-known Spridget drivers ran their cars in Lenham guise, including John Britten, Peter Slade, Mike Chalk, Geoff Weekes, Dave Paige, David Matthews and Peter May. Peter found the handling was not to his liking but transformed it by fitting a rear spoiler. Gary Wilson has enjoyed considerable success in his Special GT version.

3 Early Days of Club Racing

In the early 1960s, motor racing was growing in popularity as cars became available to a wider range of people in post-war Britain. The demand for events led to the opening in 1962 by the British Racing and Sports Car Club (BRSCC), one of the largest organizers of events, of two new circuits – Castle Combe in Wiltshire, the site of a former second world war airfield, and Cadwell Park in Lincolnshire.

Club racers, including David Pratley, say that in the early 1960s many drivers raced their everyday cars. 'You removed the spare wheel and windscreen, pumped up the tyres, bolted on a home-made aero screen and, hey presto, you had a racer.' David's first Sprite VTH 853 was, admittedly, a little more advanced than that, in that it did come with a Shorrock supercharger, to make it go faster. As he began to take his racing more seriously, the car was replaced with a Jeff Goodliffe-built, ex-Peter Cole Sprite UMW 685. This had a lightweight body, incorporating a modified Ashley front, turreted rear

David Pratley obviously concerned about John Quick's E-Type, at Copse during a BARC Silverstone meeting, August 1968

suspension and an 'A' bar locating the back axle.

222 MHY

In 1961 Roy Ashford, workshop foreman at Bristol BMC dealers Windmill and Lewis, of Merchants Road, Clifton, became one of the first people to get his hands on a new MG Midget for competition use. His employers had very good connections at Abingdon and Ashford had already raced an MGA Twin-Cam with an engine prepared by Don Moore. The firm took delivery of a Mark 1 Midget prior to the model's June announcement date. The car was registered to the Bristol garage and was allocated the index number 222 MHY. It was stripped of its interior trim and bumpers and was fitted with an aluminium bonnet and boot lid supplied by Abingdon. The hood and windscreen were also discarded, being replaced by a lightweight fly screen bolted to the scuttle. The bright red Midget was prepared in time for the start of the 1961 season.

Terry Osbourne, who later raced the ex-Ashford MGB, remembers meeting Ashford for the first time after they had both returned to Clifton after competing in the Durham Park Hill Climb. Osbourne was standing on the forecourt of the Standard Triumph dealers, where he worked as a salesman, chatting about the day's events with his pals. Roy Ashford roared by in the Midget, with a lawnmower (apparently his mother's) sticking out of the boot. Recognizing Osbourne's Herald Coupé from the event, he waved, turned round and joined in the conversation, and this was to be the start of a friendship which continues to this day.

In those days, hardly anyone had trailers, and the cars were driven to the events. Roy Ashford entered the MG Car Club Silverstone race meeting, and the regs for this event specifically prohibited trailering competing cars. Concerned that the trip from Bristol to the circuit would cause unnecessary wear on his engine, Ashford contrived to borrow the company's Land Rover demonstrator and tow the Midget on the end of a

Roy Ashford puts the Windmill and Lewis Midget through its paces at Shelsley Walsh hill climb in 1963

six-foot solid bar. After all, he wasn't trailering it, was he? The Land Rover had a diesel engine and Terry Osbourne, who had been elected to steer the MG on the downward trip, nearly passed out from the fumes. The open cockpit was just about level with the exhaust pipe of the Land Rover. 222 MHY got home under its own steam.

Windmill and Lewis originally prepared 222 MHY's engine, but as the car became more competitive the power unit was entrusted to Downton Engineering, who had already established a fine reputation for tuning the 'A' series. By now, it was running a Weber 45, which led to problems with the petrol frothing. This was cured simply by cutting an air intake slot in the bonnet to cool the carb. Ashford enjoyed a fruitful partnership with the car during the 1961 season, scoring no less than twenty top three places in circuit and hill climb events. The following year, the car was sold to John Morgan, and Ashford continued with an MGB, in which he became even better known.

ROBIN WIDDOWS

Many of those who became involved in club motor racing had previously been competitive in other sports. The British Olympic bobsleigh team was to produce two drivers who cut their teeth in Midgets before moving on to other classes. Andrew Hedges and Robin Widdows were at Innsbruck taking part in the 1964 Cresta Run; Hedges was driving for Dick Jacobs at the time. Robin Widdows had never even thought about motor racing, although he had been educated at the same school as Stirling Moss. On the top of an Austrian mountain, Robin was introduced to Lord Eddie Portman, who asked him if he had ever driven a racing car. On being told 'no', Lord Portman replied that if he would like to try it, he would buy him a little car and they could see how he got on.

Through Andrew Hedges, a brand-new Midget was purchased from Jack Barclay in Berkeley Square, complete with carpets and a heater. Once delivered, it was driven to Barwell Motors in Chessington, who had been recommended to Lord Portman. There, John Lucas and his team stripped it out, built an 1150 motor and converted it into a racer, ready for the start of the 1964 season. It was British Racing Green with a red line painted round the radiator grill, and had wire wheels and a black hardtop. During the year, the car competed at circuits up and down the country, taking a few wins and several class records. The following season, Widdows progressed to a Lotus 23, which was again prepared by Les Osbourne and Tony Fox, the two leading mechanics at Barwell. In this car, he won his class in the Autosport Championship.

In 1969, five years after Eddie Portman gave him his first chance, Widdows drove for the works Matra team at Le Mans. He moved on to Formula 2, taking the two ex-Barwell mechanics with him. Later, he was signed by the Cooper Formula 1 team. In his heyday, Widdows raced against the likes of Graham Hill, Piers Courage and Jim Clarke. He broke his back on two occasions, once in a bobsleigh and for the second time while testing the JW Mirage BRM sports car at Snetterton. When Widdows retired, Les Osbourne continued as a race mechanic, ending up at Williams.

After taking part in a Formula 2 race in Sicily, Widdows and fellow competitor Graham Hill, who were staying in the same hotel, decided to drive to a restaurant that had been recommended to them. On the way, Hill unwittingly drove through a road block. The car was surrounded by armed police, and Widdows' concern was only alleviated when Hill got out, was recognized and all was forgiven.

Early Days of Club Racing

Roy Ashford three-wheels his Windmill and Lewis-owned Midget round the recently opened Castle Combe circuit during a sprint meeting in 1962

Roy Ashford in the Windmill and Lewis MGB behind an all crossed-up Garo Nigogosian at the Mallory Park hairpin in 1968

Early Days of Club Racing

THE SOUTHEND RACING PARTNERSHIP

The green Midget ended up being sold, through a garage in Hornchurch, to Peter Beach. Beach and his friend, school-teacher Alan Daykin, raced their Spridgets as 'The Southend Racing Partnership'. A part-time business founded along with Ollie Thatcher to help fund their racing exploits, the partnership was set up at Leigh, Essex, in March 1966. They bought and sold racing cars, including John Alley Minis, and did tuning and preparation.

Beach ran the green Midget for two seasons and had one of his most rewarding outings in the BRSCC Ilford Films 500-mile race at Brands Hatch on 9 July 1966, sharing his car with Daykin. They won the up to 1150cc class in what can only be described as terrible conditions. The race was stopped after six hours, when the winning Cobra of David Piper and Bob Bondurant had only covered 464 miles (less than 750km). The two Southend drivers beat the ex-works Le Mans Sprite of David Corderoy and Mike Garton (who in fact raced it at Le Mans) into second place, after the Sprite was forced to pit to replace a diff.

The following year, Peter acquired the ex-John Ewer lightweight aluminium Midget, feeling that it had more potential than his original mount, which was fairly standard in terms of bodywork and suspension. He used this to score a number of class wins over the next three years. While he was trying to sell the Widdows car, his friend Ollie Thatcher, who usually drove the John Alley Mini, had a few outings in it.

JOHN WATSON

In 1963 a young lad in Northern Ireland, John Watson was running a Frogeye as a road car, and decided he wanted to go motor racing over the winter of 1963-64. The car was stripped and built up into a racer, complete with 1000cc Formula Junior engine. Throughout the 1964 season, Watson ran the car in Sports Car events and the handicap races that were part of the scene in Northern Ireland. He competed in the UAC meeting at Bishopscourt on 9 May, *Motoring News* commenting, 'Young J. Watson was keeping the crowds at the Esses on their toes with some very enthusiastic driving in his Sprite.' He finished 2nd in class.

Watson's best showing with the car was 2nd overall in the Holmpatrick Trophy Race at the Dunboyne road circuit, which he likens to an Irish version of the Nurburgring. He described the Sprite as 'a good little car to me, which gave me a great deal of experience'. At the end of the season it was sold to make way for a locally built Crossle sports racing car. In later years, Watson drove in Formula 1 for Penske, Brabham and McLaren.

TONY BENDING

Tony Bending, who raced his Frogeye Sprite 402 KPP from 1962 to 1969, remembers that, when he started, race entries were thirty bob (£1.50) and a set of pistons and a re-bore were £25. At the outset, competition was fairly low-key and friendly, but when BARC and BRSCC started to pay prize money, the drivers took it a bit more seriously. Bending's Sprite had a distinctive aluminium front with faired-in headlights, a bit like a mini E-Type. The car was used in all manner of events, although the 649 cam made it a bit heavy going when it came to autotests.

The Austin Healey Championship was won by Bending in 1966 and 1968. What about 1967? Well, that was the year he got married. Both bride and groom were members of the Surrey Centre of the Austin

Healey Club, and the others in the group had a collection and bought them a wedding present. This was presented to the happy couple by the Surrey President, well-known BBC motoring correspondent Raymond Baxter.

Tony Bending, along with Alan Capell, Dudley Lucas, Lynden Thorne and Chris Smith, was a member of the Austin Healey Sprite team that took part in the 1968 4-Hour relay at Croft. The night before the meeting, Bending was rebuilding his gearbox on the kitchen table while his wife, who was to feed the team at the circuit, was making a large curry, apparently her speciality. She offered her husband a taste. It was up to her usual high standard, but he did detect an unfamiliar taint and asked what she has used to fry the meat. She replied that she had used the cooking oil from the jar on the corner of the table. The jar, in fact, contained the brake fluid he had drained from the clutch slave cylinder. The curry was discarded and the team had to survive on hastily made sandwiches!

Despite the last-minute change of menu, the lads, with the help of team manager Mike Dickin, did exceedingly well. Having led at the end of the second and third hours, the Sprites went on to win the event by a margin of five laps, setting an average speed of 70mph (122km/h). There were two 1150cc and three 1300cc cars, and Chris Smith set some of the fastest laps, revelling in chucking his larger-engined car around the circuit. Dudley Lucas was running the ex-works Targa Florio Sprite EAC 90C.

RICHARD SUTHERLAND

Another Sprite victory at Croft in 1968 was chalked up by well-known Yorkshire driver Richard Sutherland. He was noted both for building and competing in Sprites, having put together his own car and those driven by Peter Smith, Mike Taylor and John Bury. Sutherland entered the Sports Car race at the Boxing Day meeting and put his 1100cc machine on the front row, which he shared with a 4.7-litre AC Cobra (Bill Wood) and a 4.2-litre E-Type (Alan Mountain). When the flag dropped, the Cobra went off in the lead, closely pursued by the Sprite. However, as they came out of Tower on the first lap, Sutherland was in the lead. He went on to win the race by a margin of 15 seconds and set the fastest lap at 76mph (122km/h).

The Sprite Team, managed by Mike Dickin, which won the 1968 Croft Four-Hour Relay, left to right, Lynden Thorne, Alan Capell, Dudley Lucas, Tony Bending, Chris Smith

At Brands on 27 April 1969, Sutherland had a race-long dice with Alan Harvey. The pair made contact, when Harvey spun at Paddock, both ending their race against the banking. Sutherland continued to compete in Modsports, campaigning a Ginetta G4 during 1970. He then moved on to long-distance Sports Car racing and was tragically killed while taking part in an event at Zolder, on 13 June 1976.

ALAN GOODWIN

Aldon boss Alan Goodwin originally started racing an ex-Targa Florio Sprite 693 LAC, in 1965. It came complete with works 1147cc engine. When the regulations changed, and non-standard bodies became banned, he bought a donor car. He and Don Loughlin stripped it out and rebuilt it, with Tony Guy glass fibre bodywork and rather radical suspension that they designed. They used the engine and gearbox from the Targa car.

Goodwin enjoyed considerable success in his so-called 'space frame' Sprite, which competed in the 1150 class. The car's debut, at a sprint in 1964, gave an indication of its potential. It set the second-fastest time, beaten only by Roy Lane's V8 Brabham. The car ended up one of the lowest Spridgets around, with a ground clearance of just 3in (75mm). During his time with the car, Goodwin set lap records at Castle Combe,

Alan Goodwin takes a glance in his mirror after rounding the Devil's Elbow at the Mallory Park Boxing Day meeting in 1965. He is driving his ex-Targa Florio Sprite 693 LAC

Silverstone and Mallory, the latter standing for three years.

Alan Goodwin's most memorable race was at Mallory in 1968. Throughout the twelve-lap Sports Car thrash, he was dicing for the lead with John Chatham's Healey 3000. He would catch him round the twisty bits, and was right on his tail through Gerrards, only to lose him down the straights. On lap 10 he took the class record, at 54.8 seconds (88.69mph/142.8km/h). On the eleventh lap, a wheel came off down the Stebbe Straight and the Sprite crashed heavily at the Esses, the resulting shunt all but destroying the car. It was rebuilt and later raced by Brian Litherland.

Another member of the Goodwin family was also well known for competing in a Sprite. Alan's late father, Alf 'Pop' Goodwin, did autocross in his immaculate 1275cc version.

ALAN WOODE

Unlike many drivers who gave up racing when they got married, development engineer Alan Woode took up motor sport after the event, because, he said, 'he had to chase *something*'. In his Frogeye Sprite, XXL 850, he took a class win at his first-ever sprint at Blackbushe on 7 June 1964. That initial season of two sprints, two races and a driving test would set Alan on the road to eight years of Spridget activity. In the early days, the wins were interspersed with mechanical

Alf 'Pop' Goodwin, father of Alan from Aldon Automotive, throws his immaculate 1965 Sprite into a corner during an autocross in 1969

reliability problems. The car had been increasingly modified and for a while the traditional Frog front was replaced with an Ashley version.

Woode was awarded the Austin Healey Club Donald Barrit Trophy for the most race wins by a club member during 1967. His tally of ten 1sts and six 2nds from eighteen starts, and three sprint wins out of three, proving that he had finally cracked the reliability problem. The only failure of the year, a broken con rod at Brands in June, which more or less totalled the engine, necessitated a month's lay-off while a new one was built.

The following year, the quest for more power led to the unreliability factor occasionally creeping back again. Woode still achieved nineteen 1sts and three 2nds from thirty-three starts in the Sprite, plus two wins and a 2nd in a friend's Diva GT. This put him third in the end-of-year tally of club race-winners compiled by *Autosport*, and netted him the Thames Estuary Automobile Club Drivers' Championship. The bright yellow car was now running as a one-eyed Sprite, with a permanent hardtop bonded in position.

The season of 1969 was without doubt Woode's most successful. The car, which had now been re-bodied as an MG Midget, with lightweight fibreglass panels, really flew. The objective was to win the Amasco Championship, but by the time of the first round on 19 January, the car was not really ready. It had the new bodywork, the old Frogeye hardtop and all the original mechanical components from the old car. It was still good enough to get pole, and Woode lined up on the front row next to Geoff Daryn's Turner and Chris Marshall in one of the Gold Seal Spitfires.

Peter Newman's 1298cc Midget led from the second row, while Woode slotted in behind Marshall for third. Newman's glory was short-lived; approaching Clearways at the end of the first lap he ran on to the grass, letting Marshall through, and Newman swerved back on to the track right in front of

Alan Woode at the wheel of his virtually standard Sprite during his first-ever race at Castle Combe 18 July 1964

Woode, causing him 'the longest racing moment' of his career. He took evasive action, the car veered from lock to lock as he tried to keep control, but it was to no avail. The Midget spun in the middle of the pack, but somehow everyone missed him. Woode puts the lack of control down to stiff steering, as a result of rust on the kingpins, which he had not had time to overhaul. His eventual class 3rd gave him two valuable points to start his tally for the championship.

The car was so quick that one or two other competitors queried whether it did in fact only have an 1143cc engine. As a result of this, Alan Woode received a letter from John Gott, the racing Chief Constable and a leading light at the time, saying he did not think he was cheating, but to be warned if he was. Woode replied that, during his last outing (Brands 15 June 1969), he had set a new joint class lap record with John Britten, and that at his next visit to that circuit he would attempt to equal or better that time. He would then present his engine for verification.

On 2 July, he duly knocked another 0.2 seconds off the time and immediately went to John Gott asking him to arrange for the Midget engine to be stripped down. He was not taken up on the offer. From that day, his car carried a sticker where the number plate would have been, with the following message – '1143cc?' No one else questioned the car's capacity.

Looking back, Woode regards 1969 as 'a very professional year when everything came together for organization, reliability and [his] driving', and the main fault was to 'change things for the sake of it'. Prior to the Croft meeting on 29 June, he went over to electronic ignition. This failed during the race, resulting in him being punted into retirement by a closely following competitor. For the Sevenoaks and District Motor Club meeting on 19 November, he changed the camshaft for one with a greater overlap. He was forced to change a wet plug on the line and only managed an uncharacteristic third place.

At the end of the season, during which he had twenty-four outings, he amassed no less than sixteen wins and, except for two retirements, never finished outside the top three in his class. He also set seven lap records, to go with the three he had established the previous year in the Sprite and Diva. Having scored the same number of Amasco points as John Gott in his Austin Healey 3000, Alan Woode won the championship by virtue of the greater number of class wins.

On the same basis, Woode came 2nd in the Freddie Dixon Series, sponsored by Chevron Oils, to Marcos pilot Chris Boulter. Woode felt that, but for the accident brought about by the ignition fault at Croft, he could have achieved the double. Despite the success, he admits that, owing to the championship pressure, the season as a whole had not been as enjoyable as 1968. With race entries costing between £7 and £14, depending on the organizing club and circuit, and Woode usually coming away with £25 to £50 prize money, he found that throughout 1968 and 1969, his racing more than paid for itself.

He had also started to do tuning work for other competitors, setting up 'Woodpecker Racing Improvements' in 1968. His woodpecker logo became well known, as other drivers, impressed by the way his own car went, soon began to use him. One of his jobs was to build a complete racing Midget for Miles Hopperton.

Having done so well in his 1150 Midget, Woode now had to decide what to move on to. He put the car up for sale, and mused on an AC Cobra or perhaps a Dulon F100 Sports Car. He was forced to wait until the following March to find a buyer for the Midget, when the car eventually went to Peter Mitchell. In the end, Woode opted to

Alan Woode's Sprite, now much modified, shared the front row of the grid with a brace of E-Types, Snetterton 28 August 1967. He won his class and was 3rd overall

replace it with an all-new, supercharged Midget.

KEITH ASHBY

The title of 'Mr Spridget' must undoubtedly go to Newbury driver Keith Ashby, who started competing in his standard Frogeye in 1964 and still races today. He bought the car, which has the original registration number 6209 AH, the previous year, from Albany Park Service Station at Kingston upon Thames. The garage was owned by Paddy Gaston, well known for his racing exploits in his supercharged Sprite, RAM 35. At Albany Park Ashby dealt with Barry Wood, who over the years raced Modsports in Sprites, Lotus Elans and Ginettas.

Two of the other lads working at Albany Park at the time were Keith McDonald and his sidekick Mick Ralph, who together prepared Paddy Gaston's racer. They subsequently formed Ram Racing, which went on to F1. The name was apparently created by abbreviating 'Ralph and McDonald', but it could have been taken from the RAM registration number of the first competition car they had a hand in – Paddy Gaston's.

Ashby's first race was at a meeting jointly organized by the Austin Healey Club, 750 Motor Club and the RAFMSA, at RAF Debden near Saffron Waldron, Essex, on 27 June 1965. By now, the Sprite had gained a one-piece, Mark II-shape, fibre front – actually, it was in three pieces when Ashby acquired it from Tony Bending, who had dis-

Keith Ashby's Mark I Sprite at Castle Combe in 1966, the familiar 'Frogeyes' removed in the interest of aerodynamics

carded it following a shunt. Money was very tight in those days. Ashby stuck it back together, made the headlights removable and cut some holes in the side to increase the airflow. Apart from this, the car was pretty standard except for a re-bore, which increased the engine capacity to 970cc. In the race, Keith came a creditable 7th out of a field of fifteen, and the race was won by another Frog, driven by Alec Poole.

Debden was a temporary race circuit set out for a few weekends a year at the RAF base of the same name, used between 1962 and 1965. Keith's first race marked the last event to be held there. During the last race, a competitor lost control of his car at the end of the main straight and ended up on the public highway, by careering through a fence and hedge. The authorities insisted that a crash barrier be erected at this point before the next event. This, combined with the proposed 1966 regulations governing the use of such temporary circuits, difficulty in getting Air Ministry permission, and the state of the tarmac surface, sounded the death knell for racing at this venue. These days, Debden Airfield is still used for sprints.

According to Ashby, everything was much more informal in those days. On one occasion, during a Marque Sports event at Brands, he had enjoyed a race-long dice with Bill Viney in his Healey 3000 (registration number HAS). Having crossed the finishing line, Ashby was all fired up and disappointed that he had not entered the next race, an all-comers event, in which Viney was taking part. Arriving back in the pits to collect his wife Carol, he voiced his regrets. She duly sprinted up to an official to see if there might be room on the grid for him and, after quickly borrowing some petrol, he lined up for his second race of the day.

The Sprite, the Ashby's only form of transport, was driven to the circuit. On arrival, tools, camping stove, food and spare clothes were all unloaded from the boot. Since the Mark I had no external boot lid, it was not unusual for something to be left in there, and this usually became obvious through an irritating rattle during practice. Ashby still owns the Frog, which now enjoys a more leisurely life as a summer weekend car.

Keith and Carol Ashby were such Sprite enthusiasts that they even had a Frogeye Sprite on top of their wedding cake. It was an Airfix kit, made up and painted with white emulsion to make it look as if it was made of icing. The cake had been made by their best man Tony Bending, chef and fellow Sprite racer. Despite being rivals on the track, the two were always great friends.

Carol, the bride, assembled and painted the Airfix model Frogeye for the Ashbys' wedding cake, made for them by fellow Sprite racer Tony Bending

Early Days of Club Racing

Ashby built his now-familiar metallic blue Modsports car in 1974. It retains quarter-elliptic springs, with an 'A' frame to locate the rear axle. Over the years, it has appeared in both Sprite and Midget guises, featuring in the top three of the STS, STP, MGCC Midget and Austin Healey championships. In 1976, he answered a 'Midget driver wanted' advertisement in *Motoring News*, and ended up driving for Robbie Gordon in his ex-John Bury car. It went so well, they nicknamed it 'The Cannon'. The next year, The Cannon was sold and Ashby reverted to his own car. He also continued to drive for Gordon in an Elan, Porsche 911 and Chevron B6, in which Keith won the Atlantic Computers Historic GT Championship.

The Ashbys were also instrumental in bringing Alan Goodman (not to be confused with Alan Goodwin of Aldon) into the Spridget racing fold. Goodman, who also lived in Berkshire, raced a TC. Whenever they met, Ashby always asked him when he was going to race a decent car. Goodman eventually succumbed to the jibes and in 1969 bought an ex-autocross Midget, in which he did one or two races. Ashby then persuaded him to acquire a space frame shell that was for sale for £60, and the mechanics and running gear from his original car were rebuilt into that. After just three events, the car was protested and banned. Goodman and Ashby cut the space framed front off and grafted back a standard Spridget 'H' frame, so that the car could race again.

The car continued to be raced in this form, but somehow Goodman never seemed to get round to spraying the bodywork properly. Having entered a race at Brands, he arranged to stay with a pal who lived in Bromley and had a double garage and a compressor. The night before the race, the two of them stayed out there till the early hours, painting the car. They finished so late, the paint was still not dry by the time they set off for the circuit. This did not impress the scrutineer, who got blue paint over his pristine white overalls. Goodman still races, now competing in the Historic Formula 3 series.

Keith Ashby in his Midget heads Mike Donovan at Thruxton in 1978

BARRY WOOD

Barry Wood had been racing his ex-Reg Venner-Pack Frogeye since 1961, the previous owner having retained his VP 7 personal plate. When Wood went to work for Paddy Gaston in 1962, it was decided to stick RAM 36 on the front and make it the 'sister car' to the governor's already well-known RAM 35. Barry continued to run his car in Marque Sports races throughout 1962 and 1963, often finding it was more reliable than Paddy's supercharged version. RAM 36 was sold at the end of the season to finance the purchase of his first Elan, from which he built the prototype of his self-designed Shapecraft Elan.

After retiring for the 1965 and 1966 seasons, in 1967 Barry heard that Sprite driver Rob Schroder was changing to an E-Type. The temptation proved too great and he bought the Sprite. He raced the car as it was for the rest of the season and decided to do things really seriously again the following year. With its new set of John Britten bodywork, the car proved most successful in the up to 1150 class. He looks back on this time with fond memories. 'It was great fun in those days and we all enjoyed it. Everyone tried to help everybody else get on the grid, even if you knew the man you were helping was likely to beat you.'

For 1969, he moved up a class, using the 1340 engine previously used by Chris Smith, to win the up to 2-litre category in the Amasco championship. He subsequently raced Ginetta G15s and a Ford Mustang.

RICHARD DOBSON AND BARRY HOPWOOD

Richard Dobson raced a Midget in 1968 and his company, Thameside Trailers, sponsored Barry Hopwood's well-known Sprite. Hopwood's engine was reputed to have Jackie Stewart's old Formula Junior crank, which had been purchased from Ken Tyrell – what a pedigree! Dobson got his first taste of motor sport as a marshal at Crystal Palace, where he found himself on duty at North Tower Bend. During the Mini race, one car spun off and the keen young marshal jumped down to help the driver out of his stricken vehicle. At that moment, four more cars came round the corner and ploughed into the first. Dobson had never been so frightened. He decided on the spot that it would be safer to be a competitor, and soon afterwards he bought the Midget.

Barry Hopwood emerges from the cockpit of his well-known Frogeye after a race at Silverstone, April 1970

Hopwood and Dobson decided that they liked the sound of a meeting in Zandvoort and, having entered, duly trailered their cars to Holland to take part. On arrival, they discovered that the race coincided with a bulb festival, and there was not a hotel room to be had. In desperation they called at the local police station, to see if they could help them find accommodation for the night. The police offered the two British drivers some very practical help. Nightfall saw them comfortably bedded down in a cosy cell, and in the morning they were even brought breakfast. The officer in charge foresaw problems getting the trailers to the track in the bad traffic, so they were instructed to unload the racers and drove to the track with a police escort!

GARO NIGOGOSIAN

Another enthusiast to progress from sprints to circuit racing was Garo Nigogosian. His brother Ara bought a 1964 Midget 9308 MT from a Golders Green showroom, and they soon started to take part in sprints at such venues as Blackbushe Airfield. The car was standard, except for a heavy-duty clutch and the removal of some trim. Garo soon assumed the role of permanent driver, his brother happy to concentrate on development of the car, so much so that it was soon taken off the road as impractical to drive on the highway.

Garo's first race was at a rainy Brands in 1966. By now the hood and windscreen had gone and the Midget had gained an aero screen and a racing mirror on the offside wing. The car and driver both progressed considerably throughout the 1967 season, during which the Midget appeared in various guises and colour schemes. It started as an open car with an Ashley Monza front and finished the year as a Lenham Coupé. (Garo's business was, and still is, car bodywork.) The final outing of the year was Boxing Day at Brands, not an auspicious occasion, with the car crashing heavily.

Undeterred by this setback, they rebuilt the car over the winter and appeared again,

Garo Nigogosian competes in his first-ever race at a sopping wet Brands Hatch, winter 1966

at Brands on 3 March 1968. Garo did not set a very good practice time, but some suspension adjustments resulted in him finishing 2nd in class, despite the car shedding its fan belt on lap 7: that's how cold it was. The registration number was now displayed as GAN 1, in deference to Abingdon's type designation for the Mark I Midget. This was to prove the car's best season; from sixteen starts Garo took ten 1sts, two 2nds and one 3rd, and set or equalled three lap records. He retired twice and non-started at Crystal Palace as a result of a shunt in practice.

Garo's most ambitious outing that year was at Brands on 21 July. Now racing as the Anglo-Armenian Racing Team, he entered two races, one for cars under 1150cc, and the sixth race for cars over 1150cc. He did both practice sessions, using his usual 1144cc engine, setting pole for the first race and getting on the second row for the last race. He led the first race from flag to flag, taking both victory and fastest lap, at 58 seconds dead. Back in the paddock, the team set to, whipped out Garo's own engine and changed it for Roger Enever's 1275cc unit. The transplant took them a little over an hour, leaving just enough time for a spot of lunch.

The sixth race resulted in overall victory for John Wilson's E-Type. He was shadowed all the way by Garo, who ended up 2nd overall taking class victory and fastest lap at 57.4 seconds. He achieved this despite an oil leak and a missed gear change while the Midget was lapping back-markers. He beat the other E-Types in the race and all the big Healeys. Class 2nd went to Rob Cox (later famous for his 'Black Brick' Lotuses) in his 1293 Midget.

Garo seemed to make a habit of doing unusual things while racing at Brands. On Sunday 26 November 1967, he had been due to compete in Event 1, Marque Sports Cars up to 1150cc and over 3000cc. During Saturday's practice, he put the Midget on the second row. Unfortunately, his tow car broke down on the way to the circuit on race day and he arrived too late to take part. Most drivers would have given up in disgust, but Garo persuaded the officials to let him take

The metamorphosis of Garo Nigogosians's Midget, leading John Britten's Sebring at Brands in 1967. The notional registration GAN 1 was the chassis number designation for the Mark I Midget

part in the Marque race for the larger-engined classes, for which he started from the back row.

Pole man Roger Enever led the field away from the flag, while Garo fought his way through the field. By lap 4 he was up to 4th and was snapping at the heels of Peter Brown in the JCB MGB. Two laps later, the grandstand crowd gasped as Garo roared past in the lead, Enever having dropped back to 3rd as a result of a misfire. Although, at the end of the eight laps, Nigogosian crossed the line first, four seconds ahead of the B, Brown received the victor's laurels; the Midget, not an official entry for that race, was ineligible for an award.

CHRIS SMITH

Smethwick driver Chris Smith, another member of the Sprite Team that took victory at the 1968 Croft Six-Hour relay, started racing in a Turner during 1965. His self-built Sprite, which he first raced in 1968, had one weakness: damper pulleys. Despite the fact that he used the large Cooper S version, the engine had a habit of throwing the things off. They would often gouge their way through the glass fibre bonnet and go into orbit. At the end of his first season with the Sprite, in which he competed in thirty-six races, Chris had amassed sixteen 1st's and ten 2nd places. He scored more wins at Silverstone than any other competitor and was awarded the John Player Gold Leaf Clubman of the Year Trophy.

Shortly after Smith started racing, John Bending brought out his ultimate space frame Midget, which was a good three seconds a lap quicker round Silverstone than any of the other Spridgets. This was hardly surprising, as it had a 1440cc engine and tipped the scales at just over 8cwt (400kg), complete with screen and hardtop. This radical machine, built by Ivan Dutton, was based on a Midget floor pan but had tubular sections with lightweight aluminium panels wherever possible and a sophisticated suspension set-up. The engine was set back almost a foot (30cm) and, although it utilized an A30 gearbox tail-piece (without a remote), the gear lever still had to be cranked back to allow the driver to change gear. At the time, Mini racer Mike Evans, a pal of Smith's, told him if he wanted to keep winning he had better get Dutton to build a car for him.

John Bending raced his lightweight version on only a few occasions. He was killed outright when he hit a marshal's post on Pilgrims Rise, which leads up to Brands Hatch Druids Bend, at the BARC meeting on 18 August 1968. Running in an undisputed fifth place, on the eighteenth lap out of twenty, he came out of Paddock Bend in an uncontrollable drift, which resulted in the fatal accident. Dutton trailered the remains of the car back to his workshop and everyone thought that was the last that would be seen of it.

This was not the case. Later in the season, Chris Smith contacted Ivan Dutton, bought what was left of the car, and got Ivan to rebuild it for him over the winter. Smith entered his new mount in a Saturday race at Silverstone on 22 March 1969 and booked a test session on the Friday. In his haste to build the engine the day before, he left out one of the rear main shells, which resulted in damage to the oil thrower scroll on the rear main cap. Undeterred, he went for a set of bearings, while Ivan stripped the engine down in the paddock, borrowed a welding set, brazed up the cap, repaired the scroll with brass and hand-scraped it to the correct profile. The engine was reassembled and put back in the car, ready for the next day's race.

Smith went out in the official practice session and put the car on pole. In the race, he was beaten off the line by the sheer power of Chris Mayman's 4.7-litre Cobra, but by the second corner Smith was all over him. The two cars continued as if tied together, until lap 8, when Smith lost his second place to hard-charging David Porter in his Ginetta G4. The Ginetta took the lead in the next lap, and the Sprite came back to second. They came into Woodcote for the last time, side by side, the commentator beside himself, both cars right on the limit of adhesion. The G4, on the inside, was the first to go. The Sprite went wide to miss it, too wide, spinning on the grass on the outside of the track.

Chris Mayman was waiting to pounce and claimed victory, while his rivals sorted themselves out, just yards from the finish line. Smith was the first to get it back together to claim second. Porter finally got started again, but the best he could manage was an up to 1150 class win. Smith had done this in his first race in a car which had brazed-up main caps!

Although, after further race victories, a number of the other drivers talked among themselves about the legality or otherwise of the car, no one actually protested it. According to Smith, that was not how things were done in those days. To help pay for his racing, he prepared other people's cars at Green Street Garage and did a bit of wheeling and dealing; at the time, he never had a proper full-time job.

In 1982, Chris Smith, by now a classic car dealer specializing in the upper end of the market, used his expertise in bolting things together to build the first Westfield Eleven. This glass fibre copy of the Lotus 11 utilized Sprite/Midget running gear. Since then, Smith has had a very full-time job as MD of Westfield Sports Cars (named after Westfield House, where he lived at the time). It is a successful British car manufacturer, producing rapid two-seaters. Inevitably, with Smith's background, a one-make racing series has now been introduced and this has proved to be most successful.

LYNDEN THORNE

Dickin Team member Lynden Thorne, an engineer from Sutton Coldfield, had started his motor sport doing night rallies, but found it was not good for his job prospects – he kept falling asleep at work the next day. He went on to use his beige 1961 Sprite, which he describes as 'my pride and joy at the time', for a few sprints, before getting the taste for circuit racing. Like many other cars of the era, his Sprite became modified beyond road use and soon became an out and out racer.

Thorne turned up for his first race in his 1275cc-engined car at the end of the 1966 season, only to be told that Frogeyes were homologated with 948cc-based engines and therefore his car was not eligible. He spent the winter fitting glass fibre Mark III shape front and rear body panels, only to find at the start of the 1967 season that the rules had changed and he could have left it as it was. By now, the car featured Donald Healey aluminium outer sills and boot floor.

As he lived in the north of England, Thorne made the occasional foray over the border to race at Ingliston. As he was returning from one such event, the wheel came off the trailer on a dual carriageway; there was no hard shoulder and he was concerned for the safety of his car. Having discovered all four studs had sheared, he lifted the trailer up on the trolley jack and slowly drove to the next junction, using the jack to keep one side of the trailer off the ground. Having parked the trailer at the side of the road, he drove for a couple of miles, found an engineer who was working and scrounged four bolts to get him home.

After he had parted with the Sprite, Thorne went on to race the F100 car built by Aldon Automotive. Although he did well, the formula did not catch on and the car was converted to a Sports Car, which he campaigned with various power units for a cou-

Early Days of Club Racing

ple of years. Some while later, like many cars of its type, the Aldon appeared as a Special GT, in Skoda guise. Thorne has long since given up racing, and taken up gliding, and is now involved in running a gliding club in Warwickshire.

MIKE DICKIN (LUBYSIL) RACING

In 1969, Chris Smith and Lynden Thorne entered as Mike Dickin (Lubysil) Racing. Dickin, an ex-Abingdon employee, fancied being a team manager and got some sponsorship from Lubysil. The only benefit Smith remembers was a pair of Firestone driver's overalls; before that he raced in jeans and a red jumper.

The BARC meeting at Snetterton on 23 March was not a good day for the team. Both cars were on the grid for the Fred W Dixon Prodsports race, Smith managing a front row position between an E-Type and a 2-litre Marcos. Under-braking on the first lap, Smith locked a wheel, going hard into the bank backwards, writing off the car, but escaping with mild concussion. Lynden Thorne, who had been displaced from third by Gabriel Konig, hit the bank and rolled at the Esses on lap 7. Thorne's car was repaired, but it really was the end of the day for the ex-Bending car.

Chris Smith had sold his original car to Worcester farmer James Tangye, who retained him as mechanic and (following the demise of the lightweight car) co-driver. They went on to compete in European endurance events in a Chevron B8.

At the beginning of May, around the time when he started to drive his old car again, Smith ceased to race under the Mike Dickin (Lubysil) Racing banner. The following month, his place in the team was taken by New Zealander John Dale, who worked for Janspeed; not unexpectedly, his car had a very quick 1316cc engine. He took a class-winning 3rd overall at his first Mallory outing, on 8 June. He went on to finish 3rd in class in the 1969 Chevron Championship and take the prestigious BARC Peter Collins Trophy for the year's best newcomer. Sprite

Chris Smith, now MD of Westfield, walked away from this heavy impact after hitting the bank at Snetterton in his ultra-lightweight Midget

Early Days of Club Racing

driver Alan Harvey was another person who was entered by the Dickin team, while Dale was later sponsored by Janspeed.

The Dickin threesome was a late entry for the 100-mile Prodsports race at Thruxton on 27 July 1969. By Spridget standards, this was almost an endurance race, although Dickin was confident that none of his cars would need fuel stops. He was, however, concerned that his drivers might dehydrate in their hot cockpits. He strapped a cyclist's drinking bottle, complete with plastic tube, to the roll cage of each car. It was a good idea, but in the thick of the action, the drivers hardly had time for a suck of liquid. Lynden Thorne, who was leading the team at half distance, retired later with a broken half shaft, but good pit signalling helped Alan Harvey and John Dale to class wins in the two smaller categories.

Mike Dickin agreed to use the remainder of the Lubysil money to hire a van so that Lynden Thorne could compete in the Nurburgring 500-km race, on 7 September 1969. Using a 15cwt Commer, they towed the Sprite to Germany. The roads were closed two days before the race and anyone could turn up, pay 10 Marks, and have a blast round the 14-mile (22.5-km) course in a road car. To help him learn the bends, Thorne paid up and he and co-driver Martin Ridehalgh trundled round in the Commer, much

Chris Smith proving that his Sprite can keep the bigger boys at bay, Woodcote corner, Silverstone, March 1969

Early Days of Club Racing

Rob Gibson scythes through the grass in his autocross Midget, circa 1968. He was to become famous in International Rallycross, driving an MG Metro 6R4

to the amusement of the local boy racers who were out in their 911s. The hire firm would have been horrified.

Thorne was concerned that if he used his usual 4.2 diff ratio, the car would run out of revs on the long straights. He managed to get hold of one of the special 3.9 ratio crown wheel and pinions that the competition department had made. During official practice, he was pulling 6,500 to 7,000rpm, which he calculated gave a speed of about 140mph (225km/h). Despite this impressive figure, he was not happy, as the steering was light and unresponsive. So he changed back to a 4.2, which, as well as stabilizing the car on the straights, made it a lot quicker through the corners.

The cars lined up in pairs behind the Mercedes pace car for the rolling start and at 1pm they were flagged away for the race, which would last for about three and a quarter hours. The Dickin team was running well in the Group 6 up to 1300cc class and finished 25th overall (there were over 120 entries), and 3rd in class, won by the Fiat-Abarth of Maurizio Zanetti.

ROBERT NETTLETON

In 1968 Robert Nettleton – another name well known today – entered the Marque Sports racing arena in an 1150 Sprite. Nettleton and David Holmes put together a car that they shared. It was powered by an overbored 'long-stroke' 1098 Midget engine, regarded by many as untunable; theirs was the later version with 2in (5cm) mains.

Nettleton retired for a couple of years, after selling the car to Ian Gorrie in 1974. He later made a comeback and has notched up many wins in both road-going and modified Sprites over the last eighteen years. David Holmes has taken on the role of chief mechanic, and the team are noted for their multi-coloured Midgets. Since his return, Nettleton, once described by a fellow competitor as the 'Alan Prost of Midget racing', has won several championships, including Donington (road-going) GT, MGCC Road-going Midget, MGCC Race-modified Midget and MGCC Cockshoot.

4 The Dick Jacobs Coupés

DICK JACOBS AND RACING

Dick Jacobs ran Mill Garage, an MG dealership in South Woodford, Essex, and was probably the best-known name for racing MG Midgets in the 1960s. He had been a racing driver of some note, but a bad shunt in an MGA at the ill-fated 1955 Le Mans race put him in hospital for four months and out of the cockpit for good. He subsequently found a niche as a private entrant, running cars for other drivers. It was in this role that he approached John Thornley at Abingdon when the Midget was announced. In an article published in the MG Car Club magazine *Safety Fast*, shortly after he retired, he described how the idea for his racing version came about. He sat at his desk with a copy of the Midget catalogue and a *Motor* road test of the Aston Martin DB 4 and evolved the basic shape of what was to become his famous MG Midget Coupé.

In an article entitled 'The Private Teams', a 1960s *Motorsport* writer stated that 'the team is run for the patron's pleasure'. This phrase was often quoted to describe Dick Jacobs' attitude towards his racing. But, much as the team enjoyed themselves, they also wanted to win. Many of the races at the time began with a Le Mans-style start (no longer used). At the drop of a flag, the drivers sprinted across the track, jumped into their cars and roared away. Jacobs decided that vital seconds could be won and lost here, so he drilled his team to perfection on a Sunday afternoon in a public car park in Wanstead. The drivers discovered how, by working out which hand to use to open the door and

The legendary Dick Jacobs on the grid at Mallory with his Andrew Hedges-driven Midget Coupé, in 1963

which leg to put in first, time was saved. Stop-watch in hand, Jacobs kept them at it till he was satisfied.

Dick Jacobs was always regarded by his contemporaries as a perfect gentleman. Mike Garton, a prolific Sprite racer in the 1960s, remembers him as a rival but also as a dear friend. He was always one of the first to come over and congratulate the winner when one of his Midgets was beaten.

JACOBS MG MIDGET COUPÉ

The Jacobs Midget Coupé was basically a production floor pan with a hand-beaten aluminium body bonded and riveted on. It had a very slippery nose cone, conceived by John Thornley, a fast-back hardtop, and weighed in at just 11cwt (560kg). Three cars were built at Abingdon but, with so many departments involved, they did not see the light of day until 1962. The engines were Formula Junior spec 995cc units, a little stronger than standard and producing 75bhp. This increase of power was aided by a twin-choke Weber, four-branch manifold and a well-worked cylinder head. To compensate for the extra power, Lockheed discs replaced the standard drum brakes at the front.

Two of these very special cars were for Dick Jacobs. Later, the third was delivered to Scot John Milne for racing north of the border. Wherever they appeared, the cars were always immaculately turned out, and the motoring press often commented on this at the time. From the fourteen races each car entered, twenty top four places were achieved, from twenty-eight starts.

THE JACOBS TEAM

Jacobs took delivery of the cars in early June 1962. As Tommy Bridger, who together with Alan Foster had driven for him in 1960, had decided to retire, he needed another driver to complete the team. Andrew Hedges, whose first race had been in a 3-litre Bentley and who had competed in an A40 against the likes of Doc Sheppard and a certain Frank Williams, came to Dick's attention. In 1961, Hedges had a number of successes in an aluminium-bodied John Sprinzel Sebring Sprite Coupé, 410 EAO, a car that obviously had similar characteristics to the Jacobs Midgets. Hedges' tally in the Sprite had included 4th overall in the Nurburgring 500km and an outright win in the Coupés de Paris.

Following a chat over lunch with Jacobs in the famous Steering Wheel Club at 47 Curzon Street, London, and a fruitful test session, 26-year-old Hedges (whose full-time job was as a sales executive for the London Bentley and Rolls Royce concessionaires, Jack Barclay) joined the Jacobs team.

On a rare visit to Britain in recent years, Andrew Hedges recalled that everyone in the team – Dick Jacobs, the drivers, and the mechanics – took part primarily for the fun of it. Pride of place on Hedges' study wall goes to an oil painting of him in the Midget, presented to him by Jacobs when the team was disbanded. He also gave him a crossed-flags trophy with the following inscription: 'To A.B. Hedges in appreciation of his team spirit and excellent driving during 1962, '63 and '64. Finished in the first three in class 42 times.'

Alan Foster, a long-time MG enthusiast, had first met Dick Jacobs when, as a customer of Mill Garage, he had bought a new car. He soon progressed to racing. He was doing particularly well in a Marque Sports Car event at Goodwood in 1956, but was forced to retire the car on the last lap. Jacobs happened to be in the paddock after the race and asked the young driver what the problem was; he was furious to learn that the car had simply run out of petrol. He asked when Foster's next event was, and announced that he would be there to run the pit for him. He then went on to prepare the car and subsequently Foster became one of the Jacobs team drivers.

The two cars, BJB 770 (Andrew Hedges) and BJB 771 (Alan Foster), were to become well known at circuits in Britain and in Europe and a force to be reckoned with for the next three and a half years. To assist the pit crews in distinguishing the otherwise identical cars, a white flash was painted across Hedges' bonnet, while Foster's had a yellow one.

Chief mechanic Gerry Neligan recalls that the team always had fun. He remembers one occasion when Tommy Bridger, who used to drive one of Jacobs' twin-cams, turned up at a meeting with his nephew in tow. The lad, Alistair, decided to make an effigy of Graham Warner's Elan, which at the time was the car to beat. Just before the start of the race, someone stuck a pin in one of the model's front wheels. To the team's amazement, and hilarity, as soon as the Lotus arrived on the grid, one of its front tyres promptly started to deflate!

THE 1962 SEASON

In the very early days, all Jacobs competition cars had been driven to and, if all went well, from the circuit. During the 1960 season, Jacobs had noticed that many of the front-running cars invariably arrived on a transporter, so he decided to get one of his own. He purchased an Austin (what else?) diesel three-ton removal lorry. Under the direction of his chief mechanic Gerry Neligan, this was converted to carry the two Midgets, one above the other. The upper car was loaded by hand-winching it up a pair of long runners made from Dexion. Only the Midgets were afforded this luxury; when Jacobs went on to run MG 1100s, he reverted to driving them to the circuits.

The Midgets were entered for the Autosport GT series and made their debut at Goodwood on Whit Monday, 11 June 1962. For some reason, which no one can remember, Foster competed in two races, whilst Hedges only took part in one. In the main event of the day, the 21-lap Whitsun Trophy Race for Sports and GT cars, Foster came

The Jacobs Team unloading in the Silverstone paddock in May 1963. Dick Jacobs and chief mechanic Gerry Neligan are at the rear of 770 BJB, while driver Andrew Hedges stands by his car. In the background is the transporter, a converted removal van

The Dick Jacobs Coupés

home 4th in the GT class, behind a brace of Marcos and a Porsche Carrera. Overall, he was placed 11th from twenty-five starters.

Both Midgets competed and finished in Event 6, a ten-lap thrash for Sports Cars up to 1200cc. Foster survived a spin on the second lap but, having got all four wheels 'off course', attracted a one-minute penalty. This was a controversial new move by the BARC, to discourage competitors from over-exuberant driving. Hedges upheld team honours by finishing 5th, while the 60 seconds added to Foster's time meant that he was classified 14th, out of seventeen starters.

It wasn't a bad debut for the Jacobs coupés, which attracted a great deal of attention in the paddock. Andrew Hedges says they were almost mobbed by MG fans, all wanting to photograph the cars. There was immediate speculation in the motoring press that Abingdon was set to introduce a production Midget GT; this, of course, never happened. Foster's spin at Goodwood was the result of a suspension malady, which meant that turning the car in for a right-hand corner produced terrible over-steer. He remembers being pleased with himself for making a really good start, then unceremoniously spinning off backwards at the end of the second lap. The cars were returned to Abingdon, where they were fitted with softer rear springs and special bushes that made them behave better.

Despite having to start from the back of the grid, Foster won the race for Sports Cars up to 1000cc at the MMEC Silverstone meeting on 23 June. This was the first of many fruitful visits to the Northamptonshire circuit for the coupé. Hedges took a 2nd the following week at Snetterton. On 22 July, they came home 2nd and 3rd in the BRSCC event at Brands. Other successes followed and by now the Racing Green projectiles were sweeping all before them on the home front.

The 1962 Goodwood Whit Monday meeting marked the first outing of the Dick Jacobs Midget coupés. Alan Foster at the wheel of 771 BJB

The Dick Jacobs Coupés

A contemporary report on the cars' appearance, at a wet meeting at Brands that August, was testament to their handling under any conditions:

'One of the outstanding features was the performance of Andrew Hedges' MG. In the pouring rain, the car seemed to be on rails, he pulled it through the field from 17th on the grid in the dry to 8th in the wet.'

Hedges still marvels today at how well the little cars handled in the wet. He won the class at an average speed of 74.06mph (120km/h), with Foster coming home 2nd, and Clive Baker's Sprite 3rd. To stamp their authority on the 1-litre GT race at Snetterton, on 19 August, the pair finished 1st and 2nd, crossing the line virtually side by side.

Dick Jacobs' previous exploits had not been limited to Britain, and he was keen to campaign the Midgets abroad. On 2 September, they formed part of the British team for the 'World Cup' at Zandvoort. The team won, assisted by Foster's 5th and Hedges' 6th place, the 995cc Midgets acquitting themselves well in the 30-lapper for cars up to 1600cc!

The season finished well, four weeks later, with the lads taking the first two class places in the Autosport Championship at Snetterton. The regs for this 3-hour event prescribed a compulsory pit stop for fuel and the last hour was driven in the dark. The team had to wait a few days for their victory to be confirmed. The lap scorers, it seems, were not used to races with pit stops, let alone watching cars circulate in the dark, so made some errors and 'lost' a few. The results were the subject of a number of protests.

The tally at the end of the Midgets' first season (actually only half a season's racing, as the cars were not ready until June) was four 1sts, five 2nds, one 3rd and three 4ths. The team also established an excellent reliability record, with neither car failing to finish the

This period shot of Brands Hatch shows the Marque Sports grid with the Jacobs Midgets in an unaccustomed position on the back

The Dick Jacobs Coupés

Andrew Hedges shares the front row of the grid at Mallory Park with an E-Type and an Elan in 1963

ten events entered that year. Although the team took in a number of rounds of the Autosport GT Championship, they had not seriously contested it. That was to be one of next year's objectives. In the races they entered, they usually managed to dominate the up to 1000cc class, Stephen Minoprio's Marcos being the only car to beat them.

THE 1963 SEASON

In October 1962 the 1098cc engine was announced, and during the course of the winter rebuild the two Jacobs Midgets were up-graded to 1140cc by using the maximum permitted over-bore. Extra breather pipes were installed and the sumps, which were baffled after testing, revealed a tendency for oil to blow out, a failing discovered by many drivers over the years. The cars were entered in the Autosport GT Championship for 1963. In the course of the season, it was discovered that running the new engine with a 948 head on it produced a significant improvement. This modification took three seconds off a lap round Silverstone, and was immediately implemented on both cars.

After early teething troubles, the new season went well, with the coupés in the hands of the same two drivers – Hedges and Foster. Conditions for the Snetterton International Meeting, on 31 March, were appalling. During the 25-lap Lombank Trophy Race for sports cars, fourteen competitors were recorded as having spun or run out of road. On lap 21, Andrew Hedges became another victim of the weather. Three-quarters of the way down the Norwich Straight, he aquaplaned and spun off into the ploughed infield, his car rolling onto its side.

Hedges had arrived at the circuit late that day and had changed for the race in a bit of a hurry. When the St John's Ambulance man arrived at the scene, he unbuttoned the blue racing overalls to check the driver over and discovered that the smart Mr Hedges, remarkably uninjured, was still wearing his business suit underneath. All was not lost for the team. Alan Foster kept it on the island, coming 3rd overall and taking a class win at an average speed of 73.85mph (119km/h), finishing two laps ahead of the next man in the class. The race was won by Graham Hill in an E-Type. At the end of the day, both the Midgets were to need repair as Foster's was damaged on the transporter. Seven days later, immaculate as ever, they took a class 2nd and 3rd at Oulton Park, a credit to the team's dedication.

The Jacobs cars often mixed it with larger-engined cars, but competition within the class was also hectic. There was an epic dice at Silverstone between Andrew Hedges and Cristabel Carlisle, having the only British race in a works Healey Sprite. This, the ultimate incidence of inter-marque rivalry, ended in tragedy when the Sprite crashed into the pit lane, fatally injuring a race official.

THE NEW DRIVERS AND NURBURGRING

Dick Jacobs had decided that the team would compete in the famous 1,000km race at Nurburgring on 19 May 1963. For this event each car would require two drivers. Keith Greene was known to Jacobs through his father Syd, whose Gilby Engineering company was a near neighbour to Mill Garage. Greene had already carried out some testing in the Midget, and, from the occasional Friday evening drink with Syd at the nearby Roundabout pub, Jacobs knew that young Keith was already an experienced campaigner in his Lotus. When asked, Greene jumped at the chance to join the team for the German Classic.

Greene looks back on those days with fond memories. He is still involved in motor sport, having followed the Jacobs path from racing driver to team manager. He ran the Renault team for the 1993 and 1994 British Touring Car Championship, owing, he considers, many of his management skills to Dick Jacobs, and using some of Jacobs' original ideas in the running of the team.

Having found Keith Greene, Dick Jacobs needed one more driver. He rang Chris Martyn and invited him to join the team for a test session at Silverstone which, as a BRDC member, Jacobs had been able to hire for his exclusive use. Martyn had all but retired from motor sport, but he had valuable experience, having raced his own Lotus 15 at the 1,000km in Germany the four previous years. Following his drive at Silverstone, he accepted the offer to partner Andrew Hedges.

That year there were only twenty-two British competitors at Nurburgring, out of a total of sixty-seven, and the Midgets were entered in the 1300 GT class. Hedges and Martyn came home 2nd in class, 2nd British car home and 13th overall, while Foster and Greene were 3rd in class, 15th overall. Chris Martyn describes the race as having a unique atmosphere: 'a sort of Sunday afternoon stroll…well, perhaps a bit harder work than that'.

Andrew Hedges in action at a wet Snetterton in March 1963, when his drive resulted in a rare retirement while lying 2nd in class. Alan Foster went on to uphold team honours by finishing 3rd overall

The Dick Jacobs Coupés

THE REST OF 1963

On its return from Germany, the team continued to enter races in Britain. The August Bank Holiday Guards Trophy Race produced a repeat of the previous year's 1-2 for the Jacobs cars, and they were then rebuilt for the Tourists Trophy meeting at Goodwood. Despite the overhauls, one car broke a crank. There was no spare engine available, so the previous year's 995cc unit was installed – not quite legal, as 1000cc was the stated minimum capacity for the event – and the car came home 5th out of nineteen starters in the up to 2-litre class. The race was won overall by Graham Hill in a Ferrari, taking a day off from driving his BRM Grand Prix car.

The end of the 1963 season saw Alan Foster take a class win (3rd overall) for the Jacobs Team in the Autosport Championship. He secured this by taking a class 2nd in the final round, the Autosport 3-Hour Race at Snetterton, on 28 September. It was a nail-biting race, as a blown head gasket necessitated about a dozen pit stops to take on water. If it hadn't been for this, Foster could have taken the overall victory, which in the end went to Roger Nathan's Elite. Both drivers had started the race with equal points.

THE 1964 SEASON

For 1964, the team looked to compete in more long-distance GT Prototype racing on the Continent and, having been denied an entry at Le Mans, readied the cars for the May event at the Nurburgring. March had seen the introduction of the 1275cc Cooper S block, which would be eligible in the Prototype class – the 1275 Midget was not introduced until 1966. The plan was to use the new blocks for events abroad, while revised 1098cc units, with the larger mains, were bored out to 1139cc for the British circuits.

Preparation for the long-distance events had included fabricating 18.5-gallon fuel tanks, upgrading the brakes, oil cooler and windscreen wipers, together with fitting stronger rear springs. As the 1964 engine was not homologated by the FIA until April, the cars were run with the smaller capacity power unit for the early part of the season. At the first outing, The International Easter Goodwood meeting, the cars took 1st and 3rd in class.

The next event saw a different face behind the wheel, Keith Greene being given the drive at the Oulton Park spring meeting. Greene was again due to share a car with Alan Foster in the forthcoming long-distance events. After, apparently, being baulked by an Elva Sebring Courier, the Midgets managed 2nd and 3rd in the class at Oulton Park, which was won by Jim Mackay in a Lotus 11 GT.

By the time of the May event at Silverstone, the new engines were 'legal'. Practice revealed problems which carried over into the race, when Foster fouled a plug on the line. The wet and windy 25-lapper was not, however, all doom and gloom, with Andrew Hedges avenging Jim Mackay's previous class victory by taking first place, beating him by almost a minute. Again, this was proof of the car's superb handling in adverse conditions.

The races in the early part of 1964 had been by the way of a build-up for the big one – Nurburgring – and the cars were now deemed ready, and shipped to Germany. For this event, the team pairings were the same as in 1963. The vast 87-car grid included just eight cars in the 1300 Prototype GT class. The Midgets came home 1st and 2nd in that category, having harried and then passed Mauro Bianchi in the works Alpine.

Andrew Hedges and Keith Greene also had the distinction of being in the first

British car home from the thirty-five that had been entered. Overall winner was the Ferrari 275P of Lodovico Scarfiotti and Nino Vaccarella. The cars, as ever, ran like clockwork; after the race, which lasted six hours, you could still have eaten your dinner off the engines. During 1963 and 1964 Chris Martyn's only races with the Jacobs team were at Nurburgring.

The coupés were to visit the famous German circuit again in August, joining up with John Milne's version to form the MG Team. Having lost out on straight line speed on their visit in May, Jacobs felt that the 4.2 diff was too high and calculated that a 3.9 would be the answer. Although the part was listed as a competition item, Abingdon did not have one available, so he had to make do with a 3.7, the standard Riley 1.5 unit. The MG Team drivers were Keith Greene, Andrew Hedges and John Milne, with Alan Foster nominated as reserve.

The 500km race for saloon and GT cars up to 1600cc saw an all-Abarth 1300 GT Prototype front row with the Midgets fourth, sixth and eleventh on the grid. It poured with rain at the start, making Jacobs regret the change of diff. John Fitzpatric's Cooper S led after the first lap, revelling in the conditions. His glory was short-lived, however, as the car succumbed to a common Mini problem – water in the ignition. By lap 3, Hedges was up to third place and he was soon pressing an Abarth for second. A pit stop by the Abarth team handed the Midget the lead but it was soon to come under pressure again.

Later in the race, as Andrew was slipstreaming the leading Abarth, they came up to lap John Milne's Midget. Milne moved over for the leading car, but failed to notice his team-mate and forced him off the road. The resulting pit stop, for attention to bodywork and replacement of a damaged wheel, demoted Hedges to eleventh place. The finish saw the MGs come home 4th, 6th and 11th, giving them 2nd in the manufacturers' team awards.

The last race for the Jacobs team coupés was their regular Autosport 3-Hour race, and the cars came home in a fitting 1-2 to provide Dick Jacobs with a storybook ending to his association with MG Midgets. This last season netted no less than fifteen top three places, and at the end the cars were prepared as if for a race and then returned to Abingdon.

JOHN MILNE

John Milne had successfully rallied, both at home and abroad, in MGAs, Minis and Healey 3000s, and was a leading light in the Scottish MG Car Club. Through the club, he got to know John Thornley, Managing Director of the MG Car Company, well, and this was how he came to be the owner of the third coupé. He competed in many events in his home country and won the 1966 Scottish Speed Championship in the MG, which, from time to time, was returned to Abingdon for service and up-dating. That year, he also came joint second in the Ingliston Championship.

During the four seasons from 1963 to 1966, Milne competed in thirty-three events and scored eleven 1sts, eight 2nds, five 3rds and three 4ths, and he was also a member of the winning team in the 1965 Croft 4-Hour relay. The car ran a variety of engines – a supercharged 1000cc unit for 1963, 1275cc in 1964 and 1139cc in 1965 and 1966. The engine may have changed, but the paintwork never did, and the car was always run in Scottish racing colours – dark blue.

Driving was not John Milne's only expertise. After the Nurburgring race in 1964, John, who was in the whisky business, insisted on buying everyone a Scotch in the nearest bar and ordered double Johnnie Walkers all round. He took a sip, and called

The Dick Jacobs Coupés

the barman over to tell him he had not been given the brand he had asked for. The barman argued but, when challenged to produce the bottle for inspection, refused to do so. He could not have known that Milne was a whisky expert, and he had picked the wrong man to argue with.

AFTER DICK JACOBS

Although not destined to appear under the Jacobs banner again, the MG coupés were entered in other events by the factory. In March 1965 they went to Sebring, where Andrew Hedges and Roger Mac (well known for successes in his ex-David Seigle-Morris Sebring Sprite 627 SKN) shared one car, and local driver Chuck Tannlund and Briton John Wagstaff the other. Part-way through the race, there was a thirty-minute cloudburst, when it rained so hard that the drains could not cope with it and the whole place was awash. Going along the straight, the drivers could see spare wheels floating down the pit lane.

Drivers of the larger, open cars had considerable difficulty but the closed Midget, with its smaller wheels, coped well in the appalling conditions. Hedges and Mac won the up to 1300cc GT class and came 12th overall, beating the two factory Bs, which came home 25nd and 32nd. The other Midget retired with engine problems.

Two months later, the Targa Florio beckoned and BMC Competitions Department partnered Andrew Hedges with none other than Paddy Hopkirk. Hedges remembers being very pleasantly surprised at the amount of money he was offered for this 'factory drive'. The pair travelled to Cerda in Sicily for the event, on 9 May, which was to prove to be the coupé's last real International showing.

The 49th running of this Italian Classic road race, which was started in 1906 by

Abingdon entered this ex-Jacobs Coupé for Chuck Tanlund and John Wagstaff to drive in the 1965 Sebring race. The car is pictured in the scrutineering queue

Vincenzo Florio, saw fifty-nine starters – twenty in the 1000–1300cc GT class. 771 BJB was the lone Midget among mainly European-built cars, including six Abarth Simcas and three Alpine-Renaults. The Friday practice session geared the drivers up for this unique event, often regarded as the toughest road race in the world. Each lap of the 45-mile (72km) street circuit took about 40 minutes to complete. Practice times were academic, as the cars started in class order, at thirty-second intervals, and the race was against the clock. The first competitor was flagged away at 8am.

Hopkirk took first stint at the wheel. He recalls spinning it during the early stages, and put his driving test (now known as autotest) experience to good use by executing a quick handbrake turn; he was soon on his way again, only losing a couple of seconds. For most of the race, the Midget ran 3rd in class, despite having to spend a while in the pits for the fitting of a cooling fan to stop it over-heating during the hottest part of the day. The green coupé made quite an impression on the Sicilian crowd and eventually finished 2nd in class, 11th overall. It was on the same lap as the race-winning Ferrari 275P/2 and only a minute behind the class-winning Abarth Simca 1300, after just over seven and a half hours of racing.

Paddy Hopkirk was well known for winning many events in various examples of BMC machinery and was particularly successful in driving tests at the wheel of Austin Healey Sprites. However, he is fairly sure the Targa marked his only race in a Midget. He was once called upon to make a detour on his way back from the 1964 Monte Carlo Rally and do a Midget demonstration drive in Singapore. He performed a series of handbrake turns in a town-centre car park that had been closed especially for the occasion, leaving most of the rubber from the almost new tyres on the tarmac.

Malcolm Beer drives the ex-Jacobs Coupé at MGCC Silverstone meeting, May 1992

Later in May 1965, one of the coupés was to make what proved to be its final International outing at the Nurburgring 1,000km. 771 BJB could only manage a class 4th in the hands of its former Jacobs pilots, Andrew Hedges and Keith Greene. Despite only entering four out of the nine qualifying events, the Midget Coupé scored a class 2nd in the World GT Constructors' Championship. This marked the end of the special Midgets' International history. The two cars were put in a corner at Abingdon and retired.

THE BEERS AND THE COUPÉS

The retirement of the cars was not, however, the end of the story. The coupés were acquired by Syd Beer, the proprietor of another well-known MG garage. Beer knew John Thornley well and had told him several times that he would be interested in buying one of the cars, should Thornley ever decided to sell. Just before Christmas 1965, Thornley rang Beer and told him that, if he still wanted one of the Midgets, he had better get to Abingdon with a trailer and pick it up. Beer did this, with Mrs Beer in the passenger seat of the tow car. After a conversation between her and Thornley, it was decided that, as they had two sons, the Beers had better come back and take the other coupé as well. The boys would then have one each.

The two green coupés were once again seen on the grids at club meetings, with one or other of the Beers at the wheel. A *Safety Fast* report on the MG Car Club's 20th Silverstone meeting, in May 1966, tells us that Malcolm Beer was second in the high-speed trial, while his brother Bruce, presumably in the sister car, was narrowly forced into the runner-up slot in the handicap race. Apparently, Bruce took the lead from Paul Langdell's TC going in to Woodcote on the last lap, but the out-braking manoeuvre resulted in him coming out wide, allowing the TC through to win by the narrowest of margins.

As Modsports began to evolve in the early 1970s, the cars once again became uncompetitive and needed radical change to stay at the head of the field. This did not happen, as the new owners did not want to chop these historic vehicles about. With the advent of wider wheels, drastic bodywork alterations would have been necessary.

All three coupés remain basically original to this day. 771 BJB took part in the celebratory 1988 Coppa d'Italia, a 1,000-mile event, entered by Syd Beer and Keith Gurrier. On this occasion the car did not run true to form, and retired on the first day. John Milne's car 138 BJB, as immaculate as ever in its original mid-blue livery, participated in the 1980 MG Car Club's Jubilee Tour of Britain. Having kept a low profile for some years, Milne attended the Abingdon Works Drivers Reunion in September 1994. Sadly, he died at the turn of the year.

Wanting to remain at the front of the Midget field, Malcolm Beer built his own modified car over the winter of 1969–70. On the club scene, this Blaze-coloured machine was to become almost as well known as the pretty little coupés. Malcolm had based it on a 1964 quarter-elliptic shell, using the know-how gained while running the Jacobs cars. At the May MG Car Club meeting at Silverstone in 1970, he had an epic dice with Ernie Foster and John Butler, in Midget and Sprite respectively. On this occasion, Malcolm came home 3rd, with less than two seconds separating the leading three cars.

1972 was Malcolm's year with this car; he drove at twenty-two meetings and came away with twenty-six awards. This fine tally gave him the MGCC Speed Championship, finishing well ahead of the opposition. He also had a class win in the Silverstone Sprint Championship. As a bonus, from only

The Dick Jacobs Coupés

Malcolm Beer's orange Midget pictured on its trailer

two starts, he came 7th in the Chevron Championship.

Although Malcolm is now better known for racing his awesome 3900cc MGB GT V8, the Beers still own the Blaze Midget and the coupés. 771 BJB appeared in the high-speed trial at the 1993 MG Car Club Silverstone meeting, lapping the new National Circuit at an average speed of 76mph (122km/h). This average speed is only 10mph slower than the fastest Modified Midget, running with a much larger engine, rear wing and nine-inch slicks!

THE END

Mill Garage, Dick Jacobs' original company, continued as a successful British Leyland dealership until 5 January 1974, when it closed its doors for the last time. Its demise, ironically, was brought about by the continued proliferation of the car in Britain, as the premises were demolished to make way for part of the M11. Dick decided to retire early and two years later published his book, *An MG Experience*. He died in November 1987, just a few days before his 71st birthday.

5 'A' Series Engine 948cc to 1496cc

The engine is the heart of any competition car, so the way in which the various sizes of 'A' series engine were developed to their maximum potential is interesting. In basic terms, the later the engine the stronger it was and, therefore, the more suitable for tuning. The exception was the Triumph-based 1500cc engine, which, some argued, proved not to be man enough for the job when stretched to the limit. The BMC practice of utilizing the same components for various models meant that Spridget drivers had a good supply of affordable, second-hand engine spares, not only from other Sprites and Midgets, but also from cars such as the Morris Minor and the Marina, the Austin A35 and A40, and later the Ital, with its much stronger 'A Plus' block.

As successive competitors searched for that seemingly elusive extra power, each basic engine size – 948cc, 1098cc and 1275cc – reached a stage when development outstripped reliability. Certainly, the early 1098cc engines (10CG serial numbers) with their 1.75in main bearings proved to be the weakest units, and when the bearings were up-graded to 2in (10CC serial numbers), they became a lot stronger. For the novice, its simple design made the 'A' series an easy engine to work on.

The original design was conceived by Johnnie Rix and Eric Bareham, who worked in the BMC engine facility at Longbridge. The cylinder head was noted for its heart-shaped combustion chamber, the brainchild of Harry Weslake. Weslake was a development engineer who had his own workshop in Rye Harbour, East Sussex, and often did work for the corporation. The 803cc unit that evolved produced 28bhp. The engine first appeared at the 1951 Motor Show, installed in the Austin A30 saloon. The car, in the words of one contemporary report, 'stole the show'.

The former Weslake building in Rye, East Sussex, where the BMC 'A' series cylinder head was developed

'A' Series Engine 948cc to 1496cc

The Midget was powered by the 948cc unit taken from the Austin Healey Sprite Mark I (Frogeye). This, in turn, was derived from the engine that powered the A30's successor – the well-proven Austin A35/Morris 1000 unit. Introduced in 1956, it produced a meagre 35bhp at 4,800rpm. When installed in the Frog, it had been breathed on a little to increase the power output to 43bhp. Most of this came from the twin inch and an eighth SU carbs, although the head did have stellited hard faced exhaust valves. To cope with the slight increase in revs, the valve springs were up-rated and the main and big end bearings were made of a higher-spec material.

The Morris 1000 and A35 had established a racing record of their own. Graham Hill and John Sprinzel had already become well known for their exploits in Austin A35s, and they, along with two others, set up Speedwell Conversions, a tuning firm that marketed kits that could be bolted on to various family saloons. The sporting motorists of the day could also buy Speedwell Supersport Austins, new cars fitted with the performance extras.

The announcement of the Midget in 1961 saw the compression ratio raised to 9:1. This, combined with twin inch and a quarter SU carbs, bigger valves with double springs, stronger crank and improved cam profile, gave an increased power output of 46bhp. The maximum over-bore increased the capacity to 1082cc, hardly a gigantic size by today's standard. Dick Jacobs did not go as far as this and used a 995cc configuration *à la* Formula Junior; this set-up was famed for its ability to rev.

Much of the development must be credited to Eddie Maher at Morris Engines, Court House Green, Coventry. It was he who evolved the Formula Junior engine upon which much of the Midget racing engine was based. Indeed, he produced the power units for the Jacobs coupés, and subsequently developed the 1275 in-line engine, which first appeared in 138 DMO, raced so successfully by Roger Enever.

The immaculate engine bay of one of the Jacobs Midgets

'A' Series Engine 948cc to 1496cc

In 1965, Mike Garton wrote the BMC 'A' series tuning manual. The book suggested that a race-tuned 948cc engine could produce 90bhp. It also stated that, in standard form, the same size unit could be revved to 6,000rpm, as it was well balanced. If the driver wanted to use 6,500rpm consistently, a 'Red' crank could be fitted, and this would take occasional bursts of 7,000rpm. Seeking any more than that would require the use of a Formula Junior item, and the block would need to be machined to accommodate it. Made from 90-ton steel and balanced, this crank would take 8,000rpm and was described as 'unbustable'.

Peter Denham, who campaigned a Lenham-bodied Sprite in the early 1970s, bought what he describes as the 'Formula Junior engine' that Barry Hopwood used to run in his racing Frogeye. This would pull up to 9,000rpm and was regularly revved to 10,000. Peter ran this 1082cc power unit without a rebuild until 1975. He had collected Hopwood's engine the day before a meeting at Brands and, having no time to fit it before the race, got a mate to bring it to the circuit, in case they had time after practice.

As it happened, he over-revved the old engine at the bottom of Paddock Bend, perhaps thinking of the spare one. He heard a noise, and thought it was the manifold coming loose, but the frantic waves from the marshals convinced him that something more serious was amiss; he pulled off onto the grass. Getting out of the car, he saw a trail of oil, which had come from a large hole in the side of the block. He made the grid, complete with new engine, but, having done two laps with one hand under the dash holding on a dislodged ignition wire, he was forced to retire.

Speedwell, already well known for tuning Sprites, soon got their expertise to work on Midgets. An *Autosport* road test by John Bolster, a noted motoring journalist of the day, reported that the firm had bored a 948cc engine out to 1080cc and fitted steel crank of standard stroke. Combined with special cam, lightening of the flywheel and rods, and a big valve aluminium head with Speedwell high ratio rockers, the power output was increased over one and a half times to 89bhp. The cost of the conversion was £250. Remember, in those days a brand-new Midget was only £599 ex-works!

Peter Denham with the Lenham, Brands Hatch, June 1975. The engine had a Formula Junior crank and was regularly revved to 10,000rpm

Announced by BMC in October 1962, the 1098cc engine, in standard form, gave 56bhp at 5,500rpm. Dick Jacobs soon had a couple of blocks bored plus 60thou, the maximum permitted under the regs, which increased the capacity to 1140cc. It was possible to get up to 95bhp out of a 1098 engine. This was achieved by over-boring and modifying the head by fitting larger valves with bronze guides; the block had to be pocketed to accommodate the valves. A 649 cam and duplex timing chain were added to the bottom end and the engine now breathed through a 45 Weber. In this guise the power unit was ideal for short club races, but it was not considered sufficiently reliable for long-distance events.

Most drivers or engineers were happy to tweak a 1098 in-line block, but a few did not want to do things the easy way, and decided that the 1071 Cooper S unit could be brought, as it were, into line. In 1967, long-time Sprite competitor John Elvers decided that this was the right way to find that extra power. He had an S block bored plus 60 and fitted with a set of modified Hepolite pistons. Meanwhile, the S crank had a flange, to take the Midget flywheel, welded on the end and he was well on the way to his 1115cc engine. The 12A 185 cylinder head was from the larger 1275 Cooper S; again it was necessary to pocket the block. At 8,500rpm it was quoted as giving just over 100bhp. To keep the moving parts well lubricated, the oil capacity was increased by deepening the sump by an extra inch and the oil pump was up-graded to a five-lobe version.

Alan Woode, one of Elver's main adversaries, followed a similar route for his 1150 engine, but could not afford the special pistons. He searched around for a cheap alternative and came up with the answer: a set of four Norton motorbike pistons, which gave a capacity of 1144cc. At the end of the day, they were not really strong enough for the job and after two blow-ups, Woode took to changing them every five races, just to be on the safe side.

Not all the innovative tweaks of the day were successful. Sprite campaigner David Pratley hit upon the idea of replacing the solid steel push rods with a set made from Titanium tube, thinking they would be lighter and much stronger. Alas, they broke after just two laps.

Tolerances are all-critical when tuning these little engines to such an extent. Some have found this out to their cost. Andy Bailey, whose Frogeye was well known in the early 1970s, bought a cam and an 1150 short-stroke crank from fellow competitor John Ling. Ling had lost his car when his garage burned down and was selling what little was left of it. Bailey built an engine incorporating these parts. He was unconcerned when he found it all a bit tight, while he was building it, but first time out it seized and a piston scored one of the bores. The crank and cam had been distorted in the heat of the fire.

All was not lost, as Bailey managed to get the crank straightened and the block linered, and the engine lived on. It was bolted back together the day before his next outing, leaving the driver with no time to run it in. To get round the problem, he loaded the Sprite on to the trailer, started the car's engine, wound up the tick-over, and left it running all the way to the circuit. He did cause a few raised eyebrows when he stopped at traffic lights, as the open exhaust system was a little 'rorty'.

The production 1275cc Midget engine emerged in October 1966. Based on the already famous Cooper S unit, this proved to be the most tunable of all the 'A' series engines. In a showroom car, it produced 65bhp at 6,000rpm, an increase of 6 brake on the old 1098 unit. It was de-tuned in the interest of production cost, the slightly lower power output enabling the material spec of some components to be reduced. Of course,

'A' Series Engine 948cc to 1496cc

The power unit is set back in the engine bay of the Heatherbourne Racing Midget; the split Webers and pipes to the boot-mounted radiator can clearly be seen

many drivers soon tuned it up to and beyond its transverse counterpart's specification. Because it was basically the same engine, Midget owners could benefit from the goodies which the specialist firms developed for the 'S'.

The cranks for the new engines were cast and machined at Wellingborough, at the same factory which produced those for the Mini Cooper S. One story goes that, during an early production run, the day shift produced a batch of cranks, complete with the flange, to which the Midget flywheel bolted. The night shift then arrived and, seeing the cranks on the bench, decided that something must be wrong, as the flange would prevent them being fitted into the Cooper S transverse block. They machined the flanges off the whole batch. Those early cranks were made of Nitrided EN 40B steel and are highly sought after by Midget racers today. The higher-spec material was much stronger and, therefore, much more able to stand up to the stresses of competition use.

Graham Paddy (now a director of Moss Europe) worked for Daniel and Bunty Richmond's Downton Engineering in Salisbury from 1966 to 1968. He remembers preparing a brand-new red 1275 Midget that arrived at their workshops in 1966. The company was to convert it for circuit racing, and he was allocated the job of building up the engine for what was to be a most successful car. Apparently, Daniel Richmond had the technical know how, but it was his wife Bunty who ran the workshop in a no-nonsense fashion. If your work was not up to scratch, you were out on your ear. The company was mainly known for tuning Minis, but they did also work on MGBs and a few Midgets.

In their heyday, Downtown did the heads and tuning for John Britten, and had a wealth of talent on the staff. Many of them, like Graham Paddy, went on to be successful with other companies, or in their own right. Ex-employees included David Dorrington (Maniflow Exhausts), Martin Goodall (Weber Concessionaires), Steve Harris (Steve Harris Motor Engineering), Paul Ivey (Race Engine Components), Richard Longman and George Toth (Richard Longman and Company), Len Lucas (GSC), and Jan O'dor (Janspeed).

Keith Ashby was looking to find more power for the Midget he bought in 1968. He managed to increase the capacity of an already over-bored 1275 unit to 1440cc, using a standard crankshaft. This was achieved by taking the block out to 75mm and using oversize Vauxhall Viva pistons, which would hardly seem suitable for the job. They were further weakened by the necessary process of boring out the gudgeon pin-holes to take the larger Midget pin. Despite this, and the thin gap between cylinders 2 and 3, this engine never blew a head gasket and even gave Ashby a number of wins.

In 1971, Graham Cooper, who ran his own tuning business (Graham Cooper Racing) in Birmingham, was among the first to take the 12CC blocked engine up to 1430cc. He used a secret boring formula and Triumph 1300 pistons to arrive at this capacity, achieved while retaining the standard-stroke crank. The engines he produced were torquey and pulled well within their 4,000 to 8,000rpm power band. Cooper favoured the Sprint cam and, although he advocated twin inch and a half SUs on his Mini engines, he found that Spridgets performed better on a 45 Weber. In those days of five-star petrol, Cooper recommended a 12.5 to 1 compression ratio, for reliability.

In 1972 David Lamyman, who had sprinted and raced a Sprite for four years, installed one of Graham Cooper's engines in his car and was very pleased with the 108bhp it produced at the rear wheels. Cooper himself ran a Sprite sprint car, for which he built a 1520cc engine. Not recommended as reliable for racing, the unit was so torquey it enabled the car to be sprinted using a 3.7 diff. Graham's ultimate feat, however, was a one-off 1556cc Mini engine for Bill Cole. It was not originally intended to be a one-off, but apparently Laystall had so many problems machining the crank that they refused to make another.

Another unique crank, of a completely different kind, was used in the Geoff Williams-designed, J.S. Whitehead Engineering-built engine, in Tony Williams' Team Ziebart Sprite in 1971. This 1297cc short-stroke engine had a special EN 25 Nitrided crank that had begun life in a BMC stationary diesel engine dating from the late 1950s. Geoff Williams saw one of these engines working while in Ireland and, having taken a couple of measurements, decided that if he could get hold of a crank it would have more than enough meat to allow it to be machined to fit a Midget block.

Through contacts he had made at Abingdon, Williams located and bought two crankshafts. The nose was about 21in long and the main bearings were 3in in diameter. This enabled him to re-grind to give the required stroke and still have enough metal to use a set of 1300 GT con rods, the larger-diameter big ends being considered much stronger than those of the Sprite. Given that the original diesel unit ran a 22:1 compression ratio, there were no fears for the strength of the finished crankshaft, even taking into account the drastic machining carried out to it. The crank was relatively inexpensive, but Williams had to pay £300 for a special set of 73.5mm Mahle pistons with the correct compression height; in 1971, this was a lot of money. The unique concept proved worthwhile, and Tony Williams took many victories and lap records with this Super Sprint cammed power unit.

The class structure was split at 1300cc. A plus 20 thou over-bore, with a standard (81.28mm) stroke, came out at 1293cc. By now, BMC Competitions Department had a whole catalogue of performance accessories available for the competitor, or for the enthusiast who wanted to improve the performance of a road Midget. The list included no fewer than five special camshafts. Most club racers tended to use the 'Sprint' or the very popular 'Race' cam, which became commonly known by its part number, 649. Many have tried the new computer-generated profiles, but have gone back to the 649, which was designed some 30 years ago, believing that it is still the best of the bunch.

In 1976, the class structure changed to 1150–1500cc. Long-time Midget competitor Chris Westell decided to build himself a long-stroke engine. Dick Skinner, who helped him with the car, worked at Abingdon and was able to buy a blank crankshaft forging. This was dispatched to Paul Ivey, who managed to find enough meat to machine it to give an 87mm stroke. Meanwhile, the block was bored to 74mm and, with Triumph pistons, a 1498cc engine was built up. Westell remembers that it had amazing torque, but was utterly unreliable, regularly blowing head gaskets. To increase performance and try to get it to stay together a bit longer, they went to Kidlington Airfield and talked someone into selling them some aviation fuel. This demon tweak resulted in the final detonation of the pistons, and it was back to the drawing board.

Gordon Howie was among the first drivers to build a big engine successfully. He got hold of some blank forgings, and his engine man had them machined. Even in those days, the total cost was £400 a crank. Now, blank forgings are almost impossible to find and steel billet cranks come out at around £1,500 each. Richard Ward, who often diced with Howie, decided the extra 50cc gained was not worth all the risk and stuck to a standard-stroke, offset-bore 1380cc engine, from which he saw 108bhp at the wheels. He does, however, admit to entering his car as a 1430, just to psyche out the opposition.

David Sheppard, who won the Modified Midget Championship in 1980 and 1981 with his Barry Chaplin-built 1485cc engine, experienced harmonic problems with his long-stroke crank. The sound waves would literally shake the starter motor to bits. To get round this, he used two very large Jubilee clips round the starter casing to stop the large Phillips-headed screw from falling out.

Personally I managed to get a blank forging and had a long telephone conversation with Paul Ivey, trying to persuade him to machine it to 87mm for me. He said that he had so many problems over the years with that length of stroke that he was not prepared to make them any more. If he were to machine it for me, 86mm was the longest I would get. As a result of his advice, my engines never exceeded 1460cc and in the main proved to be reliable.

As time went on, I learnt the hard way the dos and don'ts of building a 1275-based race engine. When looking for a block, I discovered that a thick flanged version was stronger than one with a thin flange. The one to use could be identified by the thicker flange on to which the sump bolts. If a proposed re-bore produces a capacity of over 1340cc, the bores must be offset or the very thin piece of metal between cylinders 2 and 3 will lead to gasket failure, or worse!

I remember building my first 1380 in the winter of 1979–80. One Sunday afternoon I drove, in my long-suffering company Cortina, over to Graham Paddy's fledgling Sprite and Midget Centre at Dorking, to buy a second-hand engine as a basis. I had already established it was a thick-walled block and, given the engine number was still intact, it was unlikely it had seen a re-bore: it isn't possible satisfactorily to offset-bore a block that is already over size. What I did not check was whether the oil had been drained. When I arrived home I discovered it had not, the engine had toppled over and all the oil had escaped from the dipstick hole and filled the bottom of the Cortina's spare wheel well! We learn by our mistakes.

Paddock preparation. Dave Sheppard changes the race numbers while his mechanic bolts on the aero screen. Adjacent to the nearside tyre is the aluminium air box, the larger of the two pipes at the rear of this is to let excess air escape. The unique Sheppard petrol tank is where the battery and heater are usually found on a Midget. Behind Sheppard is his trusty Marina van which could reach 80mph towing the Midget down the motorway

As the supply of Midget blocks began to dwindle, then drivers began to use the 1300 Marina item. These were reckoned to be stronger, although it was necessary to fit a sandwich plate below the oil filter in order to get take-offs for the oil cooler. The inverted filter meant that, when the engine stood from one race to the next, all the oil drained back, so I always turned the engine over with the ignition off and the plugs out to build up the pressure before putting it under load. Offset-boring a Marina block does have one problem: it is all too easy to break into an oil gallery if number 4 is set too far back.

The Marina is also a useful source of a cheap long-stroke crank. The standard Midget stroke is 81.33mm with 2in mains and 1¾in big ends. The Marina has the same stroke but with 2in mains and big ends. Having the mains offset ground to 1¾in increases the stroke to 84mm. It is not as strong as the steel item, but tuftride heat treatment does increase its life considerably. Utilizing a stroked Marina crank and a 73.5 over-bore produces an engine with a 1430cc capacity.

Lawrence Cutler, the 1992 Modified Midget champion, successfully used this format for some years. In fact, he ran his championship-winning engine, which produced 116bhp at the wheels, for twenty-one races without a rebuild. During this period, his tally was eleven pole positions, eight wins and thirteen fastest laps. This proves that it's not essential to spend a fortune on the ultimate engine in order to be successful.

The most a Midget or Marina block can reasonably be bored out is 74mm. To do this, the bores must be offset and, even if this precaution is taken, the very small amount of metal left between number 2 and 3 cylinders can lead to heat dispersal problems. This can manifest itself in a blown head gasket, resulting in loss of compression. Lucky drivers could just end up with a burnt-out piston.

The other popular engine sizes utilizing a bore of 73.5mm are 1460cc (86mm stroke)

'A' Series Engine 948cc to 1496cc

and 1476cc (87mm stroke). The 1476 has been used very successfully by Keith Ashby for many years. In fact, he used the same head, crank and rods in an engine that did about 400 events. He did have to build it into five different blocks, as the stress of the extra long stroke tended to crack the centre main housing away from the casting. This engine finally blew up on the first lap of the Midget race at Donington Park on 2 October 1988, but after 400 races he had had his money's worth.

Barry Chaplin, who built David Sheppard's engines, did once come up with a 1456cc unit. Stroking a Marina crank to 84.7mm, with 73.5mm pistons, gave this unusual size. The ultimate progression of maximizing bore and stroke is an 87mm crank (which has to be machined from a very expensive steel billet), with 74mm bore, which comes out at 1496cc. Only a superb engine builder, or a very lucky one, could get one of these to stay together for a whole season!

Steve Watkins built his engine to this format and used it to great effect in the Unigate-sponsored car that he raced from 1984 to 1987. Having done back-to-back tests on the rolling road, he found that, while both Sprint and Super Sprint profile cams gave the same top end, the Sprint gave better torque figures. He ended up with 110bhp at 6,500rpm and a maximum power output of 130bhp at 7,000rpm, all readings taken at the rear wheels. He used 1.5:1 ratio rockers and feels that these over-accentu-

Dave Sheppard with his engine-builder Barry Chaplin (left) after a win at Oulton Park, 27 June 1981

ated the overlap on the Super Sprint, which is why it did not work so well.

The engine that Steve Everitt ran from 1984 to 1987 successfully utilized a Super Sprint cam, but he only had Cooper S standard ratio rockers. It was built in an A Plus Ital block, which his friend Paul Grant polished and stress-relieved – it looked like chrome – and it had a specially made set of steel main caps to strengthen up the bottom end.

Using an 84mm or 86mm stroke crank means panel-beating the sump in order to get the webs to clear. With 87mm, the flange on the bottom of the block (the one to which the sump bolts) will probably need relieving with an angle-grinder. Incidentally, most Midget race engines have a baffled sump to prevent oil surge while the car is cornering heavily. I found an 86mm crank machined from a forging, with a 73.5mm bore, gave a 1460cc engine that was a good compromise between power (the best I saw was 121bhp, at the wheels), economy and reliability.

Since the 1275 'A' series engine first became available, various tuning firms have specialized in this particular unit. Richard Longman in Christchurch, Dorset, is probably still the best known of the old, established companies. Richard himself was a saloon car racer of some note, cutting his teeth in Minis. Brian Slark, also from Dorset, vies with the Longman company, as the maestro of the 'A' series cylinder head; his name is noted for big, big valves. Oselli Engineering in Oxford has always proved popular with all MG racers, while Jon Mowatt from North Benfleet (Mowatt started his career at Lotus, and was a very competitive Mini racer), Mountune Race Engines of Maldon, Swiftune of Bethersden, and Bill Richards of Ashford, Kent, are among other engine-builders who have constructed successful Midget engines. In recent years, Peter May Engineering from Lye, West Midlands, has established itself as the Midget specialist. Peter May started his engineering career as an apprentice at Morris and has been racing Midgets since 1979.

6 Supercharging

During the late 1960s and early 1970s several drivers, of both Sprites and Midgets, supercharged their cars – with varying degrees of success. This form of engine tuning offered tremendous advantage in terms of torque and acceleration off the line and out of corners, but reliability left much to be desired.

A supercharger is a mechanical compressor or pump, which artificially increases the pressure of induction gasses. At the time, two types were available: the Shorrock vane type and the Allard-Wade or Marshall, Rootes type. The Shorrock had a circular chamber with offset rotor hub, having blades fitted in slots, which spun round inside the cylinder, creating the suction. This was a development of the original Zola blower, which gave very high boost. If wear allowed the blade to hit the casing, the unit was prone to disintegrate. The Rootes type, invented in the USA, created its pressure from two lobes that turned round within a casing, generating a vacuum.

Both versions were available in various sizes, depending on the cubic capacity of the engine with which they were to be used. The unit was fitted on a special manifold, between the head and the carburettor, driven by a V belt from a re-designed engine bottom pulley. The belts had a habit of flying off, so most used a double pulley, with two belts, while others used a toothed belt to overcome this problem.

The RAC (now the RAC Motor Sports Association), the governing body of British motor sport, fully realized the power implications of supercharging and decided that a supercharged car had a 40 per cent advantage over a normally aspirated one. Therefore, any supercharged vehicle had its cubic capacity loaded by 40 per cent when calculating in which class it would run. A 1293cc Midget fitted with a 'blower' (as they became known) was regarded as being 1810.2cc. This was fine when the class structure had a 1301 to 2000cc class, but when the up to 1500 category was introduced, there was a decline in the use of superchargers. To keep under this limit meant blowing a 1000cc engine, which was arguably less reliable than the 1275 unit.

Having sold his well-known, 1969 championship-winning 1150 car, Alan Woode was looking for a new challenge. He decided to build an all-new supercharged Midget. He chose a Wade 1.5-litre supercharger, which he considered to be more reliable than a Shorrock. The 1275-based engine had steel main caps and ran 73mm pistons with extra deep dishes, which reduced the compression ratio to 9:1. It produced 128bhp at the wheels. The engine was not ready until some time towards the end of the 1970 season.

As well as having the engine set back 6in (15cm), Woode's new car also had the radiator moved back a similar distance. The back axle was located by four radius rods and a sliding A bar, while the chassis was beefed up in critical places to cope with the extra power. For braking, larger Ford discs replaced those at the front, while the rear drums were replaced with Mini Cooper discs.

Testing the car at Snetterton, Woode found that the engine lost power at the end of the main straight. Eventually, there was a large bang. Inspection back in the pits

Supercharging

Alan Woode's car, supercharged with the downdraught Weber protruding through the bonnet

revealed that the rubber pipes from the engine to the blower were in shreds. Despite 38mm chokes in the Weber 48-IDA carb, the car had been suffering from fuel starvation. The carburettor having run dry, the weak mixture ignited in the manifold. Replacing the fuel pump with a pair from a Jaguar cured the problem. Woode calculated that at maximum speed the fuel consumption was just 4mpg!

The car's first outing was at Silverstone on 31 August. After annexing pole position, Woode's joy was short-lived. Although the car really flew for the first five laps, leading the race, the blower jockey broke, forcing retirement. Third time out, he won the class and knocked five seconds off the class lap record for the Brands Hatch GP Circuit. The brief season finished on another low note, with the car spinning out of control into barriers at Thruxton on 11 October.

Over the winter, the body was repaired and further modified, with a fibreglass rear end and alterations to the headlights and grill surround to make the front more aerodynamic. The supercharger was also radically changed, the blower itself being moved in line with the inlet ports and the Weber changed for a 2.25in SU carb. An intercooler was added to cool the charge from the blower, the unit having its own cooling radiator and pump driven from the back of the

Alan Woode designed and made this unique front bodywork to make his car more aerodynamic

blower belt drive. Woode also decided to change the cam for the softer-profiled 731 and go for a dry sump lubrication system.

With hindsight, these modifications were too complex and the new engine failed to produce as much power as the previous year's. It also stressed everything to the limit with small initial problems, such as a stray carburettor screw and a chipped rocker, having disastrous results, and making blower and engine rebuilds necessary. After four retirements in a row, the highlight of the 1971 season was an overall win at Brands on 1 August.

Next time out, the car had another retirement, this time as a result of a failed centre main bearing. The last straw was an accident while running in the rebuilt engine at a Brands general test day. As the session was open to all competition cars, there were many different standards of driver. Woode was circulating at below racing speed and had just passed the pit lane exit when a Formula 3 car, driven by a young hot shot, came out, tapping him into a spin. The Sprite hit the bank very hard at over 70mph and the shell was written off. Woode clambered out of the wreck and collapsed in a heap.

After two days in hospital under observation, Woode contacted Peter Browning at Leyland's competition department, to see if he could secure a new shell at a discount price, but to no avail. He decided enough was enough and retired from racing.

Richard Gamble, the tall printing company director who started racing during 1973 in an 1150 Midget, won his class at Snetterton first time out, the new owner of Bob Neville's lightweight car. The following year, he fitted a Wade supercharger, with a Dellorto 45 carb, to his new 1275-based engine. He found that it was fairly competitive, when it stayed together, but it had a tendency to melt number 4 piston with frustrating regularity. The fuel metering valve was sometimes troublesome and, in fact, played up the day *Motoring News* put the car through its paces round Brands at the end of the 1975 season.

The Midget was raced under the Allard Supercharged Team banner, and in its heyday Gamble saw 160bhp at the wheels while pulling 7,000rpm. The red line had been moved back from its former destructive 8,000rpm and it had also been necessary to reduce the compression ratio from the original 9:1 to 8:1, to gain reliability. Lubrication was maximized by utilizing a dry sump system. Despite its alloy-panelled shell the car still weighed 12cwt (610kg).

Richard Gamble remembers a particular race at Mallory, in the hot summer of 1976, when the temperature got too much both for him and for the engine. Having destroyed yet another piston in practice, he cooled himself off with a swim in the lake during the lunch break, before returning home to strip down the engine yet again. There were, however, good days: at Brands on 11 August 1974 he was the meat in a Porsche sandwich, finishing 2nd, between the Ashtune- and Cartune-entered 911s.

The changes in the class structure, combined with unreliability, led to the abandoning of the supercharger. In 1976, the car was sold, in normally aspirated form, to Mike Hartley and Bob Woodley, who shared the driving. Richard Gamble went on to win, on several occasions, the big-engined class of both the BARC and BRSCC Modsports championships, in Jaguar E-Type and Marcos.

Ted Reeve currently competes in the Midget Championship and is one of the longest-standing Midget racers, having been around since 1969, when he bought Mike Bundy's car. Like all keen drivers, he wanted to make his car go faster. In 1970, he befriended fellow Spridget racer Alan Woode, who convinced him that the way to maximize power was to supercharge.

Using a block bored plus 60 thou, he added a Shorrock 1.5-litre supercharger and a Weber 48-IDA down-draught carb, which protruded through a hole cut in the bonnet. The engine, which had a standard crank and a compression ratio of 9:1, ran 14lbs of boost. The actual capacity of 1340cc, subject to the 40 per cent loading, gave a notional figure of 1876cc comfortably within the 2-litre limit of the time. The actual power output was 138bhp at the rear wheels. Reeve later changed to a 2-litre Shorrock and a Weber 45 DCOE, the side-draft version more usually found on Midgets.

Although no fuel consumption figures were ever kept, Ted Reeve reckoned that, flat out, the engine needed one gallon every three minutes. To achieve this flow, he had to bore out the needle valve with an eight drill and then dress the needle in with grinding paste. This vast volume of petrol caused severe flooding on tick over, and to get round this problem he installed a pump switch.

At the MG Car Club race meeting at Brands Hatch in April 1974, Reeve's supercharged car took pole position for both the Modsports and Spridget races. He led the twelve-lap Modsports encounter until ex-Mini pilot David Hipperson skilfully used the back-markers to get his Midget past him on lap 5. In the Spridget event, Reeve was first away at the drop of the flag and held the lead until lap 2, when second-row man Hipperson again managed to get by. For the next two laps Reeve pressed him to get his place back, but on lap 4 the V belt for the supercharger came off the pulley.

Although he was passed by Andy Bailey and Malcolm Beer, Reeve (now normally aspirated) still managed to come home 4th. David Hipperson was running the ex-Sprinzel London to Sydney Marathon car, which he bought from Charles Ivey. Hipperson says this car handled slightly better than Reeve's and he usually managed to get up the inside at the hairpin. He was also able to pass him at Clearways, but that was a waste of time, as the supercharged car was always back in front again along the start-finish straight.

Ted Reeve's first appearance with the supercharged car at a MGCC Midget Championship round was an occasion to remember. The race was at Snetterton on 13 April 1980. In practice Reeve did a 1:20.7 to get on the middle of the front row, headed only by David Sheppard who set a 1:19.9 to gain pole. After practice, championship co-ordinator Larry Quinn was inundated with protests about the Reeve car. It had been openly entered in the programme as a 1340cc supercharged Midget; other competitors were quick to point out that applying the 40 per cent rule brought it over the 1500cc championship maximum. Reeve drew their attention to the wording of the regulations, which he had construed as allowing drivers to supercharge an engine that had an *actual* capacity of up to 1500cc. The organizers had to admit that the rules were ambiguous and, as Reeve had entered in good faith, allowed him to continue with the car as it was until the end of the season, but with his points suitably loaded.

David Sheppard was involved in a start-line shunt, when a road-going class car from the back of the grid ran into his car, wrecking the aluminium rear bodywork. So Reeve won the race without the dice for which he hoped. Inevitably, with little pressure from any other driver, his fastest lap was nearly three seconds slower than his practice time.

Eventually, Reeve brought his car down a class. The smaller engine – 1070cc, which, plus 40 per cent, came out as 1498cc – just came within the limit. It utilized the same blower and carb, but the pressure was reduced by using a bigger top pulley and longer V belt. This engine was raced only three times, and at Mallory one of the push rods wore through the head. During the race, this allowed oil into the combustion chamber, resulting in the car leaving a great

Supercharging

trail of smoke around the circuit. It marked Ted Reeve's last appearance in a supercharged car.

Malcolm Beer had a brief flirtation with supercharging in 1976, when he built his green Midget. He wanted to take part in two classes in a sprint series and put together this particular version to compete in the larger class. It had coil-sprung rear suspension and a 'bloody great Wade blower' for its 1275cc engine. Malcolm's race debut in the car was at the MG Car Club winter Brands event, on 7 December. A disappointing practice for the Modified MG race, as a result of back axle problems, saw the car on the fourth row.

The diff was changed during the lunch break, and when the starter, 'Hector the Rector', dropped the flag, Malcolm was up to third by Paddock. He gained second, when Geoff Weekes retired as a result of overheating, but was not able to catch Keith Ashby, who had pulled out a comfortable lead. The later Modsports thrash resulted in Beer turning the tables on Ashby and keeping him at bay to take a win. He had to work really hard for it though; Ashby was right with him every step of the way, and his car was better sorted in the suspension department than Malcolm's, which was 'straight out of the box'. It was so close, the pair set joint fastest lap at 56.2 sec (79.43mph/127.9km/h).

Subsequently, Malcolm entered a sprint at Silverstone, one of the series for which the car had been built. On one of his timed runs, the car hit a puddle at Woodcote and rolled end over end about five times. The driver escaped with a grazed elbow but the car was destroyed. It was never rebuilt.

While the supercharged Sprites and Midgets did not always prove reliable on the circuits, drivers who used them for hill climbs found that the engines could cope better with the relatively short bursts of power needed. Russ Ward bought a road Sprite in 1965 and soon started competing in it. By 1968 it was in such an advanced state of tune that use on the highway became impractical. After seven successful years, he decided he would supercharge the car, and over the winter of 1974-75, he modified the head and bolted on a Wade RO 20 blower.

The 1293cc engine ran an 8.9:1 compression ratio and produced 145bhp at the wheels, which propelled the 12cwt (610kg)

An under-bonnet shot of Russ Ward's sprint and hill climb car, showing the supercharger

car along at a good rate. There was, however, one problem: the engine had an intermittent misfire. It came to light that, despite using thicker studs, the head was lifting slightly between cylinders 1 and 2, with the resulting water mist shorting out the distributor cap. Ward decided that he could accept losing a little coolant, so put a Mini waterproofing gaiter over the cap, which cured the problem. In 1976, the car ran the whole season without breaking a thing, netting Russ the RAC Leaders Hill Climb Championship. There was no mistaking Ward's car – to ensure the charge was cool, the Weber 48 IDA sat on a special long inlet manifold, and it perched about 14in above the bonnet.

For the following year, Ward aimed at the unlimited capacity class. Using Triumph 75mm pistons, he took the engine out to 1400cc, scaling up the boost and carb jetting from those used on the 1293. Although the car continued to do well, Ward was finding, rather like the circuit racers, that the Sprite was no match for the Elans and Davrians. It was sold to Irish driver Pat McGarrity. During the eleven years Ward ran the car, he scored over 200 class wins. He still competes, currently in a 1978 F2 Chevron with a Tuscan spec Rover engine.

Other drivers who raced or sprinted supercharged Spridgets include Steve and Jill Ashby (who subsequently turned their Midget into a Westfield); John Finch, whose car then went to Mark Hales; Keith Hartley (the ex-Gamble car); David Pratley; and Lynden Thorne. During practice for the Autosport Trophy event, at Castle Combe on 3 October 1970, Thorne put his Sprite on the second row. In the race, he made a superb start to outdrag the two front-row E-Types into Quarry. He led for the first lap and ran second for lap 2, until the second Jag managed to get by; Thorne still finished a safe 3rd.

Mark Hales recalls that his example was very noisy and had appalling handling characteristics. Coming through the old Russell bend at Snetterton in one race, right on the limit, he got it badly out of shape on the exit. Everyone signalling in the pits jumped back from the wall, thinking he would hit it, but he managed to keep it all together.

Probably the most successful of all the drivers who took the supercharged route to power was Richard Jenvey. Not only a brilliant driver, but also a very clever engineer,

Russ Ward corners hard on the hill in his multi-award-winning supercharged Midget

he was able to ensure that his engines stayed together. Richard started racing in a self-built Modsports Midget in 1971. He built his car around the shell of a road Midget that had covered just 15 miles before its unfortunate owner had written it off. He straightened the shell, built a 1275 engine and won his class at Brands second time out, taking his first overall victory in the Spridget race at a Castle Combe Austin Healey Club meeting.

This normally aspirated car was competitive within its class in Modsports races, but eventually Jenvey got bored with being the first Midget home. He decided that the only way to win outright, and beat the likes of John Fletcher's Lotus Elan, was to supercharge his own MG. He had considered turbocharging, on the basis that a turbo uses less of its own power than a supercharger. In 1972 Barry 'Whizo' Williams had done well in a turbo Mini built by Harry Ratcliffe, later of British Vita fame. However, early turbos sucked through the carbs, which created mixture problems and this, as far as Jenvey was concerned, tipped the balance in favour of a supercharger.

He bought an Allard Wade unit which he mated to a distinctive home-cast inlet manifold, which had protruding spikes to aid cooling. He fabricated a plate to bolt on the single Dellorto 48 carburettor and decided on a 597 'Sprint' camshaft. Following post-testing modifications, the engine showed 165bhp on a rolling road, the somewhat narrow power band being between 6,000 and 8,000rpm. However, Jenvey calculated that it was producing a further 50bhp, which was absorbed by the unit in driving itself. Run with just over 2-bar boost, it was driven by a toothed belt and utilized a Jenvey-designed and built exhaust manifold and 2in diameter pipe system.

Externally, the car looked much like other racing Midgets, although, to aid weight distribution, the engine had been set back some 8in (20cm) in the chassis. The body was all glass fibre, weighed just over 10cwt (500kg), and was recognisable by the holes in the flip front for the supercharger and the very short exhaust system. The pipe, in fact, exited the bodywork, just behind the nearside front wheel – there were no silencers to worry about in those days. The car was ground effect, the slots in the fabricated aluminium boot floor utilizing air from the rear-mounted radiators. A contemporary track test in *Cars and Car Conversions* was very complimentary about the car's performance.

Richard Jenvey's supercharged Midget at Castle Combe, 27 August 1973

The car first appeared in supercharged form at Brands at the start of the 1973 season and did what Jenvey expected of it: it gave the Elans a run for their money. Awarded pole for the Blue Circle Modsports race at Silverstone (beating Elans, XK 120s and a TVR), sadly he retired with a split petrol tank. He could lap the old short circuit at Silverstone in about 60 seconds, which equates to an average speed of just over 90mph (145km/h). Ten years later, the Midget lap record for the same circuit stood at 63.3. This was set by Keith Ashby, without a supercharger, but on far better tyres than those available to Jenvey.

Throughout its time in supercharged form, the car always suffered from over-heating. For a while the radiator was repositioned at the front, but this failed to provide a cure. In the end, a warped cylinder head proved to be the problem. In order to get the maximum metal to work with, Jenvey bought a brand new head. He needed to reduce the compression ratio and considered it cheaper to enlarge the combustion chambers than to buy special pistons. It turned out that it was a distorted casting, and he cured it by stress-relieving – he used a welding torch to heat it up as much as he dared and then left it to cool, before machining it. Although the new head reduced the running temperature appreciably, he still found his engine would get hotter during the closing stages of a race.

He recalls an outing one hot day at Cadwell Park, when he broke the lap record on the first (standing) lap, but the remaining lap times were marginally slower. This led him to believe that the rolling road power figures were not an indication of the true maximum, given that the power runs were always carried out once the car had been warmed up. He claims never to have blown an engine up, although he did finish one race with low oil pressure, and the resulting strip-down revealed a cracked crankshaft

The Jenvey tow car was a rather quick Austin A40, powered by a self-tuned 1275 Midget engine. Being an 'A' series car, it was occasionally cannibalized to provide spares for the racer – the disadvantage was that it all had to be put back before the team could get home. As he was competing in both the STP and Chevron championships, some weekends would see him race at Lydden on Saturday and Croft on Sunday. I have promised not to reveal the journey times quoted to me. He also used the A40 for holiday trips, and on one return journey they were running late for the ferry and averaged over 100mph (160km/h) on the way to the docks. That one still rates as the fastest road car he has ever driven.

Jenvey's Midget came second to Jon Fletcher's Lotus Elan in the 1972 Chevron Championship. Despite his continued development of the Midget, Jenvey found that the Elans were also going faster and faster, so he decided 'if you can't beat them, join them', and built his own. In 1975, he fulfilled his ambition and won the Miller Organs Modified Sportscar Championship in his Elan.

Before the Midget was sold, Allards, who had got to know Richard Jenvey well, had the car back at their works to duplicate the Jenvey-style manifold and installation kit, so they could incorporate it in their off-the-shelf kit available to other customers. The cooling spikes Jenvey had originally used were replaced by more orthodox fins in the casting. When this was done, the car went to hill climber John Hall in 1974. When I asked Jenvey which of his two racers he preferred, he answered that for sheer speed it had to be the supercharged Midget.

In theory, supercharging promised much, but in reality fitting a blower to the BMC 'A' series engine rather overstretched it. Most drivers who chose this route of tuning found this out to their cost. When all went well, the power produced was phenomenal, but reliability was always hit and miss, and this was hardly surprising given that the engine block designed for the 1952 Morris Minor was, in some cases, producing nearly 200bhp at the flywheel in supercharged form twenty years later.

7 The Abingdon Connection

BMC had an arrangement with the Donald Healey Motor Company that Healeys would race Sprites on behalf of the manufacturer, and that the works would not race any Midgets. Stuart Turner, a former Comps Manager at Abingdon, maintains that there was no need for them to race Midgets, because Healeys were doing it for them, with Sprites. He only entered Midgets in certain International rallies, in order to gain class wins.

ROGER ENEVER

At the 1964 Mallory Park Boxing Day meeting, red Midget 138 DMO first appeared on the club racing scene, in the hands of Morris Commercial Cars apprentice Roger Enever. The car went well on its initial outing, finishing 3rd in class. Enever was no novice, having raced both standard and modified MGAs. His father Syd was MG's chief engineer, and 138 DMO was the works development car, but it was entered privately by Enever. Many assumed, wrongly, that it was a works entry. Although it wasn't, the close connection with the car's manufacturer was obviously a great help to Enever's endeavours on the track.

The prototype G-AN3 (wind-up window) half-elliptic Midget 138 DMO was first registered by the MG Car Company on 7 October 1963. It was originally assigned the works registration number MG 1, but this was transferred to another factory car in 1964. John Thornley, the former general manager of the MG Car Company, subsequently had

Abingdon, October 1994. Number One Gate, and, behind it, the remaining part of A Block of the MG Car Company Works, closed in October 1981

this, the marque's ultimate personal plate, for his BGT.

Originally a production car, 138 DMO was soon modified and appeared in various guises over the next three years, but always retained its 5in wire wheels. For a while, it ran with an alloy long nose, a spare from one of the ex-Jacobs cars, an aero screen and single roll hoop over the driver's head, adding to the sleek lines of the now open car.

To assist with the development work for the GAN 4 Midget, the car was fitted with a 1275cc engine on 2 July 1965. The engine number was XSP 2195/3. The XSP identification prefix was given to all special engines built by Eddie Maher's department at Coventry – 'XSP' was short for 'experimental special purpose'. The first 1275 Midget power unit was based on a Cooper S block, complete with removable tappet chests, turned round the other way. The crank, again an S derivative, had a flange welded on the end to take the Midget flywheel.

The car was steadily developed and had a series of victories in Roger Enever's hands. The weight was reduced from 13¾cwt (700kg) on 17 August to 12¼cwt (620kg) a year later. The car went on a weighbridge once a month and they went to great lengths to pare down the weight, even going to such extremes as drilling the door handles and striker plates. Even the front brake hose lock plates were meticulously drilled with a series of progressively smaller holes.

On 22 May 1966, Enever took part in what proved to be one of his worst races, at Castle Combe. He got boxed in at the start and had to force his way back through the field. In the closing stages he was catching the class leader, Bill Bradley's Spitfire. Approaching Camp Corner on the last lap, Enever was only 50 yards adrift; he braked, lost control and spun, launching the car into a series of rolls, end over end. The Midget hit the bank hard, completely destroying the shell, within sight of his pit crew waiting at the finishing line. Enever suffered concussion and was heard to mutter instructions about digging out another car for the race the following weekend. The Midget was re-shelled and painted black, which had by

Roger Enever in the development 1275 MG Midget, 138 DMO, leads John Britten through Druids at Brands Hatch

then become the standard colour for development cars.

In 1968, Enever's last season with the Midget, he claimed five class and six overall victories, and he also established lap records at six circuits. As a result of this tally, he won the 1151–2000cc class of the Brands Hatch-based Amasco Championship, narrowly beating Rod Longton's MGB-engined TVR. Both drivers scored twenty-nine points, but Roger got the verdict as he had the higher number of class wins. He also came 2nd in class in the Freddie Dixon Championship, where drivers competed at circuits all over England. In addition, he received one of the prestigious Grovewood Awards.

During the year, Enever was finding it increasingly difficult to beat John Britten's Midget, a lighter car. In order to solve this problem, he came to an arrangement with his friend Garo Nigogosian, the owner of another very successful ultra-lightweight Midget. He borrowed Garo's car and raced it with his own 1293 engine, complete with an early 'split' 45 Weber set-up; he raced this car in this guise about five times. On these occasions, he would transport the engine in the back of his Austin 1800 to Garo's house in Muswell Hill, North London, where his brother would help with the swap. Enever also ran on his own wheels and tyres. Driving this combination of lightweight car and Abingdon-prepared power unit, Enever was able to get on terms with Britten and beat him.

The arrangement was sometimes reciprocated. On one occasion at Brands, Garo raced 138 DMO in the smaller class with his own 1150 engine installed, and enjoyed a good dice with John Britten and his teammate Gabriel Konig. While Enever was undoubtedly quicker in his friend's car, Garo found 138 DMO to be extremely stable on the corners. His own car was so light that the rear end would tend to bounce under heavy braking. Perhaps each respective driver's style really suited the other's car. It has also been suggested that Enever liked a new challenge (he did, after all, go on to drive many different cars), and that mastering Nigogosian's lightweight version was another way of putting further demands on his skill as a driver.

Neither was it unknown for Garo and Enever to swap cars and race against each other. This they did at the London Motor Club event at Brands Hatch on 24 Novem-

A rare photograph of Roger Enever driving Garo Nigogosian's Midget to an outright win at Thruxton, his reward 200 packs of Calypso cigars

Three wheels on my wagon! Although a little out of focus, this photograph illustrates the problems many drivers experienced with broken halfshafts. Garo Nigogosian at Paddock Bend, Brands Hatch

ber. Despite losing it at Druids Hairpin on lap 3, Enever just managed to pass the Nick Faure Porsche 911 in the closing stages and take a class win. John Britten was unable to find a way past the German machine and had to settle for 3rd. Garo, in 138 DMO, did not fare so well; the gearbox jammed in top and forced him to retire.

Thruxton circuit was established by the BARC at the Hampshire aerodrome at the start of the 1968 season. The club had been forced to look for a new venue to replace Goodwood, the famous Sussex track, when it was closed after 18 years by its owner, the Duke of Richmond, in 1966. The Duke had taken the decision in the summer of 1966, saying that he was fearful for crowd safety, considering the ever-increasing speed of racing cars.

Roger Enever appeared in Garo's car for the season closer at Thruxton on 13 October 1968. He headed the practice session for Sports Cars up to 2000cc, 2.8 seconds clear of the next man. He won the race, beating Gabriel Konig and bettering the lap record of her team leader John Britten into the bargain.

Garo and Enever again swapped cars for the final two winter clubbies at Brands in December. Their outing at the Mini 7 meeting was to prove successful for one and disastrous for the other. Garo enjoyed a good race in 138 DMO, winning his class and coming 2nd overall. Enever, who had held second spot for eight of the ten laps, was forced to retire on the penultimate tour with a broken half shaft. At the Christmas Trophy races Roger Enever bowed out of Midgets in style, with an overall victory. Running 4th, Garo found the Enever car stuck in second gear; not wanting to wreck his friend's engine, he was forced to ease up and in the end came home 6th.

Enever had almost pulled off an overall victory in the Alec Poole Sprite on the Silverstone Grand Prix Circuit in October. Had he won, it would have been a real turn-up for the form book. It was not uncommon to see Spridgets beat the bigger machinery on smaller circuits such as Lydden or the Brands Club, but the E-Types and others usually won on the longer tracks. At Silverstone, Enever came to the head of the field after Tom Leake, who had led from pole, spun his Aston Martin DB4GT to the back of the pack. He managed to pull out a cushion on the following Healey 3000 and AC Cobra, but a broken half shaft deprived the Sprite of eventual victory.

ALEC POOLE

Another Morris Commercial Cars apprentice, Alec Poole had started rallying his Mark I Sprite, TZA 238, in 1963. Poole's father was the Irish main dealer for Nuffield group cars, not only selling them but also importing them in CKD form for assembly in Ireland. Poole's great friend Bob Neville, also learning the business at Morris, helped him prepare the car. Neville recalls that as a result of the Pooles' unique position, young Alec was able to get a transfer to Abingdon; apart from any other benefits, this greatly assisted him in the love of his life – motor sport.

Alec Poole had acquired the Sprite during one of his visits home to Ireland. Its previous owner had found the bonnet too heavy and had part-exchanged the car for a Midget at the Poole dealership. Alec spotted the car on the forecourt and managed to get his hands on it. He brought it back to England with him and used it and abused it on numerous night rallies. Appropriately, he won the Donald Healey Trophy Rally, organized by the Austin Apprentices Association CC, on 9 and 10 November 1963, with co-driver J. Bilton. In 1964, he did a few sprints and races at Brands and immediately got the taste for racing. One day at Abingdon, he noticed a new Frogeye shell sitting in the corner of the yard and it occurred to him that this would make the ideal basis for an out-and-out racer.

He asked around and established that the shell had been there for a while. The young apprentice sought a meeting with John Thornley, the MD, at which he bowed and scraped, suggesting that, if the shell happened to be surplus to requirements, he could put it to very good use. Two days later, he was summoned back to the corridors of power and told that it was his for £5. The shell had been used as a jig by the hood manufacturers, who had returned it to the factory once the Mark II Sprite was in production. For a fiver, the body came complete with doors and a steel Frogeye bonnet.

During the winter of 1964–65, Poole was involved in the preparation of the ex-Jacobs Midgets for Sebring. In such cases, it was standard practice to replace items of running gear and suspension with new components from the production line. Poole persuaded his foreman that the old parts should be scrapped. Thus began the assembly of the legendary Alec Poole one-eyed Sprite, so named when the nearside headlamp was removed to make room for the carburettor air intake. Poole became, in his own words, 'a bit of an 'A' series Steptoe', scurrying around the factory in his lunch hour collecting second-hand bits for his project.

He even visited the Donald Healey works at Warwick in his quest for parts. Here he made his second lucky find. Among Healey's stock of used sports cars was a Mark I Sprite that had not attracted a buyer. Geoff Price, the workshop foreman, confided in Poole that the aluminum Frogeye bonnet, which in his opinion did not look quite right, was probably the reason. Poole suggested he would be prepared to swap his unused metal one for the lightweight version on the car, and the deal was done! During another visit to Warwick, he was rooting about in the yard

A brace of one-eyed Sprites at Crystal Palace: Ian Hall (91) heads Arnie Poole (93) in the ex-Alec Poole car TXA 238, at North Tower Bend, August 1969

at the back when he found a mould for a Frogeye one-piece rear; he managed to borrow and use the mould to make a lightweight rear body section for his own car.

Poole's new Sprite was now coming together very nicely. The registration plates had been transferred from the original car, which had suffered a few too many rolls on Welsh rallies. Poole's search for replacement parts had proved so thorough that only the prop shaft and pedal box remained from the Sprite that he had brought over from Ireland. He had come by a 3-gallon baffled fuel tank, and all that he needed now to complete the job was a competitive engine.

Early in 1965, Alec Poole's dad was able to persuade Eddie Maher, head of the Coventry engine department, to let them have one of the early 1275cc engines to put in the Frogeye. It duly arrived, was unpacked from its crate and bolted in. As soon as it was fired up, Alec jumped in the car and took it for a spin up the road. He was amazed at the performance – the engine had been built to full race spec.

Poole quickly honed his skills and fast gained recognition as a racing driver, scoring eight wins during the season. He enjoyed a particularly successful 1966 Whitsun, just days after returning from driving one of the ex-works Healeys at Spa. On Sunday, at the BRSCC event at Brands, his Sprite came 2nd to Bernard Unett's Alan Fraser-prepared, Sunbeam Tiger, beating John Quick's E-Type into 3rd on the Grand Prix circuit! He also set a new lap record. Monday the 31st saw him racing in the Nottingham SCC meeting at Silverstone. On the club circuit, he won outright and set fastest lap. This time it was Henry Synowiec's E-Type that was second best, the Jaguar driver narrowly beating the big Healey of Stuart Hands for 3rd. At Oulton Park on 10 July, not only did Poole take his class in the Sprite, but he also won the Alan Brown Trophy race for saloons, by four seconds, driving a Wolseley Hornet.

The Abingdon Connection

Oulton Park on 7 August was the scene of an even more audacious outing for the Poole Sprite. He harried the leading E-Type of Keith Holland for seven laps but, despite giving away 2500cc, he actually passed him on lap 8 and led for a short distance before having to give best to the larger machine. The race finished with a scrabble for the line, with the Jag getting the verdict, although the crowds were all cheering the Sprite driver home.

BOB NEVILLE

Bob Neville, a lad of 17, was looking for his first car. To repay him for his help, Alec Poole said he could have what was left of the original TZA 238. Between them, they welded up the very tired shell and acquired the missing bits to turn it back into a car of sorts. As Poole's new car was never used on the road, he lent Neville the log book to enable him to tax his car – for a short while, there were two TZA 238s. As a result of its previous hard life, Neville's road car did not last long.

Bob Neville had now become keen on motor racing. During a works visit to Abingdon, he found himself in a quiet corner of the site, where he saw two Midget shells. On his return to Morris, he wrote a letter to John Thornley, asking if, as a struggling apprentice and aspiring racing driver, he might buy one of the shells to use as a basis for a competition car. John Thornley's reply, dated 4 February 1966, told him that either of the two shells – one complete but in primer, the other painted in BRG, but minus one door – was available to him at the nominal amount of £5. He bought the green one.

The standard MG Car Company white writing paper had the company name in black and the MG octagon logo printed in red. However, John Thornley had special paper, with the octagon printed in gold. Bob Neville kept the letter and now has it framed on his office wall. The letter was addressed to him at the flat he shared with Alec's brother, Arnie Poole, at 73 Wakegreen Road, Mosely, Birmingham. This big old house, divided into flats and bedsits, was home to about ten Morris and ten Austin employees. The list of past residents reads like a who's who of MG Midget racing: Barras, Enever, May, Neville, Poole and Poole. Peter May built one of his best 1000cc engines, for his first Frogeye, in the kitchen at no 73; it was certainly no place to prepare or store food, and they all lived off chips and takeaways most of the time anyway. May later lost the Frogeye to Bob Neville in a card game, having bet it against Neville's Morris 1000 and losing: 'It was amazing what a bottle of sherry and a Mackeson would do to you in those days.' The house at no 73 has long since been demolished.

Eventually, Bob Neville got his long-awaited transfer to Abingdon and decided that it was time for him to take to the cockpit. At the time, the development department was working on a fuel-injected Mini; the shell was ready and just waiting for the special engine to be completed. Alec Poole was working on the project, and managed to get his hands on a 1275cc engine with straight-cut gearbox, which he used to get the car ready for some preliminary races, before it ran in its injected form. In 1967, Bob Neville did his first-ever competitive event – a sprint at Blackbushe – in this Mini. It was followed by two races, at Silverstone and Snetterton.

Neville's Midget was nearly ready for the track, but, in the mean time, Syd Enever suggested he have 138 DMO, as Roger would not be using it again. Neville quickly trimmed out the Midget he had built and got it registered with Berkshire County Council, who allocated it the number URX 848G. It looked impressive on its set of 5½in wire wheels and he was sure he would have no trouble selling it to finance the purchase of Enever's race-winning car. In April 1969, 138 DMO, which had been transferred to Roger Enever's name in May 1968, was sold to Neville. For a while, he was allowed to keep the car in the shop, which enabled him to tinker with it during his lunch hour, but eventually he had to move it out.

Alec Poole had raced the Sprite during 1965 and 1966 and then moved on to Minis (in which he became British saloon car champion) and MGBs. In early 1968 the Sprite was sold, partly rebuilt, to Robin Cochrane, an engineer with Girling. During the year he completely stripped the car down and reassembled it. He up-graded the front brakes with Ford Escort discs and Cortina calipers, installing an ex-Formula Junior engine, bored to 1088cc. This had an early Cooper S cylinder head, which gave a 13:1 compression ratio. The following season, Cochrane, and Alec's brother Arnie Poole, competed in over thirty club events, scoring several top three placings.

In Bob Neville's hands, 138 DMO continued to be used for development work. On one occasion, he was asked to test a new half shaft made from EN25 steel. This item was not up to the extra stresses put on it by competitive driving and broke, nearly pitching Neville into the bank at Thruxton on 30 August. This incident led to the necessary renewal of the back axle casing.

Neville had a memorable outing at the wheel of the Midget during the MG Car Club Silverstone meeting on 20 September 1969. He recalls this Sprite and Midget race vividly – a real wheel-to-wheel dice with his former flat-mate Arnie Poole in his Sprite, who was on pole. It was hectic stuff. After ten laps, they crossed the line almost side by side, but Poole just pipped Neville to take victory, the pair setting joint fastest lap at an average speed of 81.08mph (130.5km/h).

Bob Neville was one of three English drivers – with fellow Midget man Lynden Thorne and his friend John ('Plastic') Pearson, with his lightweight Jaguar XK 120 – who went to race at Ireland's Phoenix Park circuit in 1969. Another John Pearson also raced an XK, but his had steel, rather than glass fibre bodywork, hence Plastic's nickname. As a result of the ferry arriving late, the trio missed scrutineering and were worried that they might not get a race. Alec Poole, with whom Neville was staying, told them not to worry, went off and saw an official, and soon returned with the three necessary labels for the cars. The race was won by Lynden Thorne; Bob Neville came 4th and took a class win.

Neville finally sold the car in 1974, and used his knowledge gained in running the Midget to build a lightweight racing MGB GT V8, which he ran in the 1976 World Sports Car 6-hour race at Silverstone, partnered by Derek Worthington. They finished 6th overall and even beat the Jochen Mass/Jackie Ickx works Porsche, which came home 10th. The white V8 was the last MG to score World Championship points, and it is now owned and raced by Malcolm Beer.

Neville's love of speed got him into trouble when Bullingdon Magistrates Court fined him £7.50 for exceeding the 70mph limit. Under the headline 'Overtook police at 80mph', the local paper delighted in reporting that an experimental test driver for MG sports cars had committed the offence. Neville went on to race a Group 1 Triumph Dolomite Sprint and a Charles Ivey Porsche.

COMMONWEALTH CARIBBEAN CLUB CHAMPIONSHIP

Having enjoyed considerable success, in 1970 Neville was looking to sell the car and race something else. It was arranged that Alec Poole would take 138 DMO to the Caribbean to compete in the Commonwealth

Caribbean Club Championship. This was held on the South Dakota Circuit at Atkinson Field, a former US air base at Timehri, about 25 miles (40km) from Georgetown in Guyana, on 8 November 1970. The government was an active supporter of the event and this particular year had paid for the track, based on the old taxi strips, to be resurfaced.

BOAC had sponsored Alec Poole, along with Mike Crabtree in his Group 2 Willment Ford Escort, and shipped the two cars and drivers out there to compete under the banner of Team Speedbird. Poole had raced in Guyana before and ended up doing very well, in more ways than one, managing to sell the ex-works B he drove to one of the locals. It was hoped that he could repeat this with the Midget. The pair arrived in time for the Friday practice session for visiting drivers and soon recorded some quick times.

Poole scored the first victory for the team by winning the unrestricted sports car race on the long (1.98 miles/3.2km) circuit. He then got a class win in the open sports and saloon car event, which Crabtree took outright. The pair were out again in another combined sports and tin top race, in which Poole had a real ding-dong for the small class with the Downton Mini-Marcos of local man Roy Taylor. The Midget won by virtue of a demon outbraking manoeuvre on the very last corner. In the final thrash of the day, an all-comers event on the short circuit, Crabtree won and Poole came 3rd.

MORE CHANGES TO 138 DMO

Despite his array of silverware, Poole was unable to find the right buyer in Guyana for 138 DMO, so the Midget returned to Britain. By now, the shell was showing signs of wear and Poole wanted in some way to repay Bob Neville for the use of the car. Peter Browning, British Leyland Competition Director, entered the story. At about that time Browning had commissioned the building of six lightweight aluminium-panelled Midget shells, for competition purposes. They basically had steel 'H' frame, floor pan and sills, although it has been suggested that they were of thinner gauge than normal. The four flared wings, rear shroud, doors, bonnet and boot lid were all pressed in aluminium. They weighed in at 326lb as opposed to a standard shell at 430lb.

Not long after the shells were completed, the death knell sounded for the competition department, closed down by Lord Stokes on 31 October 1970. As a result, Browning's project was scrapped. Two Abingdon employees of the time remember seeing the shells, each on a trolley, sitting in a corner under a big tarpaulin. In order to recoup part of the substantial cost, the shells were to be sold off. Poole agreed to buy one for Neville in return for the use of his car.

Despite the fact that they were both employees, Poole still had to pay around £300 for the shell. On 12 December 1970, the Neville car was rebuilt into the lightweight shell using most of the bits from the original 138 DMO. The car was painted green and Bob continued to campaign it. Because of the difficult shape of the front valance pressing, the bodies Browning had made retained a steel one, but Neville managed to get his hands on an alloy valance to complete the job.

Meanwhile, Peter May, who was also an apprentice at Morris Commercial at the time, bought the original steel shell, complete with doors, one-piece fibre front, windscreen, hood and some of the running gear. He built a racer round this, putting together an engine, which ran on twin inch and three quarter SUs. He debuted his 'new' white car early in the 1971 season. In May, he finished the shell off for good in a big accident at the MG Car Club Silverstone meeting. May rebuilt the car into another shell and it

The Abingdon Connection

was sold to Teddy Arundel, whose brother Danny was a well-known club racer of the day.

During the next two years, Bob Neville enjoyed continued success with the Midget, including some excellent performances in Ireland, where the regs permitted fuel injection. He used the system developed for Mini racing. The Heron flat head, long trumpets and Lucas injection unit greatly increased the power output. When running in injected form, the power bulge was on the nearside of the bonnet. The car became noted for its two-wheeled cornering antics when competing in Ireland.

On a few occasions, the injection system was 'inadvertently' left on for an event where it was not permitted! This was stopped when MGB racer Bill Nicholson complained after an MG race at Silverstone,

Bob Neville's aluminium-panelled Midget. Note the discreet wheel arches and cooling slots in the special front panel

Roger Enever bicycles 138 DMO round Ireland's Mondello Park Circuit

during which Neville, who was running 3rd overall, managed to keep his Midget ahead of the more powerful B. Neville recalls that the race came to nothing after he ran out of fuel on the last lap, but Nicholson none the less came over to him in the paddock to complain about the injection. The injected Midget was not seen in England again.

In 1974, the Midget was overhauled, painted black with yellow pin-stripes and sold to Richard Gamble, who for a while ran it with a supercharger. When Gamble changed his allegiance to Marcos, the Midget passed to Mike Hartley. Having subsequently been owned by John Singer and Fred Boothby, the car has, since the mid-1980s, been campaigned in sprints and Midget races by Stephen Luscombe. Over the years, the front wings and bonnet have been damaged in an accident, and the car now sports a one-piece glass fibre front.

After Teddy Arundel sold the re-shelled steel-bodied version of 138 DMO to Colin Charman, it was subsequently owned by Pedro Villar, Stephen Luscombe, Ian Parkinson and Julius Thurgood. Thurgood bought it on a Thursday and the following Sunday, 6 November 1983, it was raced by Rae Davis of Moto-Build in the MGOC Allcomers Race at Brands. Despite the ten-year-old tyres, Davis managed to put it on the third row but retired during the race.

The car then appeared on the circuits in the hands of its new owner, Mike Roy. It seems he had been able to convince the DVLA that the car was the original 138 DM0 and was duly issued with a V5 registration document. Meanwhile, Bob Neville still had the old buff log book issued in 1963 by Berkshire County Council. In 1993, I spotted an advertisement for the car and tipped off Bob Neville, who wanted to be re-united with the Midget should it ever come up for sale. In partnership with his friend, ex-Mini racer Charles Dawkins, Neville has now bought and restored it.

DEVELOPMENT WORK AT ABINGDON

Abingdon was a methodical place. Every car that was used for development work had a 'department chassis record book', an ordinary blue duplicate book in which Henry Stone or Cliff Bray recorded all modifications carried out on a car. The book only contained technical information about the car, and no record was ever kept in it about how the car did in any races; after all, they were not works entries. Bob Neville now has the duplicate book for 138 DMO, and it is thanks to this that it is possible so accurately to date changes made to the car.

There was always some development work or other going on at Abingdon, all sanctioned by John Thornley or Syd Enever. While they were autonomous when it came to running MG, there were certain things they did not want people from the parent company to see. Apparently, if one of the engineers from Longbridge was due, all the racers and the record-breaking cars were conveniently hidden in the boiler-house. If any outsider were to ask why they were there, they were able to explain that it was warm and dry, an ideal place to keep such cars out of harm's way.

Another development car to see the light of day on the race track was a lightweight, but steel-bodied Midget, fitted with a full race MGB engine and gearbox. To assist the weight distribution, the 140bhp engine was set back in the chassis. Owing to changing regulations, the car was ineligible for Sports Car events and could only race as a Special GT. It was driven in one or two GT races by Guy Edwards, Peter Brown, Alec Poole and Roger Enever. Enever took it out at Oulton Park on 10 November 1968, in what was described at the time as a 'rare outing'. He spun, under-braking for Esso Bend, but was able to climb back through the field and make up most of the places that he had lost.

THE ALUMINIUM SHELLS

Of the other aluminium shells, Bob Neville bought a second one, which he and fellow Abingdon employee Rodney Line built up as a virtually street-legal racing machine, complete with ex-Formula 3 XSP engine, for Australian dentist Jeff Hinde. This white car was mainly seen at Silverstone events, sponsored by the Crown and Thistle pub. It eventually went to New South Wales with its owner, who hoped to carry on racing it in Australia.

In his last UK appearance at the Peterborough Motor Club meeting on 30 September 1972, Hinde scored two class 2nds. He also came 4th in the Vandervell Awards for novice drivers that year. The car had three outings in Australia during 1973, taking a class win on each occasion, and then the car was stored in a shed for the next twenty-one years. In 1994 it emerged having now been restored to its former glory, complete with all the original aluminium panels, prior to competing at the Eastern Creek Historics meeting on 28 January 1995, starting a new phase in its competition history.

Sussex driver Nick Ramus ran a variety of Sprites in autocross, scoring a surprise FTD at the Maidstone and Mid-Kent Car Club round of the Player's No 6 Championship on 27 April 1969. The foul weather and muddy conditions favoured his 1.3 wire-wheeled, ex-Clive Baker Sebring Sprite, 5435 WD, enabling him to beat the likes of Barry Lee, Rod Chapman and John Taylor, who found their extra power to be an embarrassment. Frank Tiedeman is now a regular Prescott competitor in this Sprite.

In 1970, Ramus moved to rallycross. He received technical assistance from the competition department at Abingdon and, through Mike Garton, was allocated one of the alloy shells to build up a lightweight rallycross Midget. He built his own gearbox and bottom end of the 1275 engine and

The Nick Ramus aluminium-bodied Midget being readied for the Six-Hour Relay at Thruxton

asked his friend Jack Cramp to do the cylinder head for him. Cramp worked at Weslakes in Rye, just down the road from Ramus; Weslakes had originally designed the 'A' series head, and Cramp came up with a really nice job. Having done a couple of rallycross meetings in his new Midget, Ramus defected to Modsports, deciding that it was really too nice a car to use on the rough. He competed in the STP Championship and, having got a taste for circuit racing, progressed to a TR7. In 1976, he sold the Midget to hill climber Martin Boulton, who appeared at Shelsley Walsh and Loton Park in 1977 and 1978.

The car was acquired by Robin Carlisle in 1979, who raced it, with moderate success, sponsored by his employers, hospitality vehicle manufacturers Club Car. He then turned his attention to saloons, racing a Toyota in the RAC Championship for a couple of seasons. During this time, Wally Agus raced and hill climbed the Midget. In 1983, Carlisle sold it to Gary Flinders, who resprayed it bright yellow and put it on the road as a street-legal car! It is now believed to be in Germany.

The Abingdon lightweight bodies were not just available to the select few. In the October 1970 edition of *Safety Fast* the special tuning department offered one for sale for £300 ono, the advertisement stating 'Cancelled works entry permits this unrepeatable offer'.

In November 1971, this remaining lightweight shell was sold to two Cheshire enthusiasts, Simon Draper and Dave Jones. After protracted correspondence with Special Tuning, they paid the asking price of £300 plus an additional £10 for delivery. It took the pair three years to build up a car, which was used at one test session and a couple of sprints at their local circuit, Oulton Park. It had a coil-sprung rear end and ran on Revolution wheels. In 1977, Jones took a job abroad, so the car was laid up in a lock-up garage, in a block at the back of a row of shops in West Kirby. In 1984 Jones was still working abroad, and the Midget remained unused in the garage. It was agreed the car should be sold and Draper advertised it in the 30 August edition of *Motoring News*, for £1,250. He received several calls, but local man Nigel Roscoe beat everyone to it and bought the Midget. Roscoe, who had previously done sand racing with motorbike and sidecar, ran the car in sprints and hill climbs during the 1985 and 1986 seasons.

In 1987, the Midget went to Angus Racing, who bought it on behalf of Charles Burt for the MGCC Midget series. Unfortunately, a coming together with the tyre wall at Silverstone's Woodcote Bend (while running as number 13), during the wet MG Car Club race meeting in May 1987, put the car out of action for many years. It was finally straightened in 1993 and is now destined for historic racing.

This accounts for four out of the six special alloy shells. When Nigel Roscoe bought his car from Simon Draper, he was told that the other two bodies had gone to South Africa. This could be true, as there has been rumour of an aluminium car, which had raced in South Africa, surfacing in Australia. However, ex-Abingdon employee Mike Garton suggests that one of the shells was irreparably damaged, and that another was used to build the Group 4 Midget in which Jerry Truit and Randy Canfield came 15th overall, winning the Sports Car class at Sebring in 1968.

Over the years, various Midgets have been described as 'ex-works cars', but were not. Had Lord Stokes not closed down the competition department, forcing Peter Browning to sell off the aluminium-panelled shells, it might have been a different story. Indeed, it seems that the six shells had been given the project designation 'GT5', which suggested the possibility of a limited production run.

WORKS ENTRIES

It seems there were a very few real Midget works entries and these were only in International events. At the beginning of 1963, BMC was looking for additional publicity in the USA for the Midget, which was already fairly popular there. Among the ten Sports Cars entered for the 22 and 23 March Sebring event was MG Midget 9252 WD. This was, in fact, a previously raced Warwick-prepared Sprite, complete with aluminium body panels, and fitted with Midget grill, badge and chrome strips.

To enhance the publicity impact, World Champion Graham Hill was signed to drive the car. It was a high-profile outing from the word 'go', with the MG and Austin Healey teams holding a party at the plush Pinecrest Country Club the evening before the event. The party was attended by the drivers, and others, including Mr and Mrs John Thornley, Donald Healey and Rod Learoyd.

Graham Hill was to compete in the three-hour race for GTs under 1000cc, the Midget's 998cc engine quoted as giving 88bhp. The two sister cars, which remained in Sprite guise, were for Pedro Rodriguez, the third designated as a spare. Sadly, not only was the Friday afternoon three-hour event at this Florida airfield circuit poorly supported, with just nine starters and five finishers, but also the two Spridgets were among the retirements. Both were sidelined within the first four laps, as a result of problems with the new limited-slip differentials.

In September 1966, two lightweight, standard-shape Midgets, driven by Timo Makinen and Rauno Aaltonen, ran in the Bridghampton 500, America's biggest East Coast Sports Car race. Aaltonen won his class and came 6th overall. Makinen, who had led his team-mate for 85 laps, was forced to pit for four laps, to have his exhaust welded up, but eventually climbed back through the field to finish 11th overall, 3rd in class.

8 Made in Britten

RAM 35 AND SS 1800

Many a young amateur racing driver, and some professionals too, has started his career in a Midget. In 1965 Hertfordshire garage proprietor John Britten, then in his mid-thirties, decided to follow this path. Inspired by a friend who had shoe-horned a Ford engine into a Frogeye, Britten began to look at the logistics of building a car. His first idea of inserting a twin-cam in a Midget was rejected. Instead, in spring 1966, he bought the ex-Paddy Gaston supercharged Sprite RAM 35, which had already established quite a reputation.

The car came with all-aluminium Sebring-type bodywork, incorporating a Perspex windscreen that was slightly smaller and more streamlined than that of similar cars. Britten remembers there was no wiper and the screen was so scratched you could hardly see through it. The 1150cc long-stroke engine had a Shorrock supercharger and the dynamo was devoid of all working parts, save for a bare armature spindle. Suspension was fairly standard, with heavy-duty dampers and a thick front anti-roll bar. Brakes were Sebring style: 8in Riley 1.5 rear drums and Girling discs at the front. The car ran on 4½in wire wheels with R5 Dunlops.

Shortly after it was bought, the Sprite was taken to a Brands test day, where Britten drove it in its 'as bought' condition. The session was open to all competition cars and he had great difficulty in pulling away from Bob Henderson's grey Minivan, a very quick, well-known vehicle with an 1100cc engine with a Fish carburettor. Britten decided the Sprite could be bettered, and he and his mechanic Oliver Ball set about rebuilding it.

Britten bought a BMC F3 engine, and, unhappy with its 999cc capacity, increased it to 1144cc by fitting a 1071 Cooper S crank. Clear in his own mind that this configura-

John Britten's original racer, the ex-Paddy Gaston Sebring Sprite RAM 35

John Britten (164) at the wheel of RAM 35, in his first-ever race at Mallory Park in May 1966, leading a brace of Triumph Spitfires into Shaws Hairpin. On lap 5 the car rolled and caught light. That was the end of the Sprite, but not of John Britten

tion would work, he got Laystall Engineering to fit a flange for the in-line flywheel. The block was bored to take a set of 73mm pistons sourced from a Swedish truck. A head modified at Downton, fed by a Weber 45, Formula 3 clutch and conversion back to the traditional wet sump, completed the job. The first-ever 1150 short-stroke engine had been built.

A ZF limited slip differential was considered a must and the car's original wire wheels were discarded in favour of a set of 6in Minilites, shod with Dunlop R6 Green Spot tyres. The makers Tech Del considered it madness to fit such wide rims on the small car; interestingly, today 10in rims are the norm. In early 1966 the car was driven to Silverstone for testing; first time out, Britten recorded times close to the existing lap record – a sign of things to come.

Some weeks later, Britten entered an event at Brands, but, as a reserve, failed to get a race. He had to wait until May 1966 to make his racing debut at the Austin Healey Club's Mallory Park meeting. The car was still in its original dark BRG Gaston livery, but Britten had added a yellow star on the roof. This was not an auspicious occasion; after starting from the middle of the grid, he was fighting through the field, overtaking about one car per lap on the entry to Shaws Hairpin. On lap 5, he was using the inside line to pass another competitor; he found out to his cost that, under heavy braking, the car needed about 18in (45cm) to allow the rear to weave from side to side. At the time, the offside rear wheel was only about 12in (30cm) from the sleepers.

The car hit the banking hard, bounced back on to the track and was tapped by another car, sending it into a multiple roll. Britten remembers being in the cockpit, counting to himself the number of times it went over: 'One, two, three.' The Midget came to rest in the middle of the track and burst into flames, which were quickly extinguished by the marshals. The driver emerged from the wreck very shaken, but otherwise unharmed.

Undeterred, Britten trailered the remains home and found that, while the shell was a write-off, most of the mechanics were all right. He bought a left hooker 1962 Midget with rear end damage for £250, and he and Oliver Ball set about the re-shell. From the ashes, literally, of RAM 35 arose what was to become the legendary SS 1800 (the registration taken from a road Midget that Britten had at the time). Resplendent in its yellow paintwork, the car sported a Lenham fastback hardtop and an Ashley fibreglass one-piece front. Suspension was modified, a self-built roll bar added and the front discs changed to the original Midget items.

Throughout his time in Midgets, Britten paid particular attention to the weight of the car, although in the interest of safety he did build his own roll cage. This hybrid item was made from two Midget exhaust systems – a cheap way of getting the correct angle for the bends. One can only hope that in 1966 they used thicker tube than today! Running a 4.5 Morris 1000 diff, the car was capable of a top speed of about 120mph (193km/h) at 8,000rpm.

Two months after the ill-fated Mallory meeting, on 10 July, SS 1800 was on the grid at Brands, where it won the MG Car Club race for Sprites and Midgets, leading from flag to flag and beating pole man David Corderoy, who made a poor start. Britten won again next time out, at the Austin Healey Club Castle Combe meeting on 23 July. Here he got fastest lap and finished 15 seconds ahead of established front-runner Alan Woode, who had to be content with second place.

The die was cast. In his first season, which in reality only comprised half a season's racing, Britten netted fourteen victories at UK circuits and took the 1150 class record at Brands. As a result, he was awarded the Peter Collins Memorial Trophy for the most promising newcomer to club racing.

The 1967 regulations for 'Marque Sports' stipulated that cars must retain their standard silhouette, making Britten's bodywork illegal, so he commissioned his own glass fibre, Midget-shape, one-piece rear end, from the Lenham Motor Company. He also carried out further lightening, even drilling holes in the handbrake lever. The car now weighed in at 10¼cwt (520kg). At the Kent Messenger Cup Car Races, on 16 April, not only did he win the small engine class, but he also came 4th overall, finishing ahead of the winners of the 2- and 3-litre classes into the bargain. He beat Roger Enever's 1293cc Midget by 4.8 seconds and lapped the Morgan Plus 4 of John House.

That year, Britten took class victory in all thirteen races of the Brands Hatch-based Amasco Championship, giving him the end of season crown by a good margin. When not competing at the Kent circuit, the car could be seen at other tracks taking part in the Freddie Dixon series. It was at one of these events, at Crystal Palace, that John was to have the only other major accident of his career, the car hitting the sleepers at 70mph (110km/h). The resultant rebuild saw the car back out in a new orange livery as it went on to take second in the Dixon championship. At the end of the season's racing, the 36-year-old garage owner had amassed twenty-eight wins, four second places and set new lap records at nine circuits.

As far as Britten was concerned, the Midget had its Achilles heel – he failed to finish several races as a result of broken drive shafts. Eventually, this weakness was recognized by the special tuning department, who produced a heavy-duty competition version, which was available as part number BTA 940. The other problem Britten encountered was the perennial one of oil leaking from the rear mains. After 10 minutes of hard use, he found oil would force its way past the rather crude thrower, get in the slipstream and smear itself over the inside of the tyre tread; obviously, this affected the handling.

Before the start of the new season, the car was displayed at the BRSCC-organized 1968 Autospeed Exhibition at London's Horticultural Halls. This year Britten teamed up with Gabriel Konig for a two-car assault on the championships. It was intended that

Gabriel Konig at the wheel of her 1150 Sebring Sprite, Silverstone 1967

John would build a 1275 motor and move up a class, while Konig would run in the up to 1150 category.

GABRIEL KONIG

Gabriel Konig had started racing during 1963 in her husband's Lotus Elite, then moved on to an Elan. She bought an aluminium-bodied Sebring Sprite, E 700, for the 1967 season. This was fitted with an old short-stroke 1150 engine, which, despite its age, won races when the car was looked after by Downton. She competed against Britten in a race meeting at Crystal Palace and scored a class 3rd. As a result of this encounter, she contacted Britten suggesting that, if he ran a two-car team the following season, he would gain a lot of extra publicity for his business. She put herself forward as the second driver.

The deal was struck and Gabriel Konig joined the team, Britten providing a Midget shell which was built up for her by ex-Chequered Flag chief mechanic Chas Beattie, who was involved in creating the Gemini Formula Junior car in the early 1960s. He designed and fabricated special front wishbones and a coil-sprung rear suspension for the Midget; unlike Britten's car, the chassis was not lightened, but it did have Britten glass fibre bodywork. Meanwhile, Chris Steele was bolting together an 1150 engine, getting George Bevan's son Peter to modify the cylinder head. The car was not ready for the start of the season, only complete in April, so Konig did the first two or three rounds of the Amasco Championship in SS 1800, setting a new 58-second lap record for the Brands Club Circuit in it.

Once the new car was running, the pair jointly carried out the development work. Interestingly, there was very little to choose between the two Midgets when they were both running in 1150 guise. SS 1800, despite its alloy body, retained the somewhat heavy original quarter-elliptic leaf springs, while the other one, with standard floor pan and coils on the rear, weighed in at 11cwt (560kg), 1cwt (50kg) more. Konig found that, in the final analysis, her car was a little more controllable in what she describes as 'stressful situations'.

Gabriel Konig racing her Midget at Crystal Palace in 1969

Britten and Konig headed the grid sheet, with the Midget of Peter Kitchen, for the up to 1150 Special Sports race at Brands on 31 March 1968. The race was possibly unique, in that, at the drop of the flag, the whole of the front row had failed to make the start. Britten, in setting pole, had broken his crank; Konig had found her legs covered in oil on arriving at the line, the result of a broken pipe; on the warming-up lap, Kitchen had a water hose give out on the Midget. This gave Roger Mould his moment of glory, with a flag to flag victory in his Sprite, leading home Peter Stewart (Midget) and Paul Butler (Sprite).

Meanwhile, a 1293 engine had been bought and over-hauled ready to be installed in SS 1800, to enable Britten to move up a class. At first, he was a little disappointed with his car's performance but this was soon traced to one of the recently acquired Dunlop 970 compound tyres, which had hardened with age. Instead of replacing it with a new one, he chose to pair it with another old tyre and the handling was back to his liking.

At the BARC meeting at Brands on 28 April 1968 the team was in typical form. Britten beat Roger Enever off the line and led him home throughout the ten laps, leaving the rest of the twelve-car field to scrap over third place. Gabriel Konig, similarly way out ahead in the small class, was mix-

John Britten's legendary Midget SS 1800 in 1988. The car ran 7.5in wheels with the 1100cc engine and 8.5in with the more powerful 1300cc unit

ing it with Colin Blyth (TVR 1800) and Peter Cox (Spitfire 1300). On lap 7, she ran wide on to the grass, but did not lift off for a moment. At the finish, despite winning the class by a considerable margin, she had to concede 4th overall to the TVR. E never mounted a late challenge, but was unable to prevent Britten from taking the flag. Britten's fastest lap in the 1293 car was exactly 3 seconds quicker than that done in his team-mate's 1150 version.

As well as interesting races with fellow 1150 runners John Northcroft and Garo Nigogosian, Gabriel Konig was constantly battling with the larger-engined Triumph Spitfires of Peter Cox and Chris Marshall. In a straight line they were quicker than the Midget, particularly Marshall's GT6 with its triple Webers, but on the twisty bits she had the upper hand. This meant Konig did well against them at circuits such as Brands and Crystal Palace, but she had to work really hard at Snetterton and Silverstone. She remembers what she describes as 'a hell of a race' at Oulton, when she managed a demon out-braking manoeuvre to get by Cox at Lodge.

Her most exciting dice with Cox, however, was when he was racing an 1150 Spitfire at Thruxton. He got off the line first but the Midget soon caught him. Being on equal terms on engine capacity, the pair circulated as one, the front of one virtually in the boot of the other. Approaching the chicane a little too quickly, Cox had the back step out, and, being so close, Konig tapped him into a car-bending retirement. Despite this, the two drivers remained friends.

When there was an exceptionally large entry for a round of the Amasco Championship, the organizers would have to allocate two races, the up to 1150 cars running against those in the 2001 to 3000cc class. On such occasions, it was not uncommon for Konig to take overall victory as well as winning the class. To do this, she needed to stay in front of the Healey 3000s of John Gott and Syd Segal, again proving the agility of the little Midget round the twisty Brands Hatch circuit.

Konig always made a point of towing her own car to the circuit; more often than not, Britten got one of the lads from the garage to bring his on the back of one of the two 'John

John Britten lines up in the paddock at Lydden, 1967. Note that the scrutineering bay and race control are both in marquees

Britten Racing Team' MG Midget pick-ups. These two unique tow barges had been made by cutting the rear deck out of 1965 and 1966 cars and fitting them with a suitably abbreviated hardtop. Both had 1098 engines and gearboxes and, even using very light Don Parker trailers, towing was marginal. Peter May used one to trailer a Midget to Brands one day and had a real struggle to get up the hill out of the old paddock on the way home. Britten also experienced problems: on more than one occasion, he stripped first gear as he pulled away.

The team had an excellent year, gaining two class wins in the 1968 Freddie Dixon Championship. Britten beat Roger Enever by a healthy twenty points in the 1151 to 2000cc class, while Gabriel Konig headed John Northcroft's Sprite by seven points in the up to 1150 category. In the Amasco series, Enever turned the tables on Britten and beat him, Britten ending up 3rd in class. Konig was widely expected to take the double and win the class in both, but Barry Wood had other ideas. The last race, at the traditional Boxing Day Brands meeting, saw him put in a stirring drive in his ex-Schroder Sprite. He beat her on the day and took the championship by just one point.

This was not Konig's only disappointment during the season. At the Mini 7 Club Brands meeting on 8 December, she got very near to beating Roger Enever, a feat which Britten had managed and she had not. On this particular day she very nearly pulled it off, despite her much smaller engine. Coming into Clearways at the end of lap 2, she changed down to slow the car and went for the brake pedal to set the car up for the exit. The nut had come off the pivot pin and the pedal was no longer where she expected it to be. The car slewed sideways into the banking, bending a wishbone and deflating a tyre.

The end-of-season tally gave Britten fourteen class wins and ten class lap records, while Konig had fifteen class wins and four lap records. She also won the British Women Racing Drivers Club's Embassy trophy, beating Jean Denton (who had taken the award

The John Britten Racing Team MG Midget pick-ups, built from Midgets that were past their prime. The boot lid and a substantial part of its surround were removed to effect the conversion, the cab being formed by cutting down a standard hardtop. Despite the lightness of Britten's racers and specially designed trailers, the 1098cc engines made towing highly marginal

Gabriel Konig's 1150 Midget leads Nigogosian's 1160 and John Britten's 1300 Midget at Brands Hatch, 1968

the two previous years in her supercharged MGB) by seventeen points. The trophy was presented at a Café Royal dinner by Cathy McGowan, presenter of ITV's *Ready Steady Go* pop music programme.

THE 1969 SEASON

As a result of these successes, Britten built two similar cars for John Northcroft and Archie Phillips. Ulsterman Phillips, the MD of local MG distributors Leslie Porter Ltd, raced the car in his home country and was always regarded as the man to beat around Mondello Park. One of his many victories came in the fifteen-lap race for Sports and Specials at the St Patrick's Day meeting in 1969. After a good dice with fellow Midget men Harold McGarrity and Jim McClements, he came to the front to win and set fastest lap.

Northcroft had a notable David and Goliath outing at the 1-mile (1.6km) Welsh airfield circuit at Llandow, on August Bank Holiday Monday 1969. He was entered in the twenty-lap thrash for Prodsports and GT cars. After early front-runners Dave McCloy and Brian Colin retired their Lotuses, John piled on the pressure in pursuit of the leading 4.7-litre Lotus 30 of Ken Wilson. He caught him and, during the last five laps, got the inside line on many corners, but had to concede victory by a scant 1.2 seconds

By now, the development of the Arkley SS – a glass fibre buggy-style car designed to go on a Spridget floor pan to replace existing rusty bodywork – was taking most of Britten's time. However, the competitive spirit was still there and 1969 saw SS 1800 re-united with an 1150cc engine and once again running in the small class. This resulted in some exciting dices with Alan Woode's similar car. Towards the middle of the season, the team found time to build a 1402cc lump and, after tweaking by Downton, it was installed in the car. Despite the increased capacity, the car still retained a 4.55 diff, enabling the driver to reach 100mph (160km/h) in third!

In the mean time, Gabriel Konig, who had previously raced her Elan at Nurburgring, entered her now 1350cc Midget in some events abroad. 'Start money' made it a worthwhile exercise, more than covering the travelling costs. In Denmark, she competed at Jyallandsbring, a small circuit that she likened to a go-kart track. This was the only place where the Midget ever ran out of brakes. Apparently, the straights were so short, the standard discs did not have time to cool before the next corner. In the end, she had to resort to putting the car sideways, in order to slow down.

Other International outings followed, including a visit to Nurburgring for the 500km on 7 September 1969, where the car went extremely quickly. This outing ended in disappointment, when terminal understeer resulted in her crashing at Brunchen half-way through the race. She also competed at Fasbourg on the North German Plain, where she achieved two victories. As a result of a meeting with Tim Schenken, the 1969 Formula Ford Champion, it was arranged for him to drive the Midget at a Brands Hatch test day. On his return to the pits, following a few laps, he expressed surprise that 'the little car seemed to be all over the circuit'. As Konig pointed out, unlike the custom-built single-seater racing car to which he was accustomed, a modified road car was a compromise and the driver simply had to learn to live with and master its shortcomings.

The Prodsports race at the Mini 7 Club meeting at Brands, in May 1969, resulted in a tremendous three-way dice between Britten, Konig and her old 1150 class adversary Barry Wood. Despite the fact that the two men were giving away 200cc to Konig, they were right with her every inch of the way. Wood got in front on lap 2, but the place was only his for half a lap, as Konig, having run neck and neck with him the length of the main straight, drove round the outside at Paddock. A grassy moment later in the race saw Britten pass Wood for second, and they finished in that order, 2.6 seconds covering the first three cars as they crossed the line. Garo Nigogosian was next home, giving Midgets the top four places.

Garo invited Konig to join him as co-driver for the 1969 Mugello event, on 20 July. This was a traditional Italian road race, which originated in 1914, run over a 41.2-mile (66km) circuit high in the Apennines, north of Florence. To prepare the car for the race, an 18-gallon fuel tank was installed, giving a range of 100 miles (160km), which meant the car had to pit for fuel every other lap. Konig came up with a wide-neck filler, which enabled 18 gallons to be taken on in about one minute. Despite the tank being bolted as close as possible to the back axle, it noticeably altered the handling, particularly when full.

The strictly amateur team was completed by Garo's mechanic Peter and his wife, working as pit crew. They travelled to the circuit in a Ford Anglia estate, towing the racer on a trailer. Garo had already discovered that those in the know arrived a couple of days before official practice and then drove round learning the circuit, while the roads were still open to the public. There were, after all, over 600 bends to be negotiated on each lap. It was not unusual to see competitors circulating at close to racing speeds, while locals carried on life as normal. Drivers would round a bend to find groups of people sitting at pavement cafés, not even bothering to move their legs as cars roared by inches away. Occasionally, the local police would flag a competitor down with 'little wooden lollipops' and give them a lecture on how to drive. However, no one ever seemed to get arrested, although the unfortunate few were subjected to on-the-spot fines. It was rumoured that the Alfa team manager had to pay over £100 for his drivers' exuberance during this pre-practice session.

Garo Nigogosian driving through the Futa Pass, Mugello 1969

Part of the circuit was over the old Bologna main road, and the highest section was over 3,000ft (900m) above sea level. In the interest of safety the maximum engine capacity for the event was limited to 3 litres. As well as catering for sports cars, the race was also a round of the Italian Saloon Car Championship. This resulted in all the local heroes going round hell for leather in their Alfas and Lancias.

The start, on the wide main road just outside Scarperia, was spectacular, as the field of 120 cars roared away in a cloud of dust. The first car was flagged off at 1pm, the others following, in class order, at ten-second intervals. There was no crowd control, not even fences to keep the spectators back on the bends. Garo came down the Futa Pass, a very steep, winding downhill section, doing about 100mph (160km/h). It was a good spectator vantage point, so the crowds were three or four deep on either side of the road. The car ahead of him had the back slide out and the mass of people weaved in and out like a giant snake, as each person, in turn, took a few steps back. The same pass also formed part of the even more famous Mille Miglia circuit.

During her stint at the wheel, Gabriel Konig rounded one corner, to find four of the saloon cars had been involved in a mighty pile-up and the road was littered with bits of Alfa Romeo. She slowed briefly, picked her way through the debris and roared off on her way. The Midget finished 5th in Group 6, 1000–2000cc class. John Britten also took part, sharing Chris Marshall's, Peter Cox-prepared 1-litre Triumph Spitfire, which came 4th in the Group 6 up to 1000cc category. Konig's Embassy award rival, Jean Denton, was also present in her MGB, which she shared with Sprite man Mike Garton.

While Gabriel Konig waved the Britten team flag abroad in 1969, Britten himself kept the honours coming on the home front. During a race at Brands on 17 August, he lowered the Midget lap record for the Club Circuit to 56.4 seconds (79.15mph/127.4km/h). This was to stand for exactly four years, being beaten by Richard Jenvey on 19 August 1973, who went round in 54.2 (82.36mph/132.6km/h). David Sheppard set a time of 51.1, on 13 September 1981, equalled by Steve Everitt two years later; it was finally beaten on 1 October 1995, by Graeme Adams, who lowered it to 50.74 (85.39mph/137.47km/h).

Gabriel Konig sold the Midget at the end of 1969 and after a spell in single-seaters, she bought an ex-works 6.3-litre Camaro, in 1972. Driving this rapid machine, she was soon dicing with the likes of Dave Brodie and the other leading saloon car contenders of the day, and getting wins in England, Ireland, and even South America. Lack of funds forced the sale of the car in 1973, and it would be nearly twenty years before the name Gabriel Konig appeared in a race programme again.

In May 1991, Peter May Engineering sponsored the Midget race at the MG Car Club Silverstone meeting. May, who knew Konig from his days working for John Britten Garages, felt it would be inappropriate to participate in a race he was sponsoring and offered her the drive in his Midget. She thoroughly enjoyed her first race on slicks, but, as she put it, she 'had been around long enough not to try and master a car after just a few laps'. She can now be found competing in the Historic Irish Tarmac Rally Championship in a 1967 Vauxhall Viva GT.

BRI 10

The reputation of the Britten Midgets was far-reaching and in 1969 Christian Favre, an apparently affluent young Swiss who had acquired the taste for motor sport through karting, approached Britten to build a car for him. For this project, a fairly standard

Made in Britten

John Britten leads the pack into Brands Hatch Paddock Bend at the start of a Marque Sports race in 1967

chassis was utilized although the rear suspension had progressed to a coil-sprung set-up. The car sat lower than SS 1800, and this was achieved by routing the exhaust system through the passenger compartment. Despite its chassis, weight was reduced to about 10cwt (500kg) by using a fibreglass body. To aid correct weight distribution, the engine was set back 8in (20cm). The car ran on 7.5in Minilites.

By the time the car was nearing completion, SS 1800 was being prepared for a long-distance event at the Ring, so Britten dug out his original 1150 power unit, dropped it in and went racing. The new Midget's debut at Brands on 18 April saw Britten come second to an E-Type and win the small engine class. BRI 10 (Bri-ten), as it was to become known, soon became a favourite with the spectators, particularly for its somewhat spectacular wheel-lifting tendencies and lurid body roll. During the Sports Car race at Thruxton on Whit Monday 1969, the car was reported to have rounded the chicane on one wheel! The coil-sprung rear, it seems, was responsible for these handling charac-

teristics, and fitting a rear anti-roll bar made the car more predictable.

Britten then commissioned Downton to build a 1402cc engine for the car and, with this power unit installed, it appeared at Brands on 17 August. The driver was Britten's good friend, Triumph Spitfire pilot

John Britten's successor to SS 1800 was BRI 10. Because of its wheel-lifting characteristics it became a firm favourite with the spectators

Richard Lloyd, who was supposedly running in the engine. Presumably he felt he had done this in practice, and went on to take a class win in the race, beating his usual Spitfire team-mate Chris Marshall, as well as Britten, who was driving SS 1800. Both Lloyd and Marshall went on to have other victories in BRI 10.

Christian Favre arrived in England to race the Midget in 1970. He came over in his left-hand drive green MGC GT, equipped with a tow bar (for the racer), and a police siren (to get him through the London traffic). He won his third-ever event, at the MG Car Club's meeting at Brands on 19 April. On this, his first visit to the Kent circuit, he led the Spridget field home with the well-known Frogeye of Barry Hopwood coming in third.

Toward the end of the season, Favre had decided to sell the car. It was advertized in *Autosport* on 15 October, the illustrated advertisement reading: 'BRI 10, one of the most successful Midgets in club racing, complete with spare short engine, wet weather wheels and tyres, to be painted in colour of purchaser's choice. Terrific value at £1,095 ono.' It seems unlikely that the car was actually sold; Favre probably took it back to Switzerland, when he returned home at the end of the season.

THE ARKLEY

To enhance the publicity for the Arkley, in 1972 John converted SS 1800 into a Modsports Arkley. By then, the model had been

Peter May racing his Arkley Modsports car, which had been converted from SS 1800

The forecourt of John Britten's premises at Arkley in 1972, showing Britten's racer now with Arkley bodywork

homologated, but he raced it just once, at Brands. For the rest of the season he entrusted the driving to his service manager, Peter May, who enjoyed some fine dices with fellow Spridget men Andy Bailey and Mike Donovan. Britten slowly slipped out of the racing scene, to concentrate on his business interests, and in 1973 sold the car to Peter May, who raced it for the rest of the season.

The following year, Peter went to live in France for 12 months and the Arkley was entrusted to Bob Neville, who, having no car of his own at the time, raced it on a few occasions. On his return to England in 1975, May successfully picked up the reins once more and won the up to 1150 class in the BRSCC Midland Modsports Championship. He sold the car to Mark Birrell at the start of the 1976 season, recalling that, when Mark came to collect it, the car still had the original Britten roll cage in it, made from two Midget exhaust pipes. Having paid his money, the new owner announced he was taking it straight to Aldon Automotive to have a proper roll cage fitted. May, who set up Peter May Engineering in 1978, specializing in competition Midgets, acquired the rights to the Arkley in 1985.

THE EX-EMPLOYEES

Chris Alford, the salesman at Arkley, is now a well-known West Sussex classic sports and racing car dealer. John Britten himself had always been a keen photographer. He gave up running the garage in 1988 and moved on to establish his Tecno Camera business. He retained an active interest in motor sport and was Richard Lloyd's partner in an endurance racing team. They ran Porsche 956 and 962 cars, scoring a 2nd at Le Mans in 1985. Britten briefly returned to the circuits in 1976 at the wheel of a Morgan Plus 8, and he is now in the computer business.

9 Sounds of the Seventies

CHANGES TO THE REGULATIONS

In 1970, the RAC changed the name of the category for sports cars specially prepared for racing, from 'Production Sports Cars' to 'Modified Sports Cars'. The new title more accurately described these vehicles, which were, after all, somewhat different from those that left the factory. The change of title coincided with the most radical revision of the regulations for many years; indeed, the rules introduced then are not far removed from those in force today. Inevitably, most people abbreviated the name of the category to 'Modsports'.

The long-standing stock block, gearbox and rear axle casing requirement was clarified, but the main change was in respect of the body shell itself. It was permitted to change the outer wings, doors, bonnet and boot lid, but the section of the monocoque between the wheel centres had to remain in the standard material – steel, in the case of Spridgets. This immediately rendered ineligible cars with alloy inner panels and any form of space frame. It did not come out of the blue; competitors were given notice of the impending changes in the previous year's rule book.

There were no changes in the four capacity classes: A – over 3000cc, B – 2001–3000cc, C – 1151–2000cc, and D – up to 1150cc. These splits meant that, in racing the Cooper S-based 1275cc engine, Sprite and Midget competitors were up against Elans, with 1600 and, in many cases, 1800cc engines. Apart from the capacity difference, the Lotus also had a more advantageous power to weight ratio and a better chassis, and there began to be an imbalance in the class structure. Spridget drivers were finding their cars overstretched in the up to 2 litre class and pressure was applied to the organizing bodies to re-align the structure. Richard Ward, who built a 1293 Midget in 1972, was a leading campaigner for the change. In each of the next three years, he had a letter on the subject published in *Motoring News*. As a result of lobbying by the drivers during the latter part of 1972, the BARC agreed to introduce an 1151–1300cc class. However, when the new season arrived, the classes did not change in the championship rounds.

WARD AND HOWIE

Some of the smaller clubs, anxious to attract competitors, did run an 1151–1300cc class in their Modsports events. These few races proved the point and led to some fine dices amongst the Spridgets. Ward himself had many a battle, particularly with Gordon Howie, who he once described in print as his 'arch rival and friend'. Howie and Ward first met on the track at Aintree in June 1974. On this and on the next four occasions when they competed against each other, Howie was to come home ahead of his rival. In three cases they were 1st (Howie) and 2nd (Ward) in class. However, at the Silverstone SUNBAC meeting in August 1974, Ward was to turn the tables in what he will always remember as 'Got Howie Day'.

Ward managed to pass Howie's car by a demon out-braking manoeuvre at Woodcote

'Got Howie Day'. Richard Ward (10) out-brakes arch rival Gordon Howie (15) at Silverstone on 31 August 1974, the first time Ward had managed to beat him

and stay in front to the flag. Howie was completely surprised and has never known how it was done. Now, all can be revealed – it was down to Ward's new driving shoes. Coming into the corner, he went to heel and toe and, at the vital moment, his foot came out of his slip-on shoe. He missed the brake pedal, and came out of the corner faster than intended, but ahead of his rival. On the next lap, he threw the offending shoe out of the window into the pits!

Nearly twenty years on, both drivers are still involved in club motor sport. Ward successfully campaigns his highly modified Elan, which he acquired in 1976. In recent years, the car has been a regular front-runner in the Castle Combe GT series. After a break of many years, Howie turned to Historic Rallying. He has stuck to a Midget and his car is, more often than not, among the top five in the premier British stage events. It certainly seems as though racing a Midget will give you a motor sport appetite for life.

THE NEW DIVISION

In 1976, a universally accepted change in the class structure was introduced – the new division came out at 1151–1500cc. This led to the leading Midget drivers searching for a way to increase their engine capacity. For the record, Gordon Howie won the 1151–1500cc class of the 1976 BRSCC Modsports Championship, but had to give best to Ian Hall's Mini Jem in the BARC series.

ALAN MINSHAW AND CHARLES IVEY

While most drivers of Sprites and Midgets competed just for fun, there were a few who used them as a grounding for bigger and better things. One well-known name in the motor sport world who had some of his early races in a Midget is Demon Tweeks boss Alan Minshaw. In 1970, he ran an ex-Alan Wood 1150 car and remembers that it was very competitive – as long as the oil stayed off the clutch. It was usually OK for four out of five laps, then there was the usual problem of oil leaking out of the rear main. To prevent the eagle-eyed 'Scrutes' chucking the car off the grid, Alan and his crew used to strap a pad of sorbo rubber under the engine to catch the drips. And I thought that was a new idea!

Today, the name Charles Ivey is synonymous with Porsche. When he arrived in England in 1967 from his native Australia, Ivey soon found a job with John Sprinzel. He worked on Sprinzel's competition cars, as well as on everyday customer vehicles, such as A35s and Sprites. When Sprinzel returned from the London–Sydney Marathon, at the beginning of 1969, with his battered MG Midget, he parked it in the workshop and got back to work. It stood there, collecting dust in a corner. Eventually, Ivey, who had raced a Holden in Australia for a year, decided the MG would make a good basis for a racer. He paid his boss what he describes as a 'nominal' amount for the car, and spent his free time over the next year converting it for this purpose.

Ivey ran the Midget in Modsports for the 1971 and 1972 seasons. In 1973, he broke his leg in a road accident and, while recovering, was a guest at a dinner party. He indulged rather too much in the wine that was flowing, and the result was that he sold the car 'far too cheaply' to former Mini racer David Hipperson.

THE FIRST WIN 1

Another well-known touring car driver had his first circuit race in a Spridget during 1971. Having tired of the constant repairs needed to his autocross and rallycross cars, in which he competed from 1964 to 1970, Win Percy was looking for a suitable vehicle to race on tarmac. He saw a picture in

A young Win Percy poses with his Midget on the forecourt of his garage. He bought the car after seeing a photograph of it having an accident in Autosport

Autosport of Brian Cutting crashing the ex-Andy Belcher car at the Thruxton season opener on 14 March 1971 and decided – 'goodness knows why' – that he wanted it.

Brian Cutting, now well known in Special Saloons, only had the one outing in the car and was amazed when he put it on the front row of the grid. He made a tardy start, but soon worked his way up through the field and was up to 5th at the end of lap 2. On the last lap, he took Brian Hough's TVR for 2nd and went off in vain pursuit of the leading E-Type of John Burbridge. In his enthusiasm, he braked too late for the chicane, spun and hit the Armco. Although he was out on the spot, he had the satisfaction of scoring the fastest lap (1:34.6), beating the time set by the race-winning Jaguar. He remembers the Midget engine had a very narrow power band – 6,600 to 8,000rpm – and that you had to keep it screaming the whole time. This was probably as a result of the special Janspeed cam in the Paul Ivey-built engine.

Fortunately, apart from the glass fibre front, replaced for £12, damage was minimal; the wishbone had broken and absorbed most of the impact. After repairs, Cutting and Percy did a deal on the car. In exchange for a Hillman Imp, an Austin 1800 and another car, together with some cash, the little racer changed hands for the third time in less than a year. The pair then went testing at Castle Combe, their local circuit. Cutting did a few laps around the 1:34 mark; when it came to Percy's turn, he remembers his times varied wildly from 1:34 to 1:50. Cutting called him in and told him that if he managed to put together more than one decent lap, he could be quite good!

Win Percy raced the car for a season, competing in events at Castle Combe (where he won his class, first time out), and Thruxton, and doing a sprint at Yeovilton. He loved racing the blue 1293cc Midget and, like many other drivers, found that its manoeuvrability enabled him to dice with the E-Types, despite the fact that the MG only came with one set of intermediates. At one Thruxton meeting, he was doing just this, when, half-way round the first lap, he spun in front of virtually the whole field, after going over the hump. He sat in the car and

Win Percy hops the chicane kerbing at Thruxton in his Midget, the first circuit car to bear the legendary WIN 1 designation

waited; somehow, everyone managed to miss him, and he was soon off again in pursuit.

The Midget was the first of many circuit cars to bear the now famous WIN 1 designation. Since those early days, Percy, who turned professional in 1974, has become British Touring Car Champion three times, and is regarded by many as the world's number one touring car driver.

BARWELL MOTORSPORT

Barwell Motorsport, who built the 1964 Robin Widows car, came back to the fore in Spridget racing during 1970, when Richard Lemmer and Paul Butler took over the company following the retirement of founder John Lucas. Barwell built the cars and, as the result of a sponsorship deal announced in July 1969, they were raced under the Medway Motor Services name. Driven by John Elvers, Paul Butler and John Nunn, the distinctive blue, white and gold Sprites soon proved themselves a force to be reckoned with. Elvers and Butler scored a class 1-2 in the Prodsports race at Brands on 21 September 1969, the pair taking 3rd and 4th overall in the race, which was dominated by an E-Type and an Elan.

Butler started racing in 1967, driving an ex-Downton Frogeye Sprite, which had been converted to a Mark II, following a comprehensive off at Brands Paddock Hill Bend. Known at the time as the last of the late-brakers, he set the outright Lydden Modsports lap record on 9 October 1970, then held it for three years. His main adversary at Lydden was the Geoff Daryn/Tony Dunderdale Turner GT, VUD 701. In 1971, Paul won the TEAC Champion of Lydden title. It was not uncommon for him to race both the Sprite and his other car, the Automex Mini 1000, on the same day. He later went on to Formula 3 and the Sprite was sold to Tony Broom. In recent years, Barwell Motorsport has been successfully revived by Richard Lemmer's son Mark, who won the VW Vento VR6 challenge in 1994.

DEAD HEAT

It is extremely rare for a race to be declared a dead heat; even if cars apparently cross the line together, they can usually be split on time. The Modsports event at Silverstone on 29 March 1972 did have joint winners, and one of them was a Midget. Gerry Ashmore's 1.6 Lotus Elan Plus 2 led for most of the 10 laps, but was pressed every inch of the way by the 1.3 Midget of Colin Lane, who tried unsuccessful out-braking manoeuvres at Woodcote virtually every lap. On the last tour, Lane tried a different tactic and tried to get by at Beckets. This resulted in a touch, which sent the Lotus into a spin.

Lane nipped by on the inside, but Ashmore made a quick recovery, catching his adversary at Woodcote. The pair dashed to the line neck and neck and the result was declared as a dead heat, both drivers being given identical race times. The Lotus was credited with the fastest lap and the pair lapped everyone up to fourth place. Andy

Ian Hall driving his well-known Sprite CAE1C at Castle Combe in 1967

Sounds of the Seventies

Bailey's Frogeye Sprite won the up to 1150 class.

IAN HALL

Sprite driver Ian Hall did just one race in his first season 1966, but, in his own words, he was 'well and truly bitten by the racing bug'. The next year he competed in thirty-seven events, driving his British Racing Green wire-wheeled Mark III Sprite, CAE 1C, to and from the circuits and, for that matter, to work the following Monday morning. His efforts led him to win the 1967 Austin Healey Championship. He went on to build a Frogeye specifically for racing, and his first car was relegated to the role of tow car, although he would, on occasions, race both cars at a meeting.

Hall acquired the taste for European races by coming home 44th, out of eighty-four starters and fifty-eight finishers in the 1969 Nurburgring 500, in a specially built Group 3 Mark IV Sprite, basically a showroom class car. The following year, he used a 14-year-old Morris Oxford to tow the Frogeye to Italy for the race at Mugello on 19 July. The journey through the Alps was quite eventful. On the way up the St Gothard Pass, he had to stop five times to allow the engine to cool; going down the other side, three halts were needed to get the brakes back to a reasonable temperature. Despite these precautionary measures, he still had to resort to the escape lane on one occasion!

He duly arrived in the centre of Florence for scrutineering and was surprised to find the street deserted, despite the fact that it was market day. When the traffic lights turned green, he soon realized he was going the wrong way up a one-way street! After scrutineering, drivers had to be examined by the circuit doctor, who was apparently much amused by the shape of Hall's legs. He had the last laugh, though, when the medic hit

This excellent period shot taken somewhere in Germany shows Ian Hall's trusty 1956 Morris Oxford towing the Sprite to the Nurburgring in 1969. The journey proved too much for the not-so-trusty trailer, which broke its back shortly after arrival

his knee to check his reflexes; his leg came up very quickly and caught the doctor in the groin.

For practice, all competitors were required to complete two laps of the 41-mile (66km) course, which only gave Hall a chance to remember 'where the really dodgy bits were'. He did derive some help from the Chevron team, who had been out the night before and painted symbols on the side of the road, indicating the severity of the bends. After returning to the paddock, Hall was approached by Mike Coombe who, having stuffed his Porsche on his first lap, needed another Group 6 car in which to qualify. Hall reluctantly agreed to lend him the Sprite, provided he took it easy. With some difficulty, Coombe eased his somewhat portly frame into the driving seat and went on his way. Having gone round in 39.5 minutes himself, Hall began to get worried when his car did not come past the pits after 45 minutes. All was well, in fact; Coombe was taking it *really* easy, lapping in just under 60 minutes.

The race saw the 103-car field start in pairs at ten-second intervals and Hall lined up beside a Ferrari Dino, which left him in a cloud of dust when the flag dropped. However, as the Sprite approached the first double bend, yellow flags were being frantically waved and the back of the Ferrari was to be seen, sticking out of the scenery. Hall found the circuit extremely bumpy, the Sprite's quarter-elliptic springs and the weight of the 15-gallon bag tank combined to give an extremely rough ride.

As his 1275cc engine had become unreliable, Hall had been forced to run his 1132cc Downton unit, which, after all the races it had completed, 'used a drop of oil'. He pitted after two laps for fuel and a couple of pints of oil before setting off again. The distinctive Frogeye appeared to cause much amusement amongst the large Italian crowd, who seemed to congregate at all the worst bends, hopeful of witnessing an incident. At the start of his fourth lap, Hall was horrified to notice that the oil pressure dropped drastically every time he rounded a corner. He was forced to nurse the car, dipping the clutch and freewheeling round the bends.

At his much reduced speed, he could see the previously amused spectators waving him on and willing him to complete the distance, which he described as 'a very moving experience'. By now, the engine was starting to tighten but, fortunately, as he approached the main straight, he was lapped by the winning car and took the flag to finish his own race after just four laps. The engine finally seized as he drove into Parc Ferme and he had to be pushed the last few yards by enthusiastic Italian spectators. Later inspection of the engine would reveal all the big end bearings had worn, one rotating in the rod and wrecking his valuable Nitrited crank.

Hall went along to the prize-giving, held in the local village hall, with a few others from the British contingent. Eventually, after about an hour of speeches, the awards ceremony started; some while later, the announcer garbled something that sounded like 'Yan Hal, Aistin Hiley', and everyone looked around expectantly, for the third time apparently. Ian Hall realized he was being called to the rostrum to receive the award for winning the Group 6 class, for cars up to 1300cc. He duly collected his trophy, together with a refund of his entry fee and £30 prize money. As well as setting the fastest lap in the class, he was, in fact, the only British winner. The class win also got him £100 bonus payments from both BMC and Castrol, and this paid for the whole trip, including a fortnight's holiday, which he and his wife went on to enjoy after the race. Second in the class went to the MG Midget of D. Andrews.

In 1972, having got the right bits on his car, Hall decided seriously to campaign the

Sounds of the Seventies

A Frogeye duo at Brands in July 1968, Ian Hall (47) leads Martin Phillis. Ian's car has one headlight removed to increase the air feed to the carburettor

Sprite in the STP Modsports Championship. His main adversary throughout the year was Barry Wood in the works Ginetta G4. At one meeting at Mallory Park, Hall's engine broke in practice. By chance, he happened to meet fellow Sprite man David Holmes in the paddock. Holmes was spectating that day, so the car he shared with Robert Nettleton was not being used. The pair quickly hatched a plan for Hall to borrow the car, so he could still score some points.

Having approached the Clerk of the Course, Hall had to get all the other drivers to sign a piece of paper allowing him to race in a different car from the one in which he had practised. They all agreed, but Hall does wonder if Barry Wood would have signed had he been present; he was not racing that day. Meanwhile, Holmes rang Robert Nettleton, who willingly agreed to the loan of their car, Hall hitched up his trailer and drove the twelve miles to collect the car from Ashby-de-la-Zouch. David Holmes checked it over before it was whisked away to be scrutineered, prior to Hall taking up his grid position. Despite never having sat in the car before, he achieved a class 3rd and scored himself some valuable championship points.

The championship went to the last round to be decided, with Hall and Wood extremely close on points. On the day, Wood broke down and was not on the grid; Hall's luck was not much better, the car stalling on the line. He managed to claw his way up through the field. Half-way through the race, it started to rain and Hall, who loved the wet, got right up with class leader Andy Talbot in his Spitfire. Urged on by the Ginetta team, who were waving fivers at him over the pit wall, the Spitfire pilot just managed to stay in front till the flag.

As a result, Hall and Wood tied on points. By virtue of his eighteen class wins to Hall's four, Wood won the class, and the pair tied for joint 3rd overall in the 1972 STP Modsports Championship. In 1975, Ian Hall went on to become even better known in a Mini Gem and subsequently a BMC-powered, rather than Imp-powered Davrian. In 1985, Bob Beaumont acquired the Sprite and, having equipped it with a Richard Longman engine, did very well in the Austin Healey Series, coming 2nd overall and winning the Modified category in 1987. Since 1989, it has been owned and driven in the same championship by tyre retailer and ex-Midget racer Nigel Bance.

Ian Hall still owns his original Sprite, CAE 1C, now in Arkley SS guise, following an altercation with an A40 in 1969. The car is now used for sprints and in 1993 he chalked up his one-hundredth victory in an 'A' series-powered car. In 1994 his son Andrew made his competition debut, finishing the season with a win in the Arkley at the Bristol Aerospace Motor Club Pegasus Sprint, under the watchful eye of Hall senior, in his new capacity as Clerk of the Course.

TONY WILLIAMS

Manchester-based Tony Williams was another club competitor who raced abroad with some success. Assisted by his twin brother Geoff, as designer and mechanic, Tony started racing a Frogeye in 1970. The following year, the car's shell assumed the standard Mark II Sprite shape and in 1973, now a Team Ziebart car, it had found form and was the holder of several lap records. Indeed, it was leading the Esso Uniflow Championship overall until the penultimate round. Overall victory eventually went to John Pearson's Jaguar XK 120, while the Williams car took class honours.

RACING IN GUYANA

The Williams sold the car to a chap in Warrington in 1973, but that is not the end of the story. They later bought the car back again and managed to get an invitation to race it in South America. They knew Gabriel Konig, by then Mrs de Freitas, living in Guyana, where her husband was the local Vauxhall importer. Gabriel was instrumental in getting Kit Nacimento, a high-ranking official in the office of the President and also a leading light in the GMRC, to invite the Williams twins to take part in the annual BOAC Commonwealth Motor Racing Championship there in 1976. Nacimento himself raced a Sprite in the series and the six club races that took place on the island throughout the year.

Drivers such as Richard Longman and Gordon Spice regularly took their Minis over and Alec Poole would invariably arrive with an MG. The series created tremendous local interest; it seems it was not uncommon for 20,000 spectators to turn out for what was basically a 'clubbie'.

The local Guyana Motor Racing Club airfield track at Timehri had two circuits, a long one, not unlike the old Silverstone Grand Prix Circuit, and a shorter, 1-mile (1.6km) club track, a bit like Brands. The longer track had three very long straights, which would see the Sprite run out of revs. The track, which incorporated one section of closed public road, was continually having sand blown on to it and was therefore extremely abrasive and hard on tyres. The championship was run on both long and short circuits, with practice one weekend and the race the next. The club was most efficient; starting at 10am, they managed to run a programme of about twenty races and still be finished by 5pm.

At the time, the islands had no television station, but there was extensive radio and press coverage, with the British drivers becoming overnight celebrities. During the week between practice and race, the visiting teams were offered lavish hospitality, with guided tours of sugar plantations and flights in private planes to visit the local waterfalls. There were parties every night and the drivers were forced to contend with the attentions of a bevy of local beauties!

On race day Tony Williams competed in several events. Afterwards the presentations took place at one of the smart local hotels, where it was almost a tradition for most of the prize-winners to be thrown, fully clothed, into the swimming pool. The Midget was then checked over and taken to the docks ready to be shipped to Barbados, for the following weekend's meeting at the Bushey Park Circuit. This was a permanent track on the site of a former airfield, best described as a 1-mile (1.6km) oval with a couple of extra bends in it. Tony Williams did well in the series, despite his standard-stroke 1300 engine. It was a fine ending to a trip that Geoff Williams describes as 'an unforgettable experience'.

ROGER SPARLING

On his return to England, Tony Williams did a few more Modsports races, before selling the car to Keith Ashby who, along with his friend Alan Goodman, briefly raced it, before selling it to Devon farmer Roger Sparling. Sparling's interest in sports cars started in 1966, when he bought a brand-new 1098 Midget from the local main dealer's showroom. He wrecked the car inside twelve months, having used it for autocross. Some years later, now settled down and married, Sparling decided to buy a boat. One weekend in 1976 he set off for Torquay in the cattle truck to look for one. He parked the truck, wandered round the boatyard and then he spied it, lurking in a corner, all shiny red fibreglass.

The yard owner had rather reluctantly taken it in part exchange, so Sparling was able to agree a good price. He manhandled it into the truck, and set off for home. When he arrived, the whole family came out to admire his new purchase; he dropped the tailgate and pushed his new toy out in front of them. It was a fine machine – a Modsports Midget, which he had been unable to resist. His wife was surprised, to say the least.

It was a nice enough car but, according to Sparling, it had been put together without too much thought, so he later sold it and replaced it with the ex-Williams Sprite. He still liked a bit of autocross. I vividly remember competing against him in a round of the Midget Championship at Brands on 22 June 1980. He had a disappointing practice session and ended up on the third row, but he made a demon start, overtaking me on the grass, before we got to Paddock, and going on to come 3rd behind Sheppard and Everitt.

When the Sprite made way for an Elan, in 1981, it went to Suffolk estate agent Robin Knight. He sprayed it cream, had distinctive knight chess-pieces painted on each door, and called it a Midget. I had another good dice with the car: during a three-way struggle for third place, Davrian driver Lorina Boughton, Robin Knight, and I managed to get round the narrow Lydden hairpin three abreast, without making contact! The car's chequered career continued, in Frogeye guise, when Tony Elsoff's driver, ex-kartist John Curtis, used it to good effect to win the 1987 Austin Healey Championship.

ERNIE FOSTER

South African Ernie Foster came to England for a holiday in the 1960s and never returned home. Between 1968 and 1978, he amassed over 120 trophies for races, sprints, hill climbs and autotests, all won driving one of several Midgets in which he competed. He was well known for towing his racer on the back of another Midget and at MGCC meetings he would also race the tow car, in the road-going event. His record for a day's motor sport was four races in two different cars.

Ernie Foster proves you can tow a Midget with a Midget, even if the rear bumper nearly touches the ground

The Heatherbourne Racing Midget of Mike Donovan and Peter Richings. The duct behind the door is the air intake for the radiator which was mounted in the boot

HEATHERBOURNE RACING

Enthusiasts of the time could not fail to remember the names of Mike Donovan and Peter Richings, whose string of successes culminated in their sharing the innovative Heatherbourne Racing Midget. As a 19-year-old BLMC student apprentice, studying at Aston University, Donovan ran a Midget in seven sprints at the end of 1972, before racing it the following season.

His first year as a racing driver resulted in five 1sts, six 2nds, three 3rds and one 5th place, the car only failing to finish twice out of seventeen outings. Having done most of his events at Silverstone, Donovan, as a novice driver, was eligible for points in the Vandervell Novice Awards, his tally giving him second place and a cheque for £100. He continued to race the car during 1974, selling it after his first event in 1975 so that he could concentrate on getting his degree.

During the winter of 1976–77, fellow racer James Thacker re-introduced Donovan to his old friend Peter Richings, who was now a near-neighbour and fellow BLMC employee. He bought a half-share in a car which Richings had almost finished building. The 1380cc Midget was completed by the pair and was debuted early in 1977. Confident after their many hours of preparation, they entered two races on the weekend of 26 and 27 March. At Oulton Park on the Saturday, Donovan came home 2nd, while the visit to Thruxton the next day produced a win. During the season, the car was the one to beat, taking six 1sts, two 2nds and two 3rd places, failing to finish three times. Among seven fastest laps, three new lap records were established.

In October 1977, at the Brands Hatch meeting that included one of the rounds of the Midget Championship, there was a cut and thrust three-way struggle for the lead between the Midgets of Donovan and Steve Everitt and Mike Chalk's Lenham-bodied Sprite. From the flag Donovan, on his first-ever visit to the Kent circuit, managed to get in front and lead the way. On lap 2, Chalk got by Everitt for 2nd place, then had a look at taking the lead. By now, they were going through corners three abreast, with bits of wheel arch flapping in the wind, as a result of body contact. To make life even more exciting, they had started to lap slower cars, which resulted in more close moments. On lap 6, Everitt got 2nd place back and was having a very serious look at taking the lead. During the final tour he got the nose of his car in front at Paddock, resulting in Donovan spinning on to the infield. Everitt beat Chalk to the line by 0.6 seconds, with Donovan coming home 3rd, not sure if he had fallen or had been pushed. None the less, he took some satisfaction from the fact that he had led for nine laps, on his first visit to the Hatch.

The Donovan/Richings car was now sponsored by Heatherbourne. It had a glass fibre body and fully rose-jointed coil-sprung rear suspension, and was rebuilt to the limit of the regs. Complete with 1460cc engine, it was ready for 1978, which would be the duo's final season in Modsports. With set-back engine and rear-mounted radiator, it had almost perfect weight distribution. Many of the lap records set by Richings and Donovan on Goodyear G50 slicks stood for nearly ten years, only to be broken with the advent of softer compound Avons. At the end of the season, the car was sold to Andrew Shilstone and the pair moved on to Clubmans Formula and ultimately Formula 3 Class B.

ANDY BAILEY

One of Donovan's regular sparring partners was Andy Bailey, whose 1150 Frogeye was

Mike Chalk in his Lenham Le Mans Sprite neck-and-neck with Steve Everitt's Midget at Brands Hatch 1977

incredibly quick, particularly in the wet. He was another driver who had progressed from sprints to racing in a car that he developed from his original road Frogeye. 1897 VX had been his 21st birthday present and his only form of transport while at university. Bailey's first racing engine and gearbox were carefully built on the bedroom floor in his hall of residence. He paid a breaker £1.50 for a 1098 Morris 1000 engine, had it bored to 1144cc, fitted a home-modified Mark IV Sprite head (12:1 compression ratio) and had it tuned to give 72bhp on the rolling road. It was revved to 7,000 and did well to do a whole season before needing a rebuild.

Bailey managed a class win in his first actual race, at Silverstone. As a novice driver, he had signed up for the Vandervell Awards, and took part in as many races at Silverstone as possible in 1972, as only races at this circuit counted. Some days, he entered both the Modsports and GT races in order to get more points. The car proved consistently quick and, having rapidly got the hang of out-braking other competitors to overtake, Bailey was soon beating much more powerful machinery. In particular, he was proving to be a thorn in the side for drivers of some 1293cc Midgets, whom he often eclipsed.

The year went fairly well. Despite missing out on entries for some of the Silverstone meetings, Bailey's final toll of three 1^{st}s, three 2^{nd}s, two 3^{rd}s and two 4th places was enough to place him 3rd in the awards. This netted him a cheque for £75, which was immediately used to reduce his overdraft. Had he not spun during his last race, he might have come 2nd. As it was, he took off Midget racer and *Autosport* scribe Peter Richings, and had to suffer at the pen of his rival in the end-of-season report on the novice series.

Bailey continued to race the car regularly throughout 1973, 1974 and 1975, taking many class wins and fastest laps in the up to 1150 category. He also continued to finish ahead of larger-engined cars. The period from March 1973 to December 1974 would see the car entered for forty-eight races, taking twenty-one class wins and only failing to finish four times (two accidents and two

Andy Bailey at Lydden Hill in 1974

mechanical problems). At that time, race entries cost between £4.50 and £6. By now, in the eyes of the media, Andy Bailey and Mike Donovan had reached 'arch rival' status, the Frogeye being variously described as 'incredible', 'standard-looking' and 'very quick'. Bailey really came into his own in the wet, admitting that he loved it. Having returned to the fray after a brief lay-off, Bailey retired and sold the car in 1979.

VIVIEN WEST

Spridget racing is not an entirely male domain. Vivien West, a prominent member of the British Women Racing Drivers Club, raced a Modsports Frogeye from 1973 to 1982, after an initial season sprinting her 1966 road Midget. Her first event in the modified car was a sprint at the Greenham Common Air Base, in September 1972. More than twenty years on, the main things she remembers about the day are losing a wheel and being transported back to the paddock on an enormous aircraft-recovery vehicle. Having returned to the paddock, she then managed to get locked in the loo!

She recalls a two-way Anglo-Irish Modsports challenge organized by the MG Car Club in 1976. The arrangement was that the Irish contingent would race at Aintree, and the following week, they would play host to the English drivers at Mondello Park. Given the proximity of Aintree to the Liverpool Docks, the visitors were told to leave their trailers behind and push the cars on to the ferry, and were assured that they would be met at the other end. Needless to say, they weren't and a few hurried phone calls had to be made.

After the day's racing, the majority of the English competitors went off home and it was left to Viv West's husband Richard, and a couple of other people who were camping at the circuit, to use their trailers to ferry the visitors back to the docks. They ran out of time and trailers, and in the end they resorted to towing the last car on the end of a rope. The Wests were, in the eyes of the Irish, real heroes, and they were to receive very special hospitality when they arrived for the return match on 28 August. Viv West remembers pushing the trailer on to the ferry and parking her tow car at Liverpool. When they arrived at the other end Don Kissaine, whom she refers to as their 'Irish godfather for the weekend', took over. The Sprite was whisked away and Viv and Richard were taken to the people who were to put them up, to leave their luggage. Then it was straight down to the pub, where the drinks were already lined up for them. They spent the evening drinking and being given advice on the best way to drive the circuit, falling out of the door at 4am the following morning.

As none of the visitors had ever even seen Mondello before, it had been arranged for them to have some familiarization laps prior to the official practice. This was not to prove advantageous, as all four Spridgets ended up having problems. Still very hung over, Viv came off worst, crashing at Duckhams. The straw bales did much more damage than she imagined possible and basically wrote off the shell. Tony Williams experienced transmission failure, while Mark Birrell's Arkley and Ian Wilkinson's Midget both had engine problems. All out before they had even passed through the scrutineering bay!

Mark Birrell approached Viv and suggested that, if she were willing, they should transfer her engine into the Arkley, then at least one of the visiting MGs could appear. Their ferry fares had been sponsored and they needed to carry out some sort of face-saving exercise. Richard West, a man prepared for all eventualities, had a folding jib which fitted on to their trailer, and this was rigged up and used to swap the engines.

Engine transplant. Richard West uses his ingenious trailer-mounted crane to change the power unit in wife Viv's Sprite, Mondello Park paddock, August 1976

When the authorities heard what was happening, they arranged for Viv to take part in the Modsports event, while the Arkley's owner was allowed out in the Sprite with the saloons, so that he at least had a race.

On their return to their Worthing base, Richard West bought Tony Bean's hill climb Midget rolling shell to see out the season. The car had been sponsored by Duckhams oils and was painted in their colours; this was ironic, as Viv's original car had been written off at Mondello Park's Duckhams bend. The following weekend, the Wests had to drive up to Warrington to collect their engine; Mark Birrell's Arkley had missed the ferry and they had been unable to swap it back on the way over from Ireland, as planned.

Two weeks after the accident in Ireland, the re-bodied car appeared at the Brighton Speed Trials. Over the winter, the Wests transferred all the original running gear into the replacement shell and it was out again, in its familiar brown and orange Frogeye guise, the next season. Viv went on to enjoy many successes in the car. Her Sprite was unique, in that it was possible to change the gearbox without taking the engine out. Richard West had fabricated a removable transmission tunnel.

In 1982, Viv West turned her attention to Formula 4, buying a Delta. She sold the Sprite to fellow Spridget racer Colin Charman, who subsequently sold it to Mike Chalk. Tony Elsoff then bought the car for the Austin Healey series and John Curtis

Sounds of the Seventies

Paul Bernal-Ryan goes over the yump at the now-defunct Bodiam Speed Hill Climb in 1985; behind is the thatched cricket pavillion

took it to victory in that championship in 1988.

Although Viv West was the most prolific of women Spridget competitors, there were others. Micki Chittenden made several Brands appearances in her husband Mike's car. Suzanne Everingham was again part of a husband and wife team; her husband Peter, an army officer, went on to run an early MGB in Historic Sports. Patti Phillips had the occasional outing in Mark Hales' car, and Wendy Black and Suzanne Richards also came out in a couple of races.

PAUL BERNAL-RYAN

Like Keith Ashby, Kent car restorer Paul Bernal-Ryan, who can often be found behind the wheel of the Charing fire engine, has raced the same car for over twenty years. He first drove his ex-Tony Santer car at Lydden Hill circuit in November 1974. He paid £350 for the Midget, and has used it at race meetings, sprints, hill climbs and even the odd autotest, every year since then. The Midget, a 1965 GAN3 model, had a competition history for most of its life, being used for rallies and autocross before being converted for circuit use in 1969. To raise the money to buy the MG, Bernal-Ryan sold his road car at the time, a Mark VI Bentley, and has no regrets, having derived so much pleasure from the Midget over twenty years.

Bernal-Ryan, who used to mechanic for John Homewood's all-conquering Hillman Imp, sponsored by Kent Messenger, tells me: 'My original reason for the whole project was to do one race, just to prove to myself that I could do it. Silly boy! One race and I was hooked, within minutes of getting home that night, I sent off my entry for the MGCC event at Brands a few weeks later. What a mistake that was. I won my class and collected a trophy; no looking back now. I just had to have more.' These sentiments would surely be echoed by many drivers.

JONATHAN PALMER AND ROBERT PARKER

In 1975 a keen young newcomer appeared in a Frogeye, introduced to racing by his father, a circuit doctor for the BARC. Medical student Jonathan Palmer's racing debut was at Thruxton on 2 March. The car, which boasted Triumph Herald front uprights, a welded locked diff and a straight-cut gearbox, had an 1120cc engine, but what the team lacked in horsepower was more than made up by the enthusiasm of the driver. His brother acted as mechanic for him, but his place was later taken by a greengrocer, whose Transit was used to tow the car to race meetings. Palmer later acquired his own van, which was driven with the same verve as the Sprite.

Palmer and Vivien West became friends. When Viv had engine problems on the first lap of practice at Thruxton on 15 November, she lent Palmer her wets for the race. As her tyres were much newer than his, he managed to climb up through the field, from 20th on the grid and was going like a train, despite the conditions. Unfortunately, it was to no avail, as he had to retire on the third lap with something hanging off the car. Palmer returned the favour the next month when he let Viv share his car at a Goodwood sprint, when her engine would not start. Having driven the car, Viv had even more admiration for his driving ability, finding the handling far from ideal.

Palmer, who had to ensure he cleaned all the oil from his fingernails before returning to medical school on Monday morning, competed in about a dozen races in the season and enjoyed some measure of success. At Brands on 2 November he finished 3rd overall, 2nd in class and also beat all the Spridgets in the 1151 to 1300cc class.

At Brands on 16 November, the Sprite appeared in a lurid shade of green. Palmer put it on pole and promptly stuck a 'For Sale' sign on it in the paddock. It was subsequently sold to Robert Parker for £385. Like Palmer, he only ran the car for one season – 1976 – basically to get six signatures on his licence.

Living in London, Parker mainly competed in events at Brands and Lydden, borrowing a friend's Mini Moke to tow. The Moke was equipped with a tow bar, but there was no socket for the trailer board, so Parker used tank tape to attach the plug to the rear panel. He recalls getting pulled up by a member of the Kent Constabulary on the way to Lydden; he was booked for having no mudguards on the trailer, which had been fabricated entirely from scaffolding tube, but the policeman did not spot that the lights did not work. Next time out, the trailer sported a pair of mudguards made from pieces of an old plastic dustbin.

Jonathan Palmer was later better known for his Modsports exploits in a 3-litre Marcos. The car was originally prepared and driven by Andy Fraser, although actually owned by John Dudley. The records show that in April 1976 Palmer won the Modsports race at Castle Combe, from the back of the grid. This, combined with other wins during the season, took him to a class 2nd in the Modsports championship that year. At last his talent was recognized and he managed to get into Formula 3. The rest is history.

WHITEGATES SERVICE STATION

To those racing during the 1970s, the name Whitegates Service Station was synonymous with a pair of immaculately prepared and well-driven Sprites. The governor, John Wilmshurst, had started racing in 1967, with an 1150 car. By 1972, there were two Whitegates Midgets, shared by Wilmshurst, Peter Moreton and Roger Redsell, who was the panel beater/sprayer at the Strood-based service station and had coil-sprung rear suspension on his car. Later on, Ian Bax, more normally seen on the grid in his Mini, had an occasional drive in Wilmshurst's car. One or other of the cars held the Brands class lap record for the whole of the 1975 season. Between them, they broke it three times in the course of the year.

Peter Vickers had joined Wilmshurst's staff as a mechanic and soon proved his expertise in building very competitive 1293 and 1380cc engines for the team cars. He perfected the use of split Webers and, had some special inlet manifolds cast to maximize the benefits of this particular modification. Vickers also drove Wilmshurst's car on occasions, scoring a few class places, particularly during 1974, when running in 1150 guise.

MEDWAY MOTORS

Geoff Weekes also raced under the Whitegates/Vickers banner. He had started his own career in 1974, when he bought one of Paul Butler's two Medway Motors metallic blue Midgets. Weekes wrecked the car at Lydden, at the end of his first season, and then bought Redsell's rolling shell (the engine having been blown up) when Redsell moved on to race a Caterham 7. With this, Weekes soon became the man to beat, particularly at Brands, his local circuit. At the MGCC meeting there on 5 December 1976, he scored two race wins. As a result of his success, he attracted sponsorship from Dodgers Diner, an American-style restaurant in Rochester. Local driver Steve Fray bought David Mercer's Midget, and raced in the same 'team'.

While lapping a road-going car during the Midget practice session at Brands, on 23 October 1977, Weekes was put off and hit the pit lane wall. Over the winter, the car was re-shelled as a Lenham but when, the following season, the Modified Midget regulations changed to allow cars to run open, he soon reverted to the Midget shape, with an aero screen. After another accident, he moved to Suffolk. Returning in 1982, he rebuilt his damaged car into the shell of Steve Fray's old Midget, and made a brief comeback for a season, before selling it to Mark Ellis for 1983. He now runs his own garage and races a BMW.

The sister car to Geoff Weekes' original Medway Motors racer went to West Sussex driver Tony Broom, who shared it during the 1972 season with Paul Barton. The pair did about twelve races in it during the season but only recall winning one pot, at Thruxton. The car was the larger-engined of the two Paul Butler cars, with 1380cc. More recently, Broom competed in the Hot Hatch series driving a Citroen AX. In the 1980s, he was the 'Mr Turner' of Modsports, owning and racing a number of examples of this now rare car, including the famous ex-John Miles/Tony Dunderdale car VUD 701.

THE LPG CAR

A unique car, in terms of motive power, appeared in 1979, when Simon Hamilton-Smith debuted the Landi Hartog Dual Fuel Systems-sponsored car. At the time, petrol was going up in price, and suddenly LPG was the in, alternative fuel; it could even be bought at some motorway service areas. As the name suggests, Hamilton-Smith's car ran on both petrol and LPG, its 1460cc engine using the normal Weber carb set-up. The car, which was the original Mike Donovan racer, went quite well, but was never a front-runner. Subsequently, the red and gold machine reverted back to petrol only, before changing hands.

10 Round Shiny Things and Sticky Black Things

When it was introduced, in 1958, the Mark I Sprite ran 145 × 13 tyres mounted on skinny 3½in rims. When the Midget came along in 1961, the wheel width remained the same. Subsequently, a 4½in wire wheel option was available, and many of the racers opted for these in order to gain the little extra grip and traction they offered.

SUERON RACING

Throughout the 1960s and early 1970s, competition Midgets had used treaded racing tyres, Dunlop CR 65 Mk III being a very popular choice. Most drivers picked them up second-hand from advertisements or from people they knew. However, with the advent of slicks for the single-seater formulae in 1970, it was not long before the Modsports cars were running on the new sticky tyres as well. The popularity of slicks was assisted by an enterprising couple called Sue and Ron Livingstone who, in 1971, set up Sueron Racing. The Livingstones purchased part-worn tyres and sold them to the club racers from the old church hall at Burstow in Surrey, the village where they lived.

Martin Ingall, who, with his friend Martin Brazil, built a Modsports Midget, recalls visiting the Livingstones' premises before the start of the 1976 season. The old hall was stacked with tyres from floor to ceiling. They knew they wanted 13in diameter, but they did not have a clue about profile or compounds. They came away with a set of Goodyear 9 × 22 × 13, which cost them £12 each. These were promptly fitted to the rims at the local tyre depot and the two Martins went off to their first meeting, at Thruxton, expecting the car to stick to the circuit without any problems. This did not prove to be the case and, furthermore, the 22in profile upset the gearing.

Telephoned the following Monday, Sueron promised to exchange the tyres if they were returned, since the wear on them would be negligible, if not non-existent. The second visit revealed why the rubber had not even got warm, let alone hot. The covers were from a Formula 1 car and were designed to last for a race distance of over 200 miles (320km). No wonder they weren't getting sticky after just ten laps at Thruxton on a windy March day. They were changed for some 20in profile Goodyear G 54s, which proved to be far better for the job. This compound was designed for the much shorter races of Formula 3 cars.

Ron Livingstone, an airline pilot who used to race Clubmans and Monoposto cars, got involved in selling racing tyres almost by accident. When John Surtees closed down Team Surtees, he had a big clearance sale. Ron went along and offered him £2 each for all of the tyres in the Edenbridge workshops. There were a large number of them as Surtees held the testing contract for Firestone, which had by then pulled out of F1. Some weeks later, with no other offers forthcoming, Livingstone's bid was accepted. He took the tyres away and began to sell them on.

Encouraged by the success of the venture, he secured a contract with Goodyear to buy all the ex-Formula 1, 2 and 3 fronts, plus a few rears that he could sell to hill climbers and Formula 5000 competitors. He continued with Goodyear until Michelin came in to F1. At this point, Goodyear decided they did not want to run the risk of any of their tyres getting into the hands of the opposition and Livingstone's supply dried up, making it difficult for many club racers to find tyres for the following season.

After a short period as the UK supplier of new Michelin racing tyres, Sueron closed in 1981. The hall reverted to the church and it is once more used for Sunday school. Repairs had to be carried out first; during the building's ten-year use as a tyre warehouse, the floor, which was a bit rotten anyway, had given way under the weight.

As Midgets moved on to wider-treaded tyres, and eventually slicks, so the style and size of wheels used also began to change. The once-traditional wire wheels soon disappeared and were replaced by four-stud fixing, wide steel rims. Drivers found that the better grip afforded by slicks put a far greater strain on the wheel, in some cases leading to failure. Certain of the early wide 'steelies' were 'banded': the maker bought second-hand standard rims, cut them in half and welded in a central band to increase the width. These were eventually outlawed for competition use, as a stronger alternative was needed.

MINILITES

Alec Poole was one of the first Spridget racers to use Minilite magnesium wheels on his car. They were made by a company called Tech Del Ltd, founded by Derek Power to manufacture equipment that he had developed to teach atomic physics. It was obvious to this astute businessman that his production equipment would have surplus capacity, and he began to look around for another commodity that could be made from cast magnesium. He came up with wheels for BMC Minis; at the time, drivers using the standard steel version in a competition environment were complaining that they cracked under stress.

The first prototype set appeared, as early as 1963, on a Radford Mini-de-Ville at the London Motor Show. Production was started the following year, the rims being sand-cast at a small Welsh foundry, then transported to Tech Del's premises in West London for machining. When the Minilites appeared on the works V8 Sunbeam Tiger rally cars, this unique new form of wheel was really brought to the attention of the enthusiasts. Suddenly, everyone wanted a set.

Power was a bit of a perfectionist and, while his wheels had proved to be extremely strong, he was not totally happy with their appearance. He ceased production while he enlisted the help of Sterling Metals in perfecting a die-cast method of making the basic rim. This new method produced a much smoother casting. Because pure magnesium burns rather fiercely, the wheels were in fact only 92 per cent pure.

In 1966, after extensive testing, the new Minilite was released and they were soon to be found on the major winning rally and race cars. They probably became most famous on the works Mini Cooper S (which, incidentally, also had lightweight sump guards made by Tech Del). After being unavailable for many years, Minilites are once again being made from a new base in Egham, Surrey.

REVOLUTION WHEELS

The aptly named Revolution wheel was one of the first to have after-market rims made of aluminium. Based originally in Surrey,

The casting machine at the Revolution Wheels Slough foundry

the company was set up in 1966 by David Newton. Keen Special Saloon car racer Pat Mannion was one potential customer. Unhappy with the heavy steel rims on his Anglia, he went to see Newton, looking for a better alternative. He concluded that, although the wheels he was shown would do the job, the quality of the sand-casting process used to produce them left a little to be desired.

In 1967 Pat Mannion purchased the patterns and name and sought out another foundry which used, he felt, a better sand-casting process. Under his ownership, the company grew and in 1971 Revolution produced their first low-pressure die-cast competition wheel. At first, only the 13in rims were cast in this way – handy for Midget racers – but by the end of the following year the whole range was being produced by the new process. To demonstrate his confidence in his revised product, Mannion enlisted the help of class-winning Escort rally exponent Roy Eyers, and set up the ultimate test.

Mike Cannon made available the autocross circuit at his Kent farm and Eyers was persuaded to do twenty laps on a set of the new Revolutions. The rear wheels had no tyres on them, and the people from *Cars and Car Conversions* magazine were there to see fair play and write an article on the result. The wheels did well in the test, and Eyers, who ran his own engine-building business, Astral Engineering, gained Revolution sponsorship for his car.

The casting was still being done off-site, but in 1976, a foundry at Maidenhead went bankrupt. Pat Mannion went to look at the premises and discovered that the firm had made alloy Mini wheels for Firestone, so they already had a low-pressure die-cast process installed. He bought the foundry from the receivers and now had the facilities to carry out every stage of manufacture within the same company. In the mean time, Roy Eyers had been persuaded to join the Revolution staff, to look after the competition side. In due course, he took on the day-to-day running of the foundry. Pat Mannion, still an active competitor in Special Saloons was now known for his exploits in a Sunbeam Stiletto, sponsored, of course, by Revolution Wheels.

The company was keen to go over to die-casting and get their own foundry; when used for aluminium products, sand-casting can result in a high degree of porosity, not good for a wheel that carries a tyre filled with air. Mannion had established that the low-pressure process was the best possible way to make wheels. He and his team further perfected the method by coming up with a special filter, which trapped the impurities from the molten metal during casting.

Revolution saw their market continue to develop and soon diversified into modular wheels. By 1980, their familiar four- or five-spoke rims in either cast (one-piece) or modular (three-piece) form were available to fit a vast range of cars. In 1984, Roy Eyers took over running the business, which was sold in 1989. It is now based near Rochester in Kent, and is part of Alloy Wheels International.

WIDER RIMS AND SLICKS

In the 1970s, most of the front-running Midgets were running 8in rims all round, but by the end of the decade 10in rims were appearing on the rear. With the arrival of the 1980s, 10in all round was becoming the norm. As rim widths increased, the modular wheel became more popular. Makers such as Compomotive and 100+ found a ready market for their products, which allowed the simple replacement of just, say, the outer rim, if it were damaged in an accident.

The advent of the slick tyre did have its disadvantage – it was necessary to have a second set of wheels and tyres for the wet. Most competitors simply used a cheap set of steel rims with the original set of treaded racing tyres and dropped the pressure a couple of pounds to make them fit the bill. Few Midget racers admit to enjoying competing in the wet, but long-time driver Ted Reeve is one of a few notable exceptions. Many other competitors have accused him of doing a rain dance to bring about a change in the weather, so he could use his demon soft wets to good effect.

It used to be very unusual to find a Modsports Midget driver racing on brand-new rubber. Several had made connections with the Formula 3 teams and were buying their cast-offs direct. I bombed up the then incomplete M25 to Woking many times to collect the season's supply in my company car; I

Revolution Wheels Slough foundry, furnaces in background and rough castings and aluminium ingots in the foreground

then had to explain to my boss why his Cortina smelt like a rubber factory! Slicks were not a problem to get hold of, but wets were more difficult, as not so many of these were used by the teams and they tended to hang on to them.

Dunlop was making a range of slicks, mainly for saloons, and had developed a small network of specialist dealers to sell their products to the clubmen. Some of the better-off, or better-connected, drivers got Goodyears from International Race Tyre Services, who traded from the old Castrol Racing building in Uxbridge. This company supplied Goodyear race rubber to all branches of the sport, except Formula 1. Goodyear originally had factories at both Wolverhampton in the UK and Akron in the USA, but at the end of the 1970s, all manufacture was transferred to the USA. IRTS felt that close liaison between themselves and factory was vital and the seed was sown for race tyres to be produced in Britain once more.

AVON RACING

In 1981, Jean Mosnier of IRTS approached Avon, well known for the manufacture of road tyres and last involved in motor sport in the 1960s, suggesting they should move into competition tyre production. He proposed that his firm would provide the marketing and technical skills, together with some equipment obtained from the closed Firestone factory at Brentford, and Avon would provide the manufacturing base. The result was that the Wiltshire-based company set up Avon Racing on part of its site in Melksham. The sales manager of this specialist department is ex-IRTS man Roger Everson.

By the mid-1980s, Avon was well established, and prepared to listen to what the competitors wanted from their tyres. This, combined with a greater amount of sponsorship money coming into the sport, resulted in many more club racers, including the Midget drivers, having access to new tyres for the first time. Like many others, I bought my first set of new slicks around this time and found they were worth two seconds a lap.

Looking back, it was crazy to spend over £1,000 building an engine and then pick up second-hand tyres for £20 each. Furthermore, the new tyres were actually designed specifically for the cars, not for a single-seater with vastly different handling characteristics. It was very often possible to ring up, order the tyres and have them fitted and balanced at the circuit. The club racer had never enjoyed such excellent service.

At the beginning of June 1984, I bought my first-ever set of new Avon slicks, which I used at the Lydden round of the Midget Championship on 10 June. I scrubbed them in during practice, setting a time of 48.7 seconds, which got me on to the middle of the front row between Steve Everitt and John Vernon. In the race, I led the pack into the first corner, and came 3rd behind Steve and John, setting fastest lap at 47.5 seconds. Afterwards, my fellow competitors told me that I had seen my moment of glory on my new set of rubber. It made me realize why the leading single-seater and saloon teams had a new set of tyres for every race. It does make a difference.

SOFTER RUBBER

A1 and A2 were the popular compounds for Midgets then, but these were superseded by A11 and A12. Today, the leading contenders run on A26, or, if money is no object, on the softer A22 rubber, which wears more quickly. Whatever the choice, the cars certainly go round corners a good deal more quickly than they did on the hard-treaded tyres of the 1960s.

11 Development of Chassis and Body

SUSPENSION

The quarter-elliptic shell has been much maligned over the years, but it is significant that the enormously successful Steve Everitt car was, and still is, based on this form of suspension set-up. To facilitate some adjustment, Armstrong, the manufacturer of the original equipment lever-arm shock absorbers, introduced an adjustable version, known as the Adjustaride, which today is extremely difficult to find.

To prevent lateral movement, an 'A' frame could be fitted to the rear axle. Two brackets welded to the central, diff-carrying part of the casing attached it via two rubber bushed arms to the floor of the passenger compartment. Later, the rubber bushes were replaced by rose joints. The BMC Competition Department introduced a lowered leaf spring, which, used in conjunction with their up-rated shorter front coils, made the car sit down. Accessory manufacturers produced lowering blocks that did the same job.

Aldon Automotive was a well-known producer of suspension modifications for Sprites and Midgets throughout the 1970s and 80s. Founded in 1969, by Alan Goodwin and Don Loughlin, two former BL design and development engineers, the company supplied a wide range. Among their more popular items were up-rated/lowered coil springs, negative camber trunions, panhard rods and 10in disc conversions. Both men had been involved in building Goodwin's rather radical Sprite in 1968. The business was founded on the back of this car's successes.

BMC's introduction of half-elliptic rear springs produced axle tramp, particularly off the start line, so the anti-tramp bar was developed. This rubber-bushed bar was fitted below the springs, but often gave ground clearance problems. In time, the bushes were replaced by rose joints, which, as well as providing a more positive location, needed slightly less ground clearance.

The ultimate set-up was the coil-sprung, five-link rear end, developed by Aldon for Phil Whitehead's car in 1973. This system completely did away with the traditional cart springs and lever arms and replaced them with vertical coils over telescopic shocks, which pivoted on the original body shell check strap mounting. The axle was now located by four trailing links, of alloy bar with rose-jointed ends, two on either side of the car. A lateral panhard rod prevented transverse movement. *Cars and Car Conversions* magazine sponsored the Phil Whitehead car, which was also driven by their Technical Editor Fred Game.

This new system transformed the handling of the car and Aldon soon added it to their ever-increasing catalogue. Installation not only reduced weight by throwing away the cart springs, but could also save even more by cutting off most of the original shell to the rear of the axle. Fabricating a small tubular space frame to support the petrol tank, and replacement glass fibre rear bodywork, completed the job.

Development of Chassis and Body

Most of today's Modsports Midgets retain very little of the original body shell to the rear of the back axle centre line. This photograph of the author's car, taken while it was being built in 1984, shows the Aldon coil-sprung back axle and the small space frame welded in to the remaining section of the shell. This carries the petrol tank and supports the removable glass fibre rear bodywork

Adjustable front lever arms were never made, although they are available in a re-valved up-rated form. The single arm tended to twist under load, causing the car to lift a wheel in a tight corner. To overcome this, drivers began to fit the double arm unit from the MGB, which required the use of a rose joint to link the arms to the king-pin. In following this route, Phil Whitehead found he had to fabricate a special king-pin and used this in conjunction with an Aldon modified lower wishbone – basically the standard pressed-steel item with rose joints replacing the usual metalastic bushes.

It was not long before furtive minds began to think in terms of using a telescopic shock absorber on the front. Indirectly, Spax came up with the answer, by manufacturing an adjustable tele for the Mini. Midget drivers soon worked out that, by bending up a couple of simple brackets, these units could be fitted on their cars. Initially, the original lever arm, drained of its fluid, was retained as the top link. This was soon refined by fabricating a second, rose-jointed arm, to prevent the twist/wheel lift syndrome. This mod first appeared on the David Sheppard car at Brands, in November 1981.

A fixed degree of negative camber was possible by fitting a modified top trunion, which gave about two degrees. Owners who retained rear cart springs and the standard front wishbones were able to stiffen them up

Aldon-modified front suspension using MGB twin lever shock absorber and extended king-pin with adjustable camber and 10in disc brake conversion

Development of Chassis and Body

by replacing the metalastic bushes with Nylatron, a self-lubricating hard nylon compound. The late Martin Lower, a Surrey metalwork teacher who joined the Midget racing ranks in 1983, established a thriving cottage industry keeping drivers supplied with these and other small machined items. His own immaculate car was rebuilt from a rusting hulk as part of a school engineering project.

With the arrival of Barry Rogers on the racing Midget scene, in 1979, came the development of many improvements to both suspension and brakes. Rogers, the director of a catering equipment firm, had fabrication facilities available to him. Soon, with the assistance of his brother Mick (the owner of a coachworks), and John Tibbs (service manager of the local Leyland dealership), he was developing his ex-sprint car. During 1981, he designed and fabricated a rose-jointed top wishbone, which, in conjunction with an up-rated mounting kit for the Spax Mini shocks, resulted in a front end giving much more positive handling.

Being rose-jointed, Rogers' top wishbone was fully adjustable, allowing a certain amount of chassis distortion to be 'dialed out'. It was often difficult to straighten the 'H' frame fully after a heavy front impact, so this fringe benefit proved very useful to several drivers over the years. Thinking I had straightened a chassis, I have occasionally found, on assembling the suspension, that the top trunion would not meet the king-pin! Rogers made duplicate sets for a few of his friends, including Dave Paige (who raced his car under the 'Barry Rogers Racing' banner), Steve Everitt, and me. When other drivers saw what he had done, they went away and copied it.

Barry Rogers stayed one jump ahead of his imitators. For the 1982 season, he came up with a rocker arm configuration, which meant that the engine had to be set back 6in (15cm) in the chassis. The two arms pivoted

The immaculate Ripspeed-sponsored car of Barry and later Mick Rogers in the Donington Park paddock, 11 April 1982. The one-piece front bodywork is a replica of the 1500 rubber-bumper Midget

on the original suspension platforms, with inboard coils and teles, located on the platform below the rack cross-member. It also incorporated a fabricated king-pin and aluminium bottom wishbone, which were both rose-jointed. A custom-made fully adjustable anti-roll bar completed the set-up. Rogers made it all up at work, in his spare time. Drivers racing in the 1960s could argue that they had seen many of these mods before, on the cars prepared by Aldon. During its time in Barry Rogers', and later in the care of his brother Mick, the car became very successful, attracting long-term sponsorship from Ripspeed.

As engine power increased, it became apparent that the Midget's 8in discs began to fall short of the mark, even when competition pads were used. Donald Healey had already introduced a wire wheel conversion kit for the Frogeye, which utilized 8.5in discs with Girling calipers. Later, he brought out a version for bolt-on wheeled cars, with a slightly larger 8.75in disc and Lockheed caliper.

Modsports soon moved on to wider alloy wheels and competitors began to look for a larger-diameter disc at a competitive price. Believe it or not, the Vauxhall Ventura provided the answer. This heavy, top of the range saloon ran 10in discs. It was a simple job to machine up an adapter plate to fit this to a Midget hub, which retained the standard bearing set. After adding a new bracket to mount the caliper on the stub axle, the Midget driver was in business.

This set-up, on the Phil Whitehead car, was track tested by Triple C in 1973. Whitehead's version was slightly more sophisticated, using Girling lightweight alloy calipers from a Formula 2 car, rather than the original heavier Vauxhall iron items. The following year, he added a dual-circuit brake system with rear discs. He used second-hand March vented discs with Cortina GT calipers. Ten years later, the Barry Rogers car had Ventura discs with Cortina calipers up front and an XR2 set-up on the rear.

In recent years, brake improvements have all been variations on a theme, utilizing parts from cars that have found their way on to the scrap heap. If discs were not vented, they were drilled to assist cooling. Some drivers, like Mike Chalk, went to AP Racing and came away with full-blown racing discs and four pot calipers, but, at £200 a corner, this is beyond the average Midget driver. No matter what the hardware, everyone had harder compound pads; Ferrodo DS 11 was popular in the 1970s and 80s, but today Mintex M1144 seems to be favourite.

OVER-HEATING AND COOLING

Over-heating is often a problem for the tuned Midget engine and even the addition of an electric fan does not always cure the problem. It is possible to squeeze a four-row core into a downflow Midget radiator, but it ends up very heavy. The introduction of the Morris Marina in 1971 provided the opportunity for a radiator transplant. You had to chop off the original Midget radiator mounting uprights and replace them with flat brackets welded across the top of the 'H' frame. The new radiator was mounted in the standard Marina rubber bushes and held vertical by one strut at the top. This saved weight and made it easy to remove.

With a bit of deviousness, the standard bottom hose could be retained and a length of convoluted rubber pipe used for the top. The Marina rad had a wider frontal area and could also be fitted with a three- or even four-row core. The ultimate lightweight job was to get a Metro Turbo or Renault 5 unit, but these alloy and plastic items were invariably a throw-away if the car was involved in an accident.

Wiltshire engineer and company director Bunny Lees-Smith started Midget racing

Development of Chassis and Body

with an ex-Mark Hales Midget in 1980. He had for many years campaigned a Mini in road rallies, but had amassed so many endorsements on his DVLA licence that he thought it safer to take to the circuits – while he still *had* a licence. He progressively developed the car and approached the cooling problem from a different direction. Purchasing a single-seater radiator from Motor Racing Services, he positioned it on brackets, so that it lay virtually flat in front of the engine. The bodywork was then modified to give a scoop to allow air in at the front, with a larger one in the centre to allow it out again. This gave the car an unusual appearance, but worked very well. Bunny Lees-Smith and I were great sparring partners during 1983 and 84; our cars were very evenly matched and we enjoyed some great dices, particularly at Castle Combe, his home circuit.

An even more drastic cooling system was utilized in the Peter Richens/Mike Donovan 'Heatherbourne Racing' car. The radiator was moved into the Midget's boot, where it was positioned over the wheel centre line. This gave a better front to rear weight distribution. Air was fed to it via ducts in each of the wheel arches, immediately to the rear of the doors. The warm air was expelled through a duct in the boot lid and was utilized by way of a large spoiler to increase downforce.

RE-POSITIONING THE ENGINE

Another modification, often carried out in order to improve weight distribution, was to move the engine back in the chassis. This operation involved altering the bulkhead and transmission tunnel, which were often replaced with aluminium, and, of course, shortening the prop shaft. Way back in 1969, John Britten re-positioned the engine 8in (20cm) back in BRI 10.

Ted Cooke, then of Bijo Sports Cars, did a job on David Lamyman's 1430 Sprite engine, setting it back 5in (12.5cm). To support the engine, he used a sheet of Dural, which he

The Bunny Lees-Smith car with modified bonnet incorporating cooling ducts for the re-positioned radiator

attached to the original mounting points, and simply bolted the original engine mounting brackets on, 5in (12.5cm) back. The gearbox remote housing was cut down, together with the rods, which resulted in the gear lever ending up roughly where Abingdon had meant it to be.

Richard Jenvey, like John Britten, opted for an 8in (20cm) set-back, while the Barry Rogers team felt that, even allowing for their rocker arm suspension, 6in (15cm) was enough. Moving engines and lowering the cars created all sorts of problems when it came to the exhaust system. Most ended up with the pipe running through the passenger footwell and exiting out of the side, either through the nearside sill or door. This kept it safe from damage in the event of the car grounding out, although obviously the regulations stated that it must be encased to prevent the driver getting burnt. Despite this, it got very hot in the cockpit, particularly if the car ran with a hardtop.

WHEEL ARCHES

Increasing wheel widths, which over the years had gone from 4.5in to 10in, resulted in a profusion of wheel arches in all shapes and sizes. Some were made from a simple sheet of metal, perhaps faired in with lots of heavy filler; some were downright ugly and did nothing at all for the car. Drivers utilized a diverse range of arches, each designed for a car other than a Midget and made by the various specialist companies. One of the most popular was the Mark I Escort 'works' rear arch, which would fit nicely on the body of a Spridget. A fussy owner who decided that the radius was a little too large could cut a couple of inches out of the middle and bond it back together again.

John Boness fell foul of a Castle Combe scrutineer the first time he took his car out with a new set of 10in Compomotives, the alert official pointing out that the tyres were not completely covered, as specified in the Blue Book. Boness, an innovative fellow, went round a few litter bins and found himself a strong cardboard box. Returning to his car, he cut it into strips and stuck the strips on his original arches with tank tape. The tyres were now covered and he was allowed to race. This 'temporary' measure stayed in place for the rest of the season.

PANELS

Both the Jacobs coupés and the so-called works shells had aluminium panels, but this material was both expensive to buy and work. From 1967 on, most Marque Sports Cars sported glass fibre panels. The one-piece, or flip front, was considered essential, both for saving weight and giving easy access to the engine. It came in standard silhouette and also in a multiplicity of different shapes and sizes from the various manufacturers, each claiming theirs was more aerodynamic than that of their rivals.

During the 1960s, a few Spridget competitors were involved in making glass fibre bodywork for their own and other people's racers. Bob Evans, later of Formula 5000 fame, turned out mouldings in the garage on the side of his mother's house. This led to the formation of Mospeed, a glass fibre and preparation business, run by Bob Evans and Mike Ordway. Evans and fellow Sprite man Peter Long raced as Team Mospeed for the 1969 season, more commonly known in the paddock as 'Mother Mospeed' because of their sponsorship deal with shirt manufacturer 'Mother Wouldn't Like It'. The cars had some progressive graphics, displayed on them.

Tony Guy from Alcester was one of the first people to sell fibreglass Midget panels to fellow competitors and, went on to set up Guy Performance, a company specializing in light-

Development of Chassis and Body

Dave Sheppard on his way to victory and double points in the Midget Race at Croft on Easter Monday 1980. The one-piece front has the air intake altered and extra holes drilled to increase cooling

weight bodywork. Guy has moved on, but Worcester-based Smith and Deakin, the glass fibre moulders, who made many of the panels he sold, still manufacture Midget fronts, rear ends, hardtops and doors to this day.

Ashley Laminates, who started making bodies for Austin 7 builders in 1954 and then progressed to making kits for Ford 10 specials, also produced Spridget panels in both standard and modified shapes. By the late 1970s Autocross Plastics of Rossendale, who sponsored John Gallagher's car, had become the leading supplier of lightweight Midget body panels. These were moulded complete with arches to cover wheels up to 10in in width.

Richard Ibrahim with his self-built Midget special GT car, based on a Mallock U2 chassis. The height to the top of the scuttle is just 23in

Development of Chassis and Body

Richard Ibrahim, who originally campaigned the ex-Gordon Howie Modsports car in 1978–79, came up with probably one of the most radical Midgets. Built in 1972, his Special GT creation was based on a Mallock U2 Mk 8 Clubmans car. It took two years to complete and stands just 23in (58cm) high, from the ground to the top of the scuttle. It has race-weight, glass fibre Midget front and rear ends, with home-fabricated aluminium scuttle and doors. This was all grafted on to the lengthened Mallock tubular chassis. Power comes from a 1549cc Ford twin-cam engine, driven through a Lotus Cortina GT close ratio gearbox. Although the front suspension utilized tubular wishbones, it did have a Midget rear axle with 3:9 diff, Mallock-style, with off-centre diff and half shafts of unequal lengths. When complete, the car weighed about 8cwt (400kg) and put out about 160bhp, a significant power to weight ratio. The most striking thing about the car was its enormous ex-Wolf F1 rear wing, which Ibrahim was advised he would need to keep him pointing in the right direction.

It seems that the spoiler was, after all, unnecessary, as the estimated 4,000lb of downforce it created, in effect, lifted the front wheels off the ground. When he removed it at the end of his first test session, the car handled. A couple of years ago, tired of the large lump of alloy taking up valuable garage space, and noticing that John Perrin was running a couple of Wolfs in Historic Formula 1, he sold it to him. It is now back in its rightful place, on a Grand Prix car.

In 1992, two long-time Midget Championship competitors, Karl Barras and Steve Westwood, each appeared in innovative cars, both incorporating an Ashley fast-back hardtop. Westwood used a raked-back cutdown windscreen to reduce the frontal area of his coupé, and a fabricated spoiler was grafted on in place of the original small Ashley boot lid. The car was very well equipped for braking with discs all round – 11in at the front and 10in rears.

Karl Barras took his development to the ultimate degree. The front suspension was a work of art, having fabricated top and bot-

With the Smith and Deakin glass fibre bodywork removed, the origins of Ibrahim's car become more apparent

159

Development of Chassis and Body

Radical engine bay and front suspension of the Karl Barras Midget in the Brands paddock, November 1992

The rear suspension detail on the Barras car; the battery and fuel tank are situated forward of the rear axle

tom wishbones with coil over shocks, the front chassis platform stiffened by aluminium bracing pieces. Again, the fast-back boot lid was replaced by an adjustable spoiler, but below that there was virtually nothing. The rear panel had been cut out to reveal the coil-sprung back axle, with battery and petrol tank forward of that.

Changes to the Fully Modified Midget Series regulations have restricted the size of aerodynamic rear wings, which will eventually be phased so that the cars retain the standard Midget profile. This tightening-up of the rules rendered the Barras and Westwood cars ineligible in 'Ashley' form. The organizers felt, perhaps, that the cars no longer looked anything like MG Midgets. Both cars are now racing in accordance with the new regs.

12 The Ark Racing Twin-Cam Sprite

JOHN BANKS

Derek Matthews, master mariner turned engineer in Willenhall, was a well-known builder of racing Lotuses. One day in 1968, he was working on a customer's Lotus 23 when a young man came into the workshop, asking if there was any chance someone could teach him to weld. Aldon Automotive had lent him a set of suspension wishbone drawings and he wanted to make up a set for a racing Sprite he was building. The car, he said, was being constructed at the nearby premises of Orwell Engineering, a small toolmakers run by his father. Matthews told him that fabrication of vital suspension components was hardly a job for a novice and suggested he came round that evening to see the project for himself.

As a result of this chance meeting, Derek Matthews spent many hours helping ex-driving test and sprint exponent John Banks, and his friends, build his car. Although rather radical, it was actually based on a proper Sprite floor pan. Banks had been persuaded by Chris Smith that he ought to take up circuit racing; to help him on his way, Smith had found him a damaged shell for £25. Banks was no engineer and he recalls that Matthews soon took control of the project, while Banks was responsible for keeping the band of helpers supplied with endless cups of tea, and masses of chips and cakes.

By the end of 1969, his first season, Banks had recorded eleven top three placings from twenty-one outings in his 1300cc Sprite. At one Silverstone meeting another competitor told him that the word in the paddock was that the Sprite's chassis had cost £2,000 to develop, and asked if this was true. He could scarcely believe the reply – that the car was based on a written-off shell and some cheap lengths of steel tube.

As a spectator at the 1968 Silverstone Grand Prix Circuit Clubmans Meeting, John Banks had watched Roger Enever throwing 138 DMO through Woodcote, right on the limit and recording record-breaking lap times of 1.52. He was convinced he would never be able to drive like that. At the same meeting, on 17 October a year later (in what was to be his last outing in this particular car), he sat on the grid, determined to make up for a poor practice time. He made a demon start from the second row, and slotted in behind the leading AC Cobra. Down the Hanger Straight, he was overtaken by Lord Cross, also in a Cobra, and demoted to third.

Shortly afterwards, the leading AC dropped out, leaving Banks and Lord Cross to dispute the lead. Lap by lap, he reeled him in. In the Woodcote grandstand, his father was shouting 'faster, faster', while his mother pleaded 'slower, slower', as Banks came through each bend more and more on the limit. He had to settle for 2nd overall, but won the class and lowered the class record to 1.50, taking 2 seconds off Enever's 1968 time. He also bettered his previous day's practice time by 3 seconds.

Banks was great friends with Richard Sutherland and recalls another Silverstone race at which they were competing against each other. Having made another of his fine starts, he looked in the mirror, to see what was happening behind. Sutherland had got off line and gone grass cutting; he cut the corner and drove straight through a hoarding. In the mirror, Banks saw the Sutherland Sprite emerging through the shattered hardboard, 'just like Desperate Dan walking through a door'.

The changes in the regulations for 1970 meant that the car was ineligible for the renamed Modsports formula. They stipulated that the monocoque had to retain standard-material, stress-bearing parts, between the wheel centres. Banks sold the Sprite via an *Autosport* advertisement to Irish driver Arthur Collier. Derek Matthews, who was still involved, suggested it was mad to pay to enter races in the UK, when, with the right car, it was possible to get paid start money to race in mainland Europe. In his workshop was an old twin cam engine, and plans for a very special Sprite began to evolve.

THE ARK SPRITE

The Ark Sprite was a totally space frame structure, the only thing Sprite about it being the Smith and Deakin glass fibre body, suitably modified for the wide wheels and extremely low profile. The frame was fabricated from both 1in and ¾in square steel tubing, and to this was added an aluminium sheet monocoque and fabricated alloy doors. It had a strengthened Ford Anglia back axle, with Hewland LSD. At the front it had modified Triumph Herald suspension with fabricated wishbones. Power came from the dry-sumped Lotus Twin-Cam 1600 engine, which formed a stressed part of the chassis, and there were Girling discs all round. The drive train was completed by a Ford racing close ratio gearbox and Janspeed were commissioned to make a special manifold. The

The virtually complete Ark Sprite space frame in Derek Matthews' workshop, January 1970

The Ark Racing Twin-Cam Sprite

project, started in January, took six months to complete. In June the car was taken to Silverstone for a full day's testing in the hands of John Banks and Chris Smith, who also had considerable previous experience in Sprites.

During the test session, the car was run without its front bodywork so that the mechanics could observe the suspension working, and it was returned to the pits for periodic adjustments. By the end of the day, it had covered a distance equivalent to ten club races and all seemed to be well.

RELAY AT SILVERSTONE

After competing satisfactorily in a number of club GT events, the car was entered for the 1970 750 Motor Club Birkitt six-hour relay at Silverstone. The other two members of the team were Jeff Simpson in his Davrian and Arthur Collier, who brought Banks's original BMC 1300cc Sprite over from Ireland. Despite what they considered to be a reasonable practice session, the team ended up with a lowly grid position. However, after 45 minutes had elapsed, Collier had worked his car up to sixth place and came in to hand over to Banks in the Ark Sprite.

Banks capitalized on the new car's excellent handling and, by the end of his stint, the team was running 3rd. Next it was the Davrian, but Simpson suffered engine problems that dropped the Ark team back to 6th again. Chris Smith took the wheel of the Ark Sprite, fought back and was in the lead, before returning to the pits for the planned hand-over to Collier.

Collier circulated in the lead for a while, but the pace took its toll and the transmission broke. He limped back to the pits, losing places on the way, before Smith took over

First outing: John Banks tests the Ark Twin Cam Sprite at Silverstone, July 1970. The car is running without the front bodywork to enable the mechanics to observe the suspension working

The Ark Racing team, 2nd in the Birkett 6-Hour Relay Race, Silverstone, 8 August 1970

once more. The Collier Sprite was soon found to be beyond immediate repair so the team was down to one car. During the last hour, Smith put in an inspired drive and snatched back third, then second place during the last five minutes of the race.

Following a check, the car was deemed ready for its first International event and the Ark team set off for the 1970 Nurburgring 500km race. They arrived in good time and were able to get in two days' practice before the official qualification session. The car, driven by John Banks, ran midfield for most of the race, but in the closing stages the crown wheel and pinion failed. The Sprite was classified as a finisher and had covered sufficient distance to come 2nd in class. It had done the equivalent of forty club races, so when it returned to base it was stripped and rebuilt, and the team also took the opportunity to modify the suspension.

Journeys to and from the circuit are not always straightforward. John Banks remembers one outing at Aintree, where the unfortunate crew had a puncture on the way to the circuit and had to change the trailer wheel. On the way back they had another flat, this time on the M6, with no spare, and began to wonder how they would get home. From his cycling days, Banks remembered a 1930s bike book that suggested, in the event of a puncture, removing the tube and filling the tyre with grass just to get home. One of the lads took off the offending wheel, while Banks pulled up grass from the verge, and, with a great deal of steam from the tyre, they completed the final part of the journey.

JARAMA

After a class 3rd in the GT Race at Thruxton on 11 October, the car was now entered for its next International outing, the six-hour event at Jarama Circuit in Spain, on 1 November. A team of six people was assembled for this mammoth trip. The Sprite was towed on the back of a white Ford Thames 15cwt van, 561 HEA, which had been nicknamed 'Gladys'. Drivers John Banks and Chris Smith were joined by Arthur Collier as nominated reserve driver, and Derek Matthews, Ray Concar and Ivan Fellows went to look after the car. They did the jour-

John Banks with trophy for 2nd in Group 6 1300 to 1600cc class, Nurburgring, 6 September 1970

ney in two days without stopping, with one driving, one navigating and keeping the driver awake, and the other four trying to snatch some sleep in the back. They were confident that the tight Jarama circuit would be ideal for the Sprite

During pre-race scrutineering, an official noticed that the car's sidelights did not function. The team already knew this, but did not speak any Spanish, and were unable to communicate with him. In the end, Smith pointed to the lights, shook his head and kept repeating 'El duffo, El duffo'; this immediately became his nickname for the rest of the trip.

The car ran well in the race, getting as high as 2nd in class, but had to retire after eighty-two laps. The thread on the front wishbone broke, scoring a big groove in the Minilite wheel. Smith struggled on with the car but had to give up because he could not steer it. As the team was loading up the car after the race, they were approached by a local garage owner, who offered them a large amount of money for the set of Minilite wheels. They turned the offer down, feeling sure that British Customs would not believe that they had lost all four wheels in one race.

That evening there was a big prize-giving ceremony at El Cerebro, a fashionable Madrid nightclub; guests included Alan de Cadenet, Jo Siffert and Pedro Rodriguez. The Ark team went along for the party and to collect their £200 start money, which they needed to get home. The organizers told them it was normal for a cheque to be sent on, but Smith was adamant: they had to have the cash to buy petrol for the return journey. The organizers relented and the Ark team was the only one to get cash on the night.

Handing over the money, the official told Smith that they were organizing a meeting at Tangier the following weekend and that, if the team could get the Sprite fixed, they would get £400 start money to take part. The lads were keen, but Smith had only been married a few weeks, and went off to ring his wife from a phone box outside the club. He was told that if he did not get home by Tuesday, he should not bother to return at all. They left for England that night, again doing a non-stop trip.

The channel crossing was particularly rough and most of the passengers were badly sea-sick. Smith, who never suffered, and ex-seaman Matthews stuffed themselves with steak, joined by the purser and head chef, the only other people left standing. They even managed to get a free bottle of red wine to go with their meal.

1971 SEASON

For 1971, a full season of International endurance racing was planned, but, owing to a change to the FIA regulations, the car became ineligible. Plans were changed to take in GT races on the home front. Parts of the car were up-graded and the front uprights, which had previously given problems, were strengthened. Having come 2nd the previous year, the Ark team's objective was to win the Birkitt six-hour race on 15 August. This was being held for the first time at the recently opened Thruxton Circuit, near Andover in Hampshire.

The plan for the Birkitt Relay was to run the Sprite, with Banks and Smith sharing the driving, for the majority of the six hours, using Fred Bootby's Lotus 17 to cover the driver change and Sprite service periods. As in the previous year, the team had a poor grid position, but Smith, who took the first stint at the wheel, made a demon start and by the end of the second lap was running in 2nd. Lap 4 saw him in the lead and, by the end of the second hour, he had a five-lap advantage over the F100 Sportscar Team.

Having been out for eighty-nine laps – two hours and twenty minutes at the wheel – Smith drove into the pits and handed over to Boothby. The next forty minutes saw fervent activity, both in the paddock and on the track. Boothby did well to maintain the lead in his less powerful car, while Derek Matthews and his crew refuelled and serviced the Sprite. At three hours, Banks took over in the Sprite, the team's lead now two laps, at half distance.

Fred Boothby did one more half-hour stint in his Lotus, while the Sprite came in for another maintenance check and the final driver change. Chris Smith drove throughout the closing stages and the team took a well-deserved victory, having done 217 laps at an overall average speed of 86.8mph (140km/h). It was the first time in the 21-year history of the Birkitt relay that the winning car had covered more than 500 miles (over 800km). They collected the *Cars and Car Conversions* trophy for the overall winner, the Speedwell Cup for the first car to exceed 500 miles, and prizes for leading at the end of the 2nd, 3rd, 4th and 5th hours. It was a clean sweep.

PHIL JEFFREYS

Further regulation changes in 1972 meant that the Ark Sprite was laid up for four years in a lock-up garage in Coventry, before being sold to Phil Jeffreys, in 1975. Jeffreys used it successfully in sprints and hill climbs, so successfully, in fact, that a number of other competitors began to question the legality of the car. To stop any further criticism, Jeffreys decided to convert it to a Special GT saloon, and run it in that category.

The car's final outing in Sprite form was at the 1978 racing car parade around the streets of Birmingham, a publicity event prior to permission being granted for the Birmingham Super Prix. James Thacker was also taking part, in his Modsports

The spoils of victory. Derek Matthews with the trophies from the 1971 Birkett 6-Hour Relay displayed on the bonnet of the Ark Sprite – Cars and Car Conversions Trophy, champagne and cap for winning the event, Speedwell Trophy for the first car to cover more than 500 miles, and awards for leading at the end of 2nd, 3rd, 4th and 5th hours

The Ark Racing Twin-Cam Sprite

Sprite to Reliant to Sprite. Mike Scott with the rebuilt Ark Racing Sprite Twin Cam, Mallory Park, 2 May 1994

Midget. Jeffreys offered him the Ark body and moulds, which would be surplus to requirements once it became a saloon. The Thacker Midget still has the original Ark bodywork.

RESTORATION

Jeffreys added 6in (15cm) to the Ark chassis, lengthened the prop by the same amount and fitted it with a glass fibre Reliant Kitten body. Regular Lydden saloon competitor Mike Scott bought the car for the 1991 season. After his first outing at Brands, he was approached by *Autosport* writer Dud Chandler, who confirmed the history of the car. Scott decided to restore it and, as a result of a small piece Chandler had written about it in the magazine, James Thacker got in touch with Scott to tell him he had the original body moulds.

The car was to remain in its Reliant guise until Scott's last race at the end of the 1993 season. He took it back to his workshop and began the painstaking task of cutting the body off. Having cut the extra inches back out of the chassis, he added Sprite bodywork, then found and rebuilt a Ford 1600 Twin-Cam, similar to the original one with which the car had raced in 1971.

As a Reliant Kitten Special GT, with a 200bhp BDA engine, it was a real struggle to get the car round the Mallory Hairpin. The first time Scott drove the rebuilt Ark Sprite Twin-Cam round the Leicestershire circuit, it handled like a dream. The lengthening of the chassis six years previously had apparently completely unbalanced the handling. The Sprite now competes in the Historic Sports Car Club RJB Mining Championship for Group 6 Sportscars. Derek Matthews saw it at Mallory and commented that it did not look very different from the car he designed and built twenty-five years ago.

13 The MG Midget Championship

THE BIRTH OF THE CHAMPIONSHIP

During 1975, the arrival of a new breed of sports car began to have a significant effect on Midget racing for the future. Throughout the season, competitors driving Midgets became increasingly disillusioned, as their cars became more and more out-classed by the likes of the Elans and Davrians. The Midget had, after all, been designed some twenty years before, and was no match for what were contemptuously regarded as the new plastic kit cars.

Meanwhile, in Essex, Gordon Cobban, general secretary of the MG Car Club, had persuaded ex-patriot Irishman Larry Quinn to take over writing the 'Midget Notes' in club magazine *Safety Fast*. Quinn, himself a budding competitor, was first published in the October 1975 edition of the magazine.

He sang the praises of racing a Midget and pointed out that, for under £50, potential competitors could buy a laminated screen, helmet, competition licence and medical. It was that easy to become a racing driver.

Over the years, the Midgets had enjoyed their own races at MG Car Club meetings, particularly at Silverstone, and there were already championships for As and T-Types. Stuart Dean, a T-Type driver, also happened to attend the Cricketers at Danbury, the same MG watering-hole as Quinn; one evening he suggested that Quinn might use Midget Notes to get a series for Midgets off the ground. The idea grew and in November 1976 Quinn organized a meeting at the Silverstone clubhouse for interested drivers. There was a very positive response.

In 1977, the Midget Competition Group was formed, with Quinn as secretary, and the Midget Championship was born. It was

Line astern: Keith Ashby (267), Dave Sheppard (273), Bunny Lees-Smith (268), Peter Nott (257) and Steve Everitt (259) at Silverstone, May 1981

run in two classes: 'A' Road-going, for virtually standard cars, and 'B' Modified, which catered for the Modsports cars. The first-ever championship race was at the Rochester Motor Club Brands Hatch meeting on 3 April 1977. During that first season, there were nine rounds and Quinn himself emerged as the Road-going champion, the modified crown being won by up-and-coming young Sevenoaks driver Steve Everitt. In those days, the two classes ran together, much as they had done at the Car Club events. Drivers were already finding that the speed and handling differentials were becoming a problem, but at least they had their own championship.

The season did not finish very well, thanks to the British weather. The Midgets were competing for the Auto Renovations Cup at the Rochester Motor Club meeting at Brands on 27 November, on one of those changeable days. It was dry when the lights went to green for the start of the combined Modified and Road-going race. On lap 3, Trevor Styles, driving the Chittenden car, rolled at Clearways and the race was stopped. By the time the track was cleared, it had started to rain slightly, with all the Modified cars on slicks. The re-start resulted in a six-car accident at Paddock on lap 1, damaging, among others, the Road-going cars of Larry Quinn and John Vernon. Again, the race was stopped.

Now it was pouring with rain but, instead of calling it a day, the organizers cleared the track and announced the remaining nine cars, half the original grid, would race over just four laps. By this time, the batteries that ran the start-line gantry were going flat, resulting in two false starts as the lights went from red to green and back to red again, without enough current to trip the relay to green. In the end, the cars were flagged away, and this caught most of the grid napping as they were still looking at the lights. This time, the race ran to the finish, despite Martin Brazil crashing at Graham Hill. Everitt lost it at Druids, but still managed to come home 2nd. *Motoring News* headlined their report on the meeting 'Disaster after disaster'. The final tally of damaged Midgets was fourteen!

Lawrence Cutler's Midget mirrored on the wet tarmac at the MGCC Silverstone meeting in May 1979

The MG Midget Championship

THE 1978 SEASON

In 1978 there was a series of ten races and, for a number of the venues, Larry Quinn had been able to liaise with the BCV8 committee and arrange for the Road-going and Modified classes to run together. This was not ideal, but better than running all the Midgets together, when the speed differential was a serious problem. Pitting the Modified Midgets against the full-race BCV8s produced some interesting results. On the shorter and twistier circuits such as Brands and Mallory, the Midgets' nimbler handling ruled supreme, but the Midgets lost out on the longer tracks such as Silverstone and Snetterton.

In its second season, the series attracted even more of the existing Modsports Midget competitors into the fold and also encouraged several drivers to build new cars or convert existing road racers into Modified cars. Over the next decade the Midget series would go from strength to strength, while Modsports was to decline and eventually become extinct. Martin Wilson, who had competed in Midgets for three or four years, became the 1978 series winner. Martin retired a couple of years later and his car was sold and went to Portugal, where it continued to win races.

As the championship progressed, drivers in each of the classes complained bitterly that competitors in the other were spoiling their racing. At one annual drivers' meeting at the famous Steering Wheel Club in Curzon Street, emotions were running particularly high. In reply to a criticism of the way Modified drivers lapped their Road-going counterparts, a not entirely serious proposal was tabled. It was suggested that Class 'A' cars should be equipped with a rear-facing passenger seat, complete with co-driver, whose responsibility it would be to tell the driver when he was about to be lapped by a Modified car! The motion was not adopted, but the resulting mirth seemed to diffuse the situation.

THE 1979 SEASON

To make motor racing more environmentally friendly, the governing body made the fitting of silencers mandatory for 1979. Midget drivers, like many others, were forced to find room to fit in a much abbreviated exhaust system. Keith Ashby and Steve Everitt were the main championship contenders this year. Ashby won and set fastest lap in the first three races, then failed to start the next, which allowed Everitt to win and get

Lawrence Cutler (99) pursues Steve Everitt (93) in vain at Brands Hatch on 17 September 1979

Following a delayed start at Silverstone on 23 May 1981, the circuit was still very wet. Spray pours from Dave Sheppard's tyres as he speeds on his way to a race win

best lap. He then did the same at the double points round at Croft. Ashby finished the year with four more wins and a 2nd, but Everitt's three wins, three 3rds and three fastest laps clinched him the championship for the second time. The race results show that, on most occasions, there were less than a couple of seconds between these two very evenly matched drivers. Lawrence Cutler was third.

DAVID SHEPPARD

Fourth place in 1979 went to David Sheppard, in the year when the Colchester garage owner moved from Road-going to the Modified class. From just five races, his tally was one 2nd, four 3rds and one fastest lap. According to Sheppard, the transition to racing a Modified car happened quite by accident, whilst he was trying to find parts for his original road Midget. In the course of his search for a spare gearbox, he had visited one of his local car-breakers in Essex. They did not have what he wanted, but told him of a motel not far away that had a racing Midget sitting in its grounds. Sheppard met Peter Beech, owner of the Silver Springs Motel, and struck a deal to run the car. When he took over this ex-John Ewer aluminium-bodied car, there was no engine or gearbox so, initially, he transferred these items from his Class 'A' car.

Soon Sheppard was running with a 1380cc engine, which had a Longman inclined valve head, and began to feature in the points. In 1980 he teamed up with Barry Chaplin, who prepared his engines, and his challenge really came good. Chaplin worked out the longest crank stroke that would keep the car within the class maximum of 1500cc, and then commissioned Gordon Allen to make him one from a billet. It cost just over £1,000, which at the time was a lot for a crank.

With his Chaplin 1496cc engine installed, Sheppard took the championship in 1980 and again in 1981. During those two years, the car lost its aluminium front and rear bodywork, which was replaced with cheaper and more readily obtainable fibreglass. While changing the body, Sheppard decided that the leaf springs had to go and converted the suspension to a coil-sprung set-up. The alloy doors remained and are still on the car to this day.

The MG Midget Championship

THE 1980 SEASON

Larry Quinn had again put double points on offer to tempt competitors to Croft, this time for the opening round of the 1980 season. Dave Sheppard was one of six Modified drivers to make the journey, scoring a very useful 14 points for a win, plus fastest lap. John Gallagher was 2nd and Dave Paige 3rd. Sheppard had also entered the Modsports race and, during practice, tangled with Tony Broom's Turner, leading to a bit of a scuffle in the paddock. A report on the meeting was so bold as to suggest that 'the highlight of the Modsports race was the bout of fisticuffs in the paddock after practice'.

John Gallagher came 2nd in the 1980 series, Bunny Lees-Smith was 3rd and I was 4th.

1981, 1982 AND 1983 SEASONS

After a three-year break from racing, Tony Williams registered for the Midget Championship in 1981. He appeared in the ex-Gordon Howie/Richard Ibrahim car, which was soon developed to the same extent as his previous car. Sadly, Tony Williams succumbed to a heart attack while leading the Midget race at Thruxton, on 30 August 1982. He had won the previous three races, at Oulton Park, Brands Hatch and Mallory Park. To commemorate his connection with MG racing, the Williams family presented a trophy, awarded to the winner of the round at Oulton Park, Tony's local circuit.

During this period, Midget racing was fairly low profile, so when Birmingham driver Malcolm Ellis appeared out of the blue in a fully sponsored car, other drivers sat up and took notice. Malcolm Ellis, like his brother Vic, had enjoyed a good record racing an MGA. In 1981 he had joined the staff

Tony Williams rounds Lodge Corner on his way to a race win and a new lap record at Oulton Park, 10 July 1982

Midgets in the rain at Silverstone 23 May 1981, leaving the grid on the warm-up lap

of the Drapkin Print Group and had only been with them a short while when he suggested that sponsoring him would be a good way to increase their customer base. To his amazement, Drapkin agreed. Sponsorship was not allowed in the MGA Championship, so Ellis sold his A and bought the ex-Alan Iles, Jack O'Newbury-sponsored Midget. This was soon painted in the Drapkin's white and red livery.

Ellis tested the car at Silverstone in March. It was so cold the radiator froze, resulting in four melted pistons. Having rebuilt the engine, he gradually developed the Midget over a two-year period, during which he persuaded his sponsors to come up with £1,500 for a Motospeed 1498cc long-stroke engine. This had a special head machined from an experimental casting and ran on a single 48 Dellorto carb, which gave 135bhp at the wheels. The car was quick in a straight line, but the braking was never ideal, despite a big disc conversion; Malcolm Ellis maintains that this was because of his short legs. The high-power output was also very hard on gearboxes, which the car got through at an alarming rate.

In 1981, runner-up to Dave Sheppard was Keith Ashby, followed by third place man Tim Cairns, in his first year in the Modified class.

In 1982 and 1983 former Road-going champion Tim Cairns took the Modified crown. The Bedford-based driver's Speedwell Blue Frogeye had won Class 'A' in 1979 and 1980, and he then bought an unknown Modified car from Hampshire. Having painted it in the same blue livery, he developed it into a winner. His Midget was one of the few front-running cars of the day not using an engine with a long-stroke crankshaft, which meant he was giving away nearly 100cc to many of his rivals.

Sponsored by Hexagon Fastenings, the Midget weighed 11¾cwt (595kg), about 1cwt (50kg) more than many of the cars on the grid, and the engine was quoted as putting out 160bhp at the flywheel when pulling 7,800rpm. Cairns had one terrible piece of bad luck at Donington, on 29 August 1983, when the engine failed during practice, pitching the car backwards into the bank. Examination in the paddock revealed not only severe body damage, but also a rod through the side of the block.

Barry Rogers came 2nd in the 1982 Midget Championship, driving his well-developed car, whilst Steve Everitt was 3rd. Everitt was runner-up to Cairns the following year (by

Tim Cairns (1) dicing with Steve Everett (3), one of many such battles enjoyed by the pair during the 1982 and 1983 seasons

just one point), with third place going to Devon driver Peter Nott.

The Modified Midgets were still racing with the Modified BCV8s at a number of meetings, but in 1982 Mike Chalk re-wrote the form book, which hitherto had given the Midgets the edge over the BCV8s on the shorter circuits. Chalk, who started racing a Frogeye in 1970, was a very experienced driver who raced a great number of different cars.

Following a season in single-seaters, Chalk decided to go back to MGs and, having looked carefully at the technical regulations for Modified MGBs, decided that none of the cars in the championship was exploiting them to the full. He built an innovative no-expense-spared MGB, which became known as the 'White Tornado' and was soon the class of the field. Much to their chagrin, Mike was beating the Modified Midgets round Brands and Lydden. Having cleaned up in his car, he sold it to Martin Dell and the following season was out in a Sprite once more.

In 1983, a few of the Midgets appeared in a non-competitive role at a Grand Prix meeting. That year, Brands Hatch hosted the Grand Prix of Europe, which was held on 24 September. The MG Car Club was called upon to provide a cross-section of open cars from the marque, to parade the GP drivers round the circuit half an hour before the big race.

Mick Rogers, in brother Barry's car, chauffeured Michele Alboreto (Tyrrell); Dave Paige, Jean Pierre Jarier (Ligier); Tim Cairns, Piercarlo Ghinzani (Osella); and Larry Quinn and his wife Dorothy had Roberto Guerrero (Theodore) aboard their Irish-registered road Midget. The MG procession gave the 67,000-strong crowd a chance to see each of their favourite drivers go past them at a reasonable speed. This event also marked the Grand Prix debut of former Sprite racer Jonathan Palmer, in the third TAG Williams. He qualified 25th but finished 13th, two laps down on the winning Brabham of Nelson Piquet.

1984–1987 SEASONS

Castrol Oils and *Auto Performance* magazine (the one-time Link House sister publication to *Triple C*) joined forces to sponsor the Midget series in 1984. While this gave Quinn and his organizing committee a lot of paperwork, to register the championship officially with the RAC Motor Sports Association (which was obligatory with a series sponsor), it did considerably raise the profile. During the year, the magazine did two double-page spreads on the series (one of which marked my own first published piece of motoring journalism). Unfortunately, the arrangement was short-lived, as the magazine ceased publication and was incorporated in *Cars and Car Conversions*. This magazine already had other sponsorship commitments and was unable to continue the deal. Nevertheless, the year under the Link House umbrella elevated the Midgets from the 'just another one-make series' category.

By this time, the number of competitors had grown and it was becoming difficult to get a place on the grid. Until now, both classes had continued to be run in the same race, but in 1984 the series was divided into two completely different championships, each with their own calendar. At last, the Modified drivers no longer had the problem of lapping the slower Road-going cars. On occasion, the Modified grids did not come up to scratch and the organizing clubs sometimes put the Midgets together with some strange bedfellows. I was once a mixed grid with Jaguar saloons, and being in a 10cwt 'plastic' MG on the inside of a 2-ton Mark 10, going round Druids at Brands, was not my idea of fun. We also had one race with the

Anglo/Trans Am Challenge cars, again at Brands. They proved twice as difficult to lap as a Midget on road tyres, since they were twice as wide.

Over the next four years Steve Everitt ruled supreme, winning the crown from 1984 until his untimely death in 1987. During his reign, he occasionally came under a lot of pressure from Steve Watkins, but nearly always managed to stave him off. Watkins gave him a run for his money and beat him fair and square at least once each year, often claiming the extra point for fastest lap. The rivalry between them was friendly and the commentators loved talking about 'the two battling Steves disputing the lead'. It was made even more confusing for the crowd, when Steve Millard also made the front row of the grid. One announcer, in his pre-race preamble, suggested that the only way to be competitive in Midgets was to have the name Steve.

From 1985 to 1987, Watkins and I were to end up 2nd and 3rd in the championship table and we also enjoyed some good dices. After Everitt's death, perhaps Watkins felt that, if he carried on in Midgets and won the series, it would be a hollow victory. He moved on to race the ex-Colin Blower TVR 3000S for David Gerald Sports Cars.

1988–1991 SEASONS

Steve Watkins sold the Midget, which probably had the most reliable, powerful engine at the time (reputed to put out just over 130bhp at the rear wheels!), to Graeme Adams, who came 2nd in 1988. The result was a close-run thing, with both he and Mike Chalk going to the last round at Donington in October with a chance of overall honours. In the end, Chalk finished one place ahead of Adams, which, after Adams dropped his worst score, put them even on 60 points each. The regulations state that in such circumstances the number of race wins should be used as a decider. They had three apiece. Resorting to the number of second places to break the tie gave it to Chalkie by the narrowest of margins. It was certainly one of the most cliff-hanging of seasons' ends since the series began.

In 1989 Alvin Heaton won the championship in his first year. Heaton emerged in the Tarporley Garage car, closely attended by Geoff Williams, who had prepared his late twin brother Tony's car for so many years. It seems that the car Heaton drove was a Sprite originally built by Richard Sutherland, acquired and rebuilt by Geoff Williams for Ray Grimes to race. The out-

Steve Watkins edges up the inside of the author on the exit of Druids at Brands Hatch

come of the championship that year might have been a different story if Ed Reeve, who won the first two races and then missed most of the others, had finished the season. As it was, Adams again came 2nd, just ahead of David Brooker-Carey. Having cleaned up, Heaton swiftly moved on to Fiestas.

Mike Chalk had now built his Midget version of the 'White Tornado'. This was based on the immaculate Chris Tolchard car, which was subsequently raced by Nigel Bance. The car was very radical, having four pot calipers on each corner, with rear suspension and bodywork such as no one had ever seen before. The back was completely open; looking under the raised rear wing revealed the axle, battery and petrol tank. This latest creation from his Danbury stable was to come out on top in 1990. It was, however, a down-to-the-wire last race, again with Graeme Adams. This time, there were two points in it.

In 1991 Adams finally fulfilled his aspirations and took the championship, beating long-time competitor Lawrence Cutler into second place by two points. This made it third time lucky for Adams, who has the distinction of being a member of the only father and son racing team in the Midget brigade. His father Don occasionally competed in the ex-John Warren car (in which Graeme first started racing), when not mechanic-ing for his lad. Ed Reeve, who had raced Midgets for 20 years, was 3rd.

LAWRENCE CUTLER

Thirty years on from the first appearance of the Dick Jacobs cars, Modified Midgets were still going strong. Lawrence Cutler, who has raced Midgets on and off since 1975, emerged as the top man for 1992. Like Everitt's, his car was another ex-David Strange machine, bought in 1977 for £380, including trailer. He enjoyed some epic dices with Everitt during the early 1980s.

After comprehensively wrecking his car at Silverstone's original Woodcote corner, in August 1978, Cutler was having trouble finding a second-hand shell that was not a rot box. In desperation he rang Abingdon, and spoke to John Kerswill, the Special Tuning Sales and Marketing Manager. Cutler explained what had happened and, stressing the publicity Midget racing was getting the marque, asked if it would be possible for him to buy a shell. He was delighted to receive a call two days later, telling him they could take a 1500 shell off the line for him and the

Mike Chalk's Swiftune Midget, complete with sill side skirts, on the way to a win at Snetterton, October 1990

The MG Midget Championship

cost would be £150. As ever with these 'special competitor deals', he was to keep the price to himself.

When he arrived at the plant with his trailer to collect the shell, he was surprised to see that it was complete with front wings, doors, bonnet and boot lid, which, of course, he did not need for Modsports. The car was re-shelled and the surplus panels sold off, so that at the end of the day the new body had cost him virtually nothing. Over the years the extra box sections, needed for the rubber bumpers, were removed to reduce weight, and the car now sports a fibreglass rear.

Cutler's Silverstone accident had happened right in front of his then girlfriend Nicki, spectating in the Woodcote grandstand with, among others, Martin Ingall. The distraught young lady was immediately comforted by the chivalrous Mr Ingall, who, having just changed the plugs on my car, left black fingerprints all over her white T-shirt. When the story got out, there was much amused speculation in the paddock as to quite how much he had comforted her. Some claimed to have seen oily handprints in embarrassing places on her white clothing, although this was strenuously denied by both parties.

The rebuild of the car was completed in time for the last race of the season, but becoming a property owner in 1981 meant an enforced four-year lay-off for Cutler. During this time, the racer, which had the newest shell on any grid, filled up with water and threatened to rot away as it stood in the front garden. Sadly, an original set of 10in Minilites, lying in the cockpit at the time, also suffered oxidization. But old Midgets never die and the car was to re-emerge.

Motivated by his ex-Mini 7 and Ford 2000 racing brother Julian, Lawrence Cutler repaired the shell and eased his way back into the series with a few races in 1985 and 1987. When he first reappeared, his car was

Racing in the Halfords Midget Challenge is close, as illustrated here by Ted Reeve (3) coming under pressure

177

painted Speedwell Blue like Tim Cairns' car, 'just to keep the boys on their toes'. He started doing the championship in earnest again in 1988 and took four years to get back to the top. Cutler was one of the few Midget drivers to run in an aero-screened car with an open-face helmet and goggles, looking like the Red Baron.

In the 1992 season Cutler took the championship by winning four out of the nine races, three victories going to Steve Westwood's unique coupé version, and two to Graeme Adams. At the end of the day Westwood came 2nd and Peter May 3rd in the series.

1993, 1994 & 1995 SEASONS

As is so often the case, 1993 was a bad year for the previous season's champion. Cutler had three non-classifications during the early part of the season, although he may have drawn some consolation from getting fastest lap before retiring in two of the races. The year would see a two-way struggle for honours between Steve Westwood and Ted Reeve, who, despite his many years' racing, has never won the Midget Championship. At the half-way stage, Westwood was ten points clear of his rival, but Reeve caught up during the second half, despite a blown engine at Pembrey on 15 August, two laps from home.

It was all down to the last event in the calendar, the Steve Everitt Memorial Race at Brands on a very wet 13 November. Reeve, known for liking the wet, put his car on the middle of the front row, while his rival could only manage the outside of row three. This was as a result of a water-induced misfire, despite the distributor being wrapped in a plastic carrier bag. Chris Montague annexed pole in his all-new car.

When it came to the race, Reeve made the cleanest start, but Montague was in front at Paddock. By lap 4 Westwood, now running on all cylinders, was up to 3rd behind Reeve; he, in turn, was shaping up to have a close look at Montague, who he managed to get by on the following tour. If he could stay up front for the five remaining laps and keep Montague's white car between him and Westwood, who was now running a distant 3rd, he would take the championship. It was not to be. Montague hit the front on lap 8 and stayed there, putting some back-markers between himself and his rival on the last lap, just to make sure. By coming home 3rd, Westwood secured the crown by just one point. It was a typical nail-biting finish to another Halfords MG Car Club Modified Midget Series.

Lawrence Cutler made up for a poor start to the 1994 season and came through to take the championship. Chris Montague made a strong start, winning three races in succession, early in the year, after Graeme Adams had claimed victory in the championship opener at Cadwell. The fifth round at Silverstone saw Cutler out with his new Peter May-built 1460cc engine, which gave him a win straight out of the box. He missed the next round at Lydden (being godfather at a christening), and then went on to take three wins and fastest laps in a row, to have the series in the bag before the final round.

Having qualified on the front row in the final round, Cutler's transmission disintegrated on the line, leading to retirement before his familiar blue car had even turned a wheel. Chris Montague, using his spare engine, having blown up at Mallory the race before, went on to win from lights to flag. He was quite grateful not to have the extra power of his big engine, given the appalling conditions. This win just got him 2nd in the series by one point from Ted Reeve, who in turn beat Adams for 4th by just one point. Had Adams not chosen to race his BGT in the combined Midget and BCV8 race at Silverstone, and lend the Midget to former owner Steve Watkins, he would surely have come in 2nd at the end of the year.

In 1995 Cutler mounted a late start to his defence of the title. This enabled David Shannon, in his well-prepared Bill Richards-engined car, to establish an early lead in the series, which he was not to relinquish. Graeme Adams was 2nd and Cutler eventually finished 3rd.

COLIN CHARMAN

Midget drivers come and go; some start racing in the Road-going class, then move on to Fully Modified, possibly taking in a year or two in the Race Modified category on the way. However, Tenterden-based driver Colin Charman has proved during his eighteen years of involvement that everyone is different. He started racing Modsports in a Midget in 1977, joining the MGCC Midget Championship from 1978 to 1985. During this time, he raced ex-Graham Smith, Peter May/Ted Arundel, Fred Taylor and Vivien West cars and had one brief period of retirement. His first car was destroyed during the Modsports race at the Rochester Motor Club Brands meeting, on 27 November 1977. He came into Clearways to find that a journalist having a guest drive in the very rapid Janspeed Datsun 240Z had lost it. The Datsun spun once and Charman thought 'Oh good, I've missed him', but then he spun a second time and could do nothing but plough into the other car. Having loaded the remains of his car onto the trailer, Charman was approached by John Wilmshurst, who told him he knew the whereabouts of another rolling shell.

After phoning the owner, Ted Arundel, and going to see the shell, Charman realized he would have to borrow some money to buy it. He limped into his bank two days after the accident, still black and blue. The concerned bank manager asked how he had got in such a mess and Charman told him that it was the result of wrecking his racing car the previous Sunday. After explaining the purpose of the loan, Charman was delighted to be granted the loan immediately. He says he puts it down to Black Horse power!

RACING OVERSEAS

The British Spridgets ventured abroad and acquitted themselves well during the 1960s and 1970s, and the tradition continues. Since 1989, regular Midget Championship contender David Brooker-Carey has regularly taken his car to Belgium's famous Spa Circuit, to compete in the Trophée des Ardennes. This two-day event, first run in 1987, takes place in May and is a feast of historic motor racing, offering a unique atmosphere for competitor and spectator alike. Encouraged by Brooker-Carey, fellow Midget drivers Malcolm Johnson and Steve Westwood have also taken part.

Midgets are eligible for the MG/British Sportscar Challenge, which is also open to Jaguars and replica Cobras. The Midget fares better than one might think against the larger machinery over the sweeping 4.3-mile (6.94km) track. Brooker-Carey found that his lap times were better than those of full-race Cobras, which had more than 400 horsepower available. Over the years that he has raced there, he has consistently finished around 10th overall, from between fifty-five and sixty starters, always beating many cars in the larger-engine capacity classes.

In 1993, Brooker-Carey won his class at an average speed of 84.7mph (136.4km/h), and the previous year his lap time (2:59.0) would have qualified him for the Steierberger Supersports Race for ex-Le Mans cars, just behind a 5700cc Lola T70. It's an impressive performance from a 1460cc car with just over 120bhp gross. Following in

David Brooker-Carey (5) and Steve Westwood (51) share the grid with some exotic machinery at the Trophée des Ardennes, Spa, May 1991

Larry and Dorothy Quinn in the Halfords hospitality unit at the Midget Challenge 20th Anniversary meeting at Donington Park, August 1996

the footsteps of the Dick Jacobs Team nearly thirty years before, MG Midgets continue to give more powerful machinery a run for its money at international level.

MODIFIED MIDGETS TODAY

Despite the formation of the Historic Modsports Association, Modsports races are no longer a feature of British club racing. A few Midgets compete in the Special GT Series, but in the main the MG Car Club Championship is where Modified Midgets find action today. For the past five years, the series has enjoyed backing from Halfords, the high-street motorists' store.

Twenty years after calling the first drivers' meeting at Silverstone, Larry Quinn still runs the Midget Competition Group with the help of his wife Dorothy. Like anyone who organizes a voluntary body, he has attracted some criticism, but without him there would have been no championship. He has not raced his own car since it was damaged in a multiple accident at Brands Paddock Bend in 1977 – the current RAC Motorsports Association rules prohibit any championship official from competing in his or her series. His Midget has now been returned to its former glory after five years' work.

MGCC MODIFIED MIDGET LAP RECORDS

Class A

Location	Driver	Time	MPH	Date
Brands Hatch	Graeme Adams	50.74	85.39	01.10.95
Cadwell Park – short	Steve Westwood	1.19.0	67.26	09.08.92
Cadwell Park – long	Graeme Adams	1.38.38	79.40	06.08.95
Castle Combe	Steve Everitt	1.07.7	97.84	08.08.87
Croft	Dave Shannon	1.12.39	89.52	18.06.95
Donington	Lawrence Cutler	1.21.52	86.43	28.06.92
Lydden	Graeme Adams	44.2	81.44	01.05.94
Mallory Park	Chris Montague	50.22	96.77	06.05.96
Oulton Park – Fosters	Graeme Adams	1.08.61	86.78	08.04.95
Pembrey	Graeme Adams	1.03.9	82.02	18.07.92
Silverstone	Graeme Adams	1.08.58	86.56	25.05.91
Snetterton	Lawrence Cutler	1.20.6	87.19	11.06.95
Thruxton	Steve Westwood	1.28.65	95.67	31.05.93

Class B

Driver	Time	MPH	Date
Chris Montague	53.0	81.75	15.11.92
Peter Tipper	1.21.2	65.43	09.08.92
Steve Hyde	1.43.5	75.47	07.03.93
Malcolm Johnson	1.13.6	90.00	01.04.91
Marcus Fellows	1.16.13	85.12	18.06.95
Chris Montague	1.23.13	84.76	28.06.92
Philip Mayne	48.4	74.38	31.07.94
Chris Montague	52.2	93.10	20.09.92
Philip Mayne	1.16.75	78.58	08.04.95
Peter May	1.08.1	76.96	09.09.90
Peter Tipper	1.10.64	84.03	22.05.93
Peter May	1.26.4	81.33	06.10.91
Steve Hyde	1.34.53	89.72	31.05.93

Compiled by Lawrence Cutler

14 Half-Way House

Once separate grids for the Road-going and Modsports cars had been established in the MG Midget Championship, it was found that the Modified class could not always come up with enough cars to justify its own race. At the outset of the championship, in 1977, it was the full-race cars that were in the majority but eight years on the opposite was true, when several drivers, including Tim Cairns and Steve Watkins, successfully made the transition from one class to the other. However, with the fully modified cars becoming more advanced, there began to be a lack of new competitors coming into the series in that class.

For 1985, in an attempt to attract more drivers, Larry Quinn introduced a Semi-modified class. This allowed owners to carry out some mods to their vehicles, but prohibited the more expensive items such as long-stroke crankshafts, glass fibre rear bodywork and doors, and fancy suspension set-ups. Wheel width was restricted to 6in, enabling cars to run on Sports 2000 slicks, relatively cheap and easy to get hold of second hand. So that spectators could recognize those in the new class, the regulations prescribed that they had to run with a full windscreen and hardtop.

The new regulations meant that a driver could take a standard MG Midget, build a tuned engine, bolt on a set of 6in wide, slick-shod wheels and come out and take part. The average Semi-modified car had a 1340cc engine running on a single 45 side-draft carb; again, in the interest of cost, larger or split carburettor systems were not allowed. Most cars in this new class still put out around 100bhp at the wheels. Barry Coghlan built both 1293 and 1380cc engines for his car. These two units produced 112 and 116bhp respectively. It soon became obvious that the best of this new breed were not much slower than the Fully Modified cars, as they were now called.

The class was slow to get off the ground, with only Tony Dowler's car appearing in the 1985 season opener at Castle Combe, and at the next two rounds. Tony was a former Road-going competitor concerned at the potential development costs of building a full-race car, and just the sort of person at whom the new class was aimed. At the following two meetings, Dowling's place as the single entry was taken by Graham Robson, and the organizers began to wonder if this had been such a good idea.

By June, the numbers had increased to just four, and even Larry Quinn was beginning to have second thoughts. That first season eventually saw Tony Dowler come out the winner, just beating John Prince by two points. In the end, nine different drivers came out in the new class, whilst twenty-eight competed in the Fully Modified section.

The following year, the number of entrants increased to thirteen. Most were former Road-going men, except Mark Ellis and Colin Charman, who had previously competed in Fully Modified cars. Peter May, the MG specialist from the West Midlands, achieved a runaway victory, beating Tony Dowler into second place by forty-five points. He managed to take nine wins from nine starts and set the fastest lap in seven of those races.

The 1987 season was a battle royal between two former Road-going champions,

Robert Nettleton and Jon Simpson. Nettleton netted eight wins and five fastest laps, to Simpson's seven wins and six fastest laps. This gave Nettleton the championship by three points after a very close season's racing. Peter May, who only did half of the races, came home 3rd. He found that his success the previous year had led to so much extra preparation work on customers' cars that his own racing had to take a back seat.

Mark Ellis managed to beat Peter May by just one point to win in 1988, driving the ex-Geoff Weekes Modsports car, which he had de-tuned to make it eligible for the category. This particular year, Class B, now renamed 'Race Modified', saved the series, with fifteen competitors; there were just nine Fully Modified cars. Karl Barras, another Morris Motors apprentice turned Midget racer, was 3rd. The following year he came 2nd to Steve Westwood, who was in his second season in the class having also come from Road-going.

The old firm of May and Barras was towards the head of the next year's table, but both had to give best to Malcolm Johnson who filled the number one slot. Peter May could, however, take some comfort from the fact that his company had built Johnson's winning engine. May himself had another runaway win in 1991, coming home twenty-nine points clear of Rob Lea. The year also saw virtually the same number of cars competing in each of the two classes.

The end of the 1992 season went right down to the wire for the Class B cars, with both Ian Stagg and sometime Sports 2000 driver Barry Coghlan going to Brands with a chance of overall victory. Coghlan, who had only to record a finish to win, drove what was described as a 'tactical race', and took the spoils. Stagg was 2nd and racing returner Chris Montague 3rd. Montague, who had in the past raced in Minis and Formula 3, found it attractive to compete in a Race Modified Midget, and his car was immaculately prepared.

Peter May again rose to the top in 1993, this year finding time to compete in most of the rounds. Kent driver Philip Mayne came

Peter May kicks up the dust in his car during the MGCC two-driver race at Snetterton in October 1990. He shared his car with fellow Midget man Mark Ellis

2nd, with Ian Stagg 3rd again. It might have been Steve Hyde's year, but an unfortunate accident at Snetterton forced him to sit out the rest of the season, and he had to be content with 4th.

Phil Mayne came second again the following season, scoring wins and fastest laps at both Lydden and Brands. His car had the handling for the shorter circuits rather than outright power for the longer ones. Ken Tempest was the winner, with three race wins to his credit, while Ian Stagg finished 3rd yet again. Stephen Edmed was 5th while newcomer Jon Paul Ivey, son of noted engine-builder Paul Ivey, scored three wins and fastest laps at the end of the season to take fifth spot.

In 1995 it finally came good for Phil Mayne, who established a points cushion early in the season and had the Race Modified crown in the bag with two races left to run. Ian Stagg came 2nd for a change, while Stephen Edmed had to be content with 3rd after destroying his car at Cadwell Park and missing the last four rounds of the series. Up to that point, he had been giving Mayne a run for his money.

The class has proved successful as a 'half-way house'; both Steve Westwood and Karl Barras moved from it to Fully Modified cars in 1992, and Chris Montague has also built a sophisticated Fully Modified car, in which he has scored a good number of race wins. However, most of the Class B runners are happy to stay where they are, enjoying low-cost racing, conceived for the driver who wants to carry out a little more tuning and run his car on slick tyres.

The Clubs

Enthusiasts wishing to obtain information about racing Austin Healey Sprites and MG Midgets can find out more by contacting the following clubs:

The Austin Healey Club Limited
(Secretary: D.Ross)
33 Derwent Way
White Court
Braintree
Essex
CM7 8UH

The Historic Sports Car Club
(Secretary: Steve Lydon)
Silverstone Circuit
Silverstone
Towcester
Northants.
NN12 8TN

The MG Car Club Limited
Kimber House
PO Box 251
Abingdon
Oxon
OX14 1FF

The MG Owner's Club
Octagon House
Swavesey
Cambridge
CB4 5QZ
Tel: 01954 231125

The Midget Competition Group
(Secretary: Larry Quinn)
1 Dalwood
Thorpe Bay
Essex
SS3 8UP
Tel: 01702 582560

15 Purely Personal

I bought my first Spridget, a Frogeye, in 1967 and promptly wrapped it round a lamp-post on third-party insurance the following year. I kept the remains which, after living in various barns over the years, are now about two-thirds of the way through a rebuild and re-shell. I then bought a 1967 Sprite Mark III which was sold in 1972 when I got my first company car, a Marina Coupé – a model which, twenty years on, has gained classic status!

I first got to know fellow Sevenoaks estate agent Martin Ingall as he was running a Midget on the road and, in 1976, he offered me a part share in the Modsports car that he and a friend had built together. I had always been fascinated by motor sport; the first racing car I ever saw in action was the Tony Dunderdale Turner, at a Lydden meeting. I suppose that it was logical, therefore, that I should end up racing a Modsports car, and a Midget at that.

We discussed figures for the purchase of my third of the car, but I insisted on driving before parting with my money. I had a medical, obtained my licence and turned up at the Brands open practice session the following Wednesday morning. The car was warmed up for a few laps by Ingall and then it was my turn. I was strapped in the closed car and sent on my way. In those days, you just needed a restricted licence and no experience to drive in one of these test sessions.

My first lap was at a snail's pace and I remember passing the pits to find my pit crew leaning over the wall, waving me on to go faster. Apparently, they were worried that my lack of speed would cause an accident. Having built up to a half-decent pace, I was amazed at the way Paddock Bend fell away so steeply – this was the life. I was a racing driver, and I was hooked. I was jolted back into the real world as I was lapped by the late Nick Whiting in the All Car Equipe Escort; he passed me on the main straight like I was standing still.

It was fitting that my race debut should be at Lydden, which, despite its shortcomings in facilities, has always been a friendly circuit and a nice one to drive. I entered the West Essex Car Club's meeting on 10 July 1977, having joined the BARC, one of the invited clubs, the week before. I was down for the Modsports event, but as there were only five entries – two Turners, a Ginetta G4, a Porsche Carrera and my Midget – the race was combined with the next on the programme, just for Porsches. This was unfortunate for the Carrera driver, who had entered both races, but lucky for me as I would now get twenty laps instead of ten.

After practice I was on the back row of the grid, which I shared with a 356A driven by an American named Wayne Hardman. During the lunch break, Martin Ingall taught me how to heel and toe. I knew nothing about this but Ingall considered it vital, if he were to have a gearbox left for his next race the following weekend. I was also taught start procedure – arrive at the grid, clear the gate, put it in first when the starter moves to the front of his rostrum, bring the revs up to about 4,500 then drop the clutch as the man drops the flag. 'Sounds easy', I thought.

I lined up, and went through the procedure that I had been taught, dropping the clutch as soon as the starter's arm twitched. The whole field roared away leaving me on

Purely Personal

the line; I had forgotten to put it in gear. I passed the 356A on the second lap and made up one other place during the race. In the paddock afterwards, I spoke to Wayne Hardman who was delighted that his virtually standard classic Porsche, which he had driven to the circuit, had beaten my full-race car off the line!

West Essex Car Club seems to have started a trend; when I raced at Lydden with them later that year, the Porsches were again in with the Modsports. By now, I had graduated to the second-to-back row and had learnt to put the car in gear for the start. On this occasion, one of the start-line marshals came over to tell me that John Piper in the 911 in front thought I ought to know that, as his car was an automatic, it might be a bit slow off the line.

That race was one of the best I had during my early days in the sport. I was pressurized almost throughout by Adrian Yeates-Smith in a 911. On each lap he would catch me on the straights, but he could not get past me on the corners. Yeates-Smith had driven his car to the circuit carrying a set of split-rim wheels with slicks on a roof-rack. Before scrutineering, he changed wheels and stripped the passenger seats and carpets out of the car.

I withstood the onslaught for eight laps and on the last tour, having failed to get inside me at the hairpin, he tried to go round the outside at Paddock. I have seen very few people get away with this manoeuvre at Lydden and the 911 was to prove no exception. It hit the bank hard, rolled out of contention, and the driver had to find a lift home. Basking in my own glory shortly after the race, I was concerned to hear my name called over the tannoy, being requested to attend race control. Convinced that the other driver had protested me for some reason, I stood before the secretary of the meeting, only to be told that my David and Goliath performance had been the best dice of the day so far and I was to get a special award. Thus, young Baggott won his first trophy.

While my racing exploits had their high points, like everyone else I also had my low moments. One piece of bad luck happened on my first visit to Croft, in 1979. As the circuit was a good seven hours' drive from home, we went up on the Saturday and booked overnight accommodation at a guest-house in the middle of Darlington. There was no car park so we left the tow car, racer and trailer in the road outside, the proprietor assuring us it would be all right. While I was getting ready for breakfast the next day, Martin Ingall went down to his Capri to load up our luggage.

He came back to the room to tell me that I would not, after all, be racing, as both the Midget and trailer had gone. I only believed him when I saw it with my own eyes. We reported the crime, gave a description of the car to the police, and proceeded to the circuit to try and get my entry fee back. The meeting was being covered by the local radio station and I pestered the press box until the sports reporter came out to see me. He agreed to broadcast a description of the car in his programme and, there being nothing else we could do, we returned to Kent.

As soon as we got back, we rang Darlington CID to learn that the car had been found by a woman out walking her dog just half an hour after we had left the area. The police towed it back to the station and locked it in the duty inspector's garage until we could go back and fetch it. Apparently, the inspector was on holiday and, anyway, they were sure he wouldn't mind as he liked a bit of motor racing. We went to work on Monday and drove back up to Darlington to collect the car on Tuesday. When we arrived, the crime prevention officer who was dealing with the case could not find the keys to the garage, so he and I had to use the tools in the tow car to pick the lock.

Left to right, the author, Geoff Wright and Steve Gardiner service my original racing Midget after practice at Donington Park, June 1983

My visit to Castle Combe for the season opener on 1 May 1978 was hardly an auspicious occasion: the sump plug fell out during practice and it rained so hard during the race that visibility was negligible. I finished well down the field. As I had not had time to fit a tow bar to my new company car and Martin Ingall was unable to mechanic that day, I hired a Transit. Long-time friend Peter Cope agreed to accompany me, suggesting that we could combine the trip with a visit to his parents who lived just outside Cardiff, staying the night with them and then taking a short run down the M4 on Sunday morning.

We arrived at the Cope residence in Lisvane, one of the more salubrious areas of the city, and parked the van and trailer on the drive. Peter Cope had not told his parents about our mode of transport, and they seemed less than impressed. His mother said it made her feel as if she had tradesmen in, and his father was not happy when the van left a deposit of oil on his newly surfaced drive.

A more worthwhile outing during my early days in the sport was another David and Goliath battle. This time, Goliath was haulage boss Garry Charlwood in his Ford Capri, into which he had shoe-horned a 5.3-litre Jaguar engine. We ended up beside each other on the front row of a Special GT grid at Lydden, on 4 July 1982. With all that power, he got the jump on me at the start, but there then followed a nine-lap cat and mouse game, where he pulled away from me on the two short straights, only to have my much nimbler Midget snapping at his heels as soon as he backed off for the corners.

Purely Personal

On two occasions, I managed to get inside him at the Devil's Elbow, but he still managed to come out just in front and then pull out a meagre margin going up the hill to the Hairpin. Sensing the possibility of beating him, I decided to make a final effort at the Elbow on the last lap. I was still accelerating into the corner in third as he was braking; when I got inside him I changed down to second, ready to beat him out of the corner. There was a dull thud, the engine lost power, the oil light came on and I immediately switched the engine off. I was going so fast that I managed to coast up the hill and down the other side to come home 3rd. Graham Smith, driving Colin Charman's Midget that day, just got by me on the last bend. Apparently, TVS showed some video footage of the race in a South East sports review in 1991; I would love to see it again.

I thought I may have melted number 4 piston and put the car on the trailer. When I went over to congratulate Garry Charlwood and chat about the race, he told me that his trucks went all over the country and offered to pick up any bits I needed for the engine to help me get back on the circuit. It was typical of the camaraderie that existed in club-level motor sport at the time.

The next evening my mechanic and I took the engine out. As I passed the rope round to attach the lump to the block and tackle, one of my fingers disappeared into a hole. 'Good job I have a spare sump', I thought. When the engine was up in the air, it became apparent that I would need more than that. It turned out that the iron crank, a Marina item that had been re-stroked, had broken, taking with it two rods, three pistons, camshaft, distributor drive, two valves and the block. Now seemed to be a good time to invest in a steel crank.

Every Midget driver wanted to beat Steve Everitt. In all my years of competing against him I only did it once, and the weather did give me a helping hand. He was a brilliant driver; his car had a quick engine but the suspension was not that sophisticated. My chance to beat him came when we were both caught in the rain on slicks at our local circuit, Brands, in September 1984. Everitt was on pole, sharing the front row with John Vernon and me. Steve Millard, whose Sprite was to play a significant part in the proceedings, was on the inside of the third row.

Everitt led from the start, but began to slow as it started to rain during the second lap, when Steve Millard and I were disputing second place. He was in front and, as I caught him, he was reeling in Everitt. The three of us were tied together at Paddock, on lap six, but as we approached Druids Millard managed to get inside Everitt and get by, perhaps gaining some extra grip from his brand-new slicks. I promptly followed him through. By now, the rain had eased slightly but, if anything, the track was getting more slippery.

I had a look at taking the lead, but there was now no traction to be had off the racing line. Having just repaired my car from a previous shunt, I decided to opt for nine points from what appeared to be a safe second place rather than risk getting no points and another bent car. All three of us got a lap of honour on the Brands Hatch Capri and Steve Millard collected his race winner's hat, an honour that was always to evade me. After the race Steve Gardiner, who was now mechanic-ing for me and had helped build the new car for the 1984 season, told me that I could never again use the excuse that I did not like the rain.

I have made many friends in the many years I have been racing Midgets. I've also had a few accidents, including one roll at Combe, on 2 May 1983, while dicing with long-time competitor James Thacker. As a teenage marshal in 1962, Thacker enjoyed a lap of Mallory as a passenger in the course car and decided there and then he wanted to take up racing. He moved from an MG TC to

Lap of honour on the Brands Hatch Sierra, left to right, Steve Millard, the author and Steve Everitt, 16 September 1984

a Sprite in 1970, when he and his cousin, Edward Thacker, bought the former Alec Poole car from Rob Cochrane. My most serious accident, which necessitated a re-shell, was at Castle Combe in 1989. I recall lying in the ambulance, which was waiting at Quarry Bend for radio clearance to return to the medical centre. As the vehicle turned, I let out a yell and the doctor leant over me and asked where the pain was. 'In my bloody wallet,' I replied, for I had just seen the remains of my car through the window. He sensibly told me, 'You can always replace the car, lad, but the driver's a different story!'

Within a week of the accident, still on crutches and contrary to my physiotherapist's instructions, I drove to Norfolk to look at another shell, and ended up buying one just up the road, in Bromley. Steve Gardiner and I rebuilt the car and I was back on the

Purely Personal

James Thacker's Spridgebits-sponsored car in the paddock at Silverstone May 1982. It has the original glass fibre bodywork from the Ark Sprite

track in two months; that's how hooked I was. Unfortunately, there was some internal damage to the engine that I did not spot, so we were plagued with reliability problems for the rest of the season.

Although I came 3rd in the Fully Modified class of the Midget championship three years running, I never won a race. Martin Hunt, my father-in-law, drew a cartoon for me: it is a Midget grid at Brands, Murray Walker is leaning out of the commentary box window, mike in hand, and in the bubble are the words, 'John Baggott, 28-year-old estate agent, racing for 19 years and still looking for his first win!' I always gave my age as 28 on the commentary sheet, and I never managed to score a race victory. Perhaps I should have gone all out at that wet Brands meeting? Even without winning, I thoroughly enjoyed racing with such a friendly bunch of drivers.

In the final race of the 1988 season I needed a finish to take 3rd in the championship and broke the gearbox on the last lap of practice. I had a spare with me but, seeing it in the back of the tow car, mechanic Steve Gardiner had pointedly asked how I proposed to change it on my own should the need arise. The only way to get the gearbox out of a Midget is to remove the engine first. We took off the rad and carbs and, as we started to unbolt the engine, a group of my fellow competitors gathered round. By the time the engine was ready to come out, they were back. One had a rope, another found a bulk of timber in the camping area. I was pushed aside while the rope was tied round the block, which, with the aid of the length of wood, was lifted out by six of them. They went off to have lunch telling us to be sure to give them a shout when it was ready to go back in.

Purely Personal

Two shots from a Steve Jones motor-drive sequence of the author destroying his car at Castle Combe in May 1989. The car was re-shelled and back on the track in eight weeks

They did come back and help me finish the job, and I even had time for a bite to eat before the off. I was to discover that the spare box, which had never been used, jumped out of first. From 4th on the grid I came home 7th, thanks to a poor start, but I still finished 3rd in the championship by just two points. I still have the lap chart for that event. In the remarks column Gardiner had written 'gearbox change at circuit: £65 please'. I should clarify that he, like all the other mechanics, assisted for the love of the sport, a few beers and, in my case, the excellent chicken rolls my mum used to make for the day's outing.

The ultimate in sportsmanship must be down to John Boness, the racing Reading postman who ran Rupert Russel's former car from 1980 to 1985. During an ill-fated practice session at Snetterton, on 14 June 1981, he melted a piston, Steve Everitt did his gearbox in and Barry Rogers cracked his cylinder head. Having removed the head from his own car to discover his piston problems, Boness lent it to Rogers. When word of this reached Everitt, he came along and before long Boness had removed his engine to get the box out for Everitt. With his mechanic Dave Woodgate, Everitt managed to fit it in his own car in time to take up his grid position, on the outside of the front row.

The race was won by pole man David Sheppard, with Keith Ashby 2nd and Everitt, complete with the borrowed gearbox, 3rd. Barry Rogers came home 6th so, despite not getting a race itself, parts of Boness' car took two places in the top six. Later in the day, Sheppard had a puncture as he was about to go out for the Garelli Modified Sportscar event, and he took a class win with a pair of Boness' wheels and tyres on the front of the car. Boness was a typical member of the Midget crowd, always ready to help out a fellow competitor.

16 Steve Everitt

Steve Everitt was probably the best-known MG Midget racer of all time and someone it was impossible not to like. He was born in Sevenoaks on 12 May 1952 and was, sadly, killed at the wheel of a four-wheel-drive vehicle on a Greek island. He had gone there with his sponsor Chris Bunch, just days after winning what was to be his last-ever race at Snetterton, in October 1987. He was a bachelor, with more than his fair share of female friends. His philosophy on motor sport was never to let it get him down, win or lose (although he usually won), and, most importantly, to enjoy a beer in the clubhouse with the lads after the race.

Educated at Bethany School in Goudhurst, young Everitt, who was dyslexic, protected himself with his sense of humour when the going got tough in the classroom. He became the class comedian, very popular with his classmates but not always with the teaching staff. From an early age, he had a strong interest in cars, and he went on to take a City and Guilds Motor Vehicle Technicians course at the West Kent College in Tonbridge. By now, he had passed his driving test and was looking for a car of his own. Peter Denham, who raced a Lenham Midget, recalls that Everitt was very keen on one of his sisters. In order to impress her, he offered to give her a lift home from school. He had a spare key cut for his father's car and then, without his father's knowledge, borrowed the car from the commuter car park at Sevenoaks Station, where it stood all day. He then returned it to the same parking space afterwards, locked it up and walked home.

Victor's laurels for Steve Everitt, Castle Combe, May 1980

Steve Everitt

I first met Steve Everitt in 1974; at the time my secretary was his girlfriend and he drove a Morris 1000, with a tuned 1275cc engine, wide wheels, flared arches and hideous tinted windows. It was given to him by his grandmother and I am sure she did not recognize it once it had been given it the treatment. The Morris was soon well known throughout the Sevenoaks and Tonbridge areas, particularly to the local constabulary, who seemed keen to stop its driver and find out what made it go so fast! Eventually, it was rolled into a ball in Oak Lane, Sevenoaks, and despite coming to rest against a wall, Everitt and his two female passengers were able to walk away from it. He bought another Morris 1000 (WNJ 33) as a replacement, and although he tuned the engine and lowered the suspension, he had now decided that tinted windows and wide Escort arches attracted too much unwelcome attention. These modifications were not incorporated in the Mark II version, although it did have a fibreglass bonnet and up-rated suspension.

Having joined the local Sevenoaks and District Motor Club, Everitt did his first event, the Valence Hill Climb, in July 1975. Driving the Morris, he was sixth fastest out of thirty in his class – a sign of things to come. This well-known hill is up the drive of a special school at Westerham; as well as raising funds for the establishment, the event also provides a great day out for the children.

During his college sandwich course, Steve worked at Bluebird Garage in Sevenoaks, where he became friends with Tony Mason and Dave Woodgate. He then used his motor trade qualifications to get a job with the local 'U Drive' car hire firm. While working there, he met the local Lombard North Central rep, who told him the vehicle finance group were looking for someone to cover the East Sussex area. Everitt was successful in getting the job, and stayed with the company for the rest of his working life.

His second Morris made way for a company car and, without a road vehicle of his own to maintain, he began to think about having a go at motor racing. He thought about Special Saloons, but eventually ruled this class out on the grounds of cost. He finally decided a Modsports Midget was the

Mean Machine: Steve Everitt's Morris 1000 on south Bank at Brands Hatch. It was in this, his everyday road car at the time, that he took part in his first competitive event, the 1975 Valence Hill Climb

logical choice, given he had already acquired considerable knowledge about the 'A' Series while tuning his Morris.

At the end of 1975, he was spectating at the Sevenoaks and District winter clubbie at Brands and saw a 'For Sale' sign on the David Strange Midget, which had just come 4th in the up to 1300cc Modsports event, in which Jonathan Palmer had come 2nd. Everitt looked round the car in the paddock, went to see the owner the following weekend, and bought the car for £900. The Midget had a 1275cc Longman-prepared engine and ran on 8½in Revolutions. Having nowhere to keep the car, Everitt talked Martin Ingall into letting him have some space in a barn he rented on the Weald farm next to his cottage. Over the winter, he rebuilt the car and made his race debut in the British Racing Green Modsports Midget in the Modified Sportscar Championship event, at Thruxton on 4 April 1976.

This event marked the beginning of a most successful twelve-year car and driver partnership. During that time, he amassed a tally of some seventy 1st places and took the Modified Midget Championship no less than six times, was runner-up twice, 3rd once and 4th twice. Despite a couple of accidents over the years, the car retained the same pre-1964 quarter-elliptic body shell, as it does to this day, now owned by Ted Reeve, who bought the car at the beginning of the 1988 season.

Everitt's early days had the inevitable teething troubles. He qualified 28th from thirty-one starters in that first race at Thruxton and finished 20th overall, 7th in class. His next outing was at Lydden Hill Circuit near Dover, a disastrous occasion when both the clutch and gearbox disintegrated. The gearbox was rebuilt with help from Tony Mason, the first of many occasions when Mason would assist with rebuilds. At the end of the first year, it had become obvious to Everitt that the car, although competitive in 1975, was now being outclassed. Having decided more power was needed, he had the engine bored out to 1380cc.

Originally, Everitt competed in the STS and STP series, taking in any other Modsports races at his two local circuits, Brands and Lydden. He moved to the Midget series in 1977, its inaugural year, and was the first Modified champion. Lawrence Cutler recalls that Everitt kept his defection to the one-make series quiet; the first that most people knew of it was when the race results were published in *Motoring News*. Cutler and other STP Midget drivers followed him into the MG Car Club Championship, but even in those early days, Everitt was the man to beat.

Everitt had one memorable battle, in more ways than one, at the MG Car Club Brands meeting on 4 December 1978. Having already won the Midget race earlier in the afternoon, he was on the front row for the Modsports encounter, which was Race 4. Fellow front row man Dave Bettinson, in his much-modified Caterham Super Seven, known as the 'Black Brick', led from the start but Everitt successfully challenged for the lead at Druids. Bettinson tried hard – too hard – to get back at Bottom bend, spinning and narrowly being missed by Ian Mason's Aston Martin. And there were still nine laps to go.

By lap 4, the fast-recovering Bettinson was back up to 3rd, having powered past the big Aston. On the next lap he took Lawrence Cutler for second place. On the eighth tour the Caterham caught up with the Midget at Druids and re-took the lead along the start-finish straight at the beginning of the ninth. Everitt was having none of it and, on the last lap, again used the hairpin to get by the more powerful car. Bettinson countered by squirting the Caterham back in front round the outside at Clearways, but he cut in too early and collected the Midget, the impact

Steve Everitt

The controversial Steve Everitt/Dave Bettinson dice that resulted in a Modsports win for Everitt after the pair made contact on the last corner. Brands Hatch, 4 December 1977

spinning his car into the armco within sight of the flag. Everitt kept his engine running and made it to the line to win, despite his deranged bodywork.

Having joined the Midget Championship, Everitt was one of a small band of drivers who made the long journey north for the first round of the 1980 series, at Croft on 7 April. After two laps of practice, the distributor moved and the change in timing resulted in two burnt-out pistons and retirement on the spot. He had had a sixteen-hour round trip for just two laps of practice, and was forced to sit on the sidelines and watch Dave Sheppard win the race from John Gallagher. Even this cloud had a silver lining, however: not having a car to look after in the race, Everitt's mechanic Dave Woodgate was able to find a good vantage point and take photographs, some of which are used in this book.

David Sheppard and Steve Everitt enjoyed great on-track rivalry from 1978 to 1981, but were invariably found in the bar together after the race. Their first real dice was at Brands in November 1977. This was a combined race for Road-going (in which Sheppard was competing at the time) and Modified Midgets. Half-way through the race, it started raining and Everitt, being on slicks, had a job to control his car. The two drivers changed places a couple of times and at Clearways, on the last lap, Sheppard got by and stayed in front to take overall victory, previously unheard of for a road car.

After the race, Sheppard commented to Everitt that his car must have been a bit dodgy in the wet, on slicks with all that power. To which Everitt, who had never seen Sheppard in his life before, replied, 'Yes, it was, but I'm sure that bastard in the blue car that beat me didn't have a standard engine.' There followed a discussion on what was legal and what was not, and Everitt realized that he was talking to the man who had just won the race. This was the start of a friendship that lasted well beyond the time when Sheppard gave up racing Midgets.

The two drivers were to have many epic battles, but two races were exceptional. By some coincidence, both drivers were a bit late getting in their entries for the Midget race at the BRSCC Sportscar Festival, at Mallory on 26 May 1980, and ended up as reserves. After practice, which saw John Gallagher awarded pole with a 55.3, Sheppard was fastest on 54.3, while Everitt turned in a 55.2; both would have had front-row grid positions. However, as reserves, they were lined up at the back, on the basis that they would start only if two other drivers dropped out.

They did the warm-up lap then formed up on the back row and waited, expecting to be pulled off the grid at any moment. When the flag dropped, no one stopped them and off they went, working their way up through the field. By the end of lap 2, Sheppard was 4th and Everitt 7th, climbing to 6th next time round. Lap 6 saw Sheppard take the lead from David Humphries, only to spin it all away on lap 7. Meanwhile, Everitt caught John Gallagher and took him for 2nd on lap 8; could he possibly catch David Humphries, who seemed to have an unassailable lead? Fate took a hand, and on the same lap Humphries coasted to a halt, handing Everitt first place. He had gone from 22nd on the grid to the front of the field in eight laps of the circuit!

After the race, the organizers realized their 'mistake'. Victory was awarded to John Gallagher, and the results showed that Everitt and Sheppard had both been excluded, along with Graham Bell, who had been third reserve. Both were philosophical about what happened – despite not gaining any championship points, they had enjoyed their race. It was not entirely a wasted day, as both drivers did, officially, get on the grid for the later Modsports event. Everitt came 3rd overall, winning the class and Sheppard finished 4th in class, 6th overall. Third place in class went to the other car excluded from the Midget race, that of Simon Hamilton-Smith, this time at the wheel of his LPG-powered car that had previously been driven by Graham Bell.

Dave Sheppard leads Steve Everitt during their epic dice at Brands Hatch on 14 September 1980

In September 1980, Everitt and Sheppard had another head to head, this time at Brands Hatch. The meeting was organized by the MG Car Club and the practice times saw the two friends once more next to one another on the front row. Everitt made a disappointing start from pole, allowing Sheppard to take the lead, but Everitt was soon up to 2nd for a race-long duel, the likes of which had not been seen for a long time. Most laps saw them side by side down the Brabham straight, with the lead changing at least once. On the third tour, they swapped positions three times as things really heated up. The hectic action continued till lap 9, when the two cars touched at Paddock Hill bend, resulting in Everitt's Midget spinning out into the catch fencing and coming to rest embedded in the front wing of a marshal's car that was parked on the infield.

Sheppard took the victory and set the fastest MG lap of the day (79.47mph/128km/h). It was not all bad for Everitt, who was awarded the then traditional Brands Hatch 'driver of the day' award and the £50 cheque that went with it.

As he told commentator Brian Jones at the presentation, the money would buy the next round, and help to pay for his damaged bodywork. Incidentally, the marshal whose car he had hit sought Everitt out after the race to ask him if he had any insurance to cover the cost of repairing the car's wing. Everitt's response is unprintable.

During the ten laps of the race, the lead had changed no less than twenty-one times. Afterwards, Brian Jones said he had not seen such an exciting race for ten or fifteen years. The two were going at such a pace that second-place man John Gallagher finished thirteen seconds behind, Malcolm Ellis was third in the smart Drapkin Print Group car.

The November 1980 edition of *Safety Fast* described the encounter thus: 'Even though coachwork scuffing occurred, this tremendous duel was not a ragged, vicious scrap, but a gentlemanly conflict executed with mutual respect.' Everitt bore no malice, saying that the accident was just 'one of those things'. In any case, the tables were turned later that month at Donington Park. Sheppard, having set pole, retired on lap 4 leav-

Everitt (179) leads Sheppard (181) at Brands Hatch Club Circuit on 14 September 1980. The lead changed twenty-one times during the ten laps

ing Everitt to finish 2nd to a very much on-form Keith Ashby.

At about this time, Modsports cars were sprouting rear spoilers, some of rather large proportions, so Everitt decided he really should have one. He fabricated his masterpiece from the aluminium roof of an old caravan he found in the yard of one of the garages with which he dealt. A track test in *Cars and Car Conversions* in 1980 quoted Everitt as admitting its main advantage was in 'psyche value' against the opposition.

One of Everitt's other major sparring partners was Warlingham driver Lawrence Cutler. They always made a point of doing the winter clubbies at Brands, enjoying the unique end-of-term atmosphere that prevailed at these meetings. Invariably, the day would finish with them having a session in the bar after the presentations, usually in the company of Brian Jones.

Like all of us, Everitt had his silly moments, both on and off the track. I recall an MG Car Club meeting at Silverstone, when we all lined up for practice without him, although I knew he had set off, because I had passed him at a petrol station in Sevenoaks. He eventually arrived at lunchtime, too late to qualify, even out of session. He told us he got to Lewisham before realizing that he had left his crash helmet and race licence behind. So that he could drive back home as quickly as possible, he unhitched the trailer, left it on the side of the road, and persuaded his long-suffering girlfriend, Jill, to stay and guard it. When I expressed concern (for her), Everitt replied: 'Well, mate, I couldn't leave the car unattended there. It's a bit of a dodgy area, isn't it?'

One of his early tweaks was an air box for the carbs, fabricated from an old one-gallon Duckhams can, to keep the Webers supplied with cool air. The only problem was that when the car was trailered to the circuit in the rain, the trumpets tended to fill with water. Everitt soon came up with an answer to this, he went to a builder's merchants and bought two rubber bath plugs, tied them together with a piece of string and stuck them in the trumpets. Unfortunately, at one meeting he arrived a bit late and started the car without removing the plugs; the engine sucked in the 'O' rings!

MG Car Club secretary Gordon Cobban presents Steve Everitt with his Brands Hatch race-winner's hat on 11 September 1981

Everitt was one of the first Midget drivers to use a set of split Weber 48 carbs, getting them soon after they came out. He did not want his fellow competitors to know where his extra power came from, and there was a risk they would, since drivers habitually wandered round between practice and race, looking at everyone else's car. When he installed his new carburettors, he unbolted the top covers from his old set of 45s, which, being the same size, he was able to fix on the top of the new ones. Anyone looking under the bonnet would see '45 DCOE' stamped on the top and not know that he was in fact using 48s.

There was, at the time, much mystique about what went into Everitt's engines. The chassis on his car was quite basic. It still had the adjustable Armstrong lever arm shock absorbers, now rare. Long-time friend Mike Oldfield, who worked with him at Bluebird Motors, helped build the racing engines and gearboxes, while the machining was done by former autocross champion Paul Grant. Grant spent many hours polishing and stress relieving the blocks Everitt used. In common with most of his contemporaries, he progressed from 1275 (as it was when he bought the car) to 1380, 1430 and 1460cc engines.

It was impossible to get a straight answer from Everitt about the power output, but really his success was more a result of his total commitment behind the wheel than of how many brake horsepower his engine gave. He used a Bryan Slark big valve head and, having tried a Reece corrected profile, his quickest engine ended up running a Leyland AEG 595 Super Sprint cam. Somehow, he got it to work with a long-stroke engine, using solid steel main caps to help it stay together.

One winter, Everitt decided he wanted a more aerodynamic front on his car and, having taken stock of what was around, decided on the Lenham shape. He managed to persuade Peter Denham to lend him the Lenham front from his car, so that he could take a mould from it; it was ideal as it already had wide arches. Having bought a supply of glass fibre matting and resin, Everitt requisitioned his parents' garage to do the work. He moved most of the clutter to one side but had to leave the freezer where it was.

He managed to take the mould and remove Denham's original without even cracking the paint. After that, making his own front was easy, and it was soon painted and fitted on the Midget. A week later, he sat down to Sunday lunch with his parents, and they all tucked in to roast beef. His mother commented that the meat had rather a sweet taste to it, and Everitt realized that it was resin. The lid seal on the freezer was slightly defective and the contents had been tainted by Everitt's work. He kept quiet about it.

Peter Nott, a fellow competitor, well remembers the Donington meeting at the start of the 1981 season. He towed his new blue car up to the circuit on the back of his new VW Transporter van the day before. Having laid out their sleeping bags in the back of the wagon, he and his crew adjourned to the Redgate Bar, chuckling to themselves that none of the other Midget lads would recognize either the racer, or the tow barge. They emerged from the bar at closing time, climbed in the back of the VW and went to sleep. A little while later, Nott thought he heard giggling, and later still he was awakened by a scratching noise, which continued to disturb his sleep for the rest of the night. Getting up in the morning, he saw six empty lager bottles on the roof of the van, evidently a present from the Everitt crew.

Although 1982 was Everitt's worst year ever, he still beat Peter Nott for second place in the Midget Championship. He started the season well, with two wins, but then had two retirements with 'fuel problems'. At Cadwell the pump packed up, and when it was examined in the paddock after the race, it was so corroded that everyone was surprised it worked at all. Disaster struck again the next week at Castle Combe. While leading, he ran out of petrol on lap 8. The car had lost its fan belt in practice and they were busy sorting this out. Everitt remembered just as the two-minute board was displayed on the grid – too late, of course! The bad luck continued when he crashed heavily at Silverstone as a result of a deflating tyre.

As a leading Midget driver Everitt was one of the people invited by Larry Quinn to take part in the MG GP drivers' parade at the 1983 Brands Hatch Grand Prix of Europe. Everitt was due to chauffeur Jacques Laffite, the number two Williams driver, who, unfortunately, had failed to qualify for the race. Everitt and mechanic Dave Woodgate drove along the back of the pit lane garages to the Williams pit to collect their driver. They were told that, as Laffite was not racing, he had already left the circuit. They thought they were about to miss out on their moment of glory, but just at that moment Angela Webb, wife of circuit supremo John Webb, was marshalling all the cars out of the pits for the parade. Everitt, whose sponsor was in the crowd, shouted to Dave Woodgate to jump in, as they were going anyway. That is how Woodgate came to do a lap of the track impersonating Jacques Laffite, waving at the crowds and shrugging Gallic-style at the bemused marshals.

Everitt's determination to race and win, no matter what the setbacks, is well illustrated by what happened during practice for the Midget race at Brands, on 5 August 1984. In the closing stages of the session, during which he qualified on pole, he came into the pits to report a bad vibration from the engine. Back in the paddock, the engine was removed – as this was his local circuit, there were plenty of friends to help – and it was discovered that the flywheel had broken. With the engine out, a large amount of oil was visible in the transmission tunnel; removal of the gearbox revealed that lubricant was escaping from a crack in the tail

Brands Hatch Paddock, August 1984; left to right, Mike Oldfield, Tony Mason and Steve Everitt prepare to replace the engine after changing the flywheel

shaft housing. At this stage, most other people would have given up. Not Everitt.

He rang Tony Mason, who lived 45 minutes' drive away near Hastings and was about to go out for a day's sailing with his wife. He agreed to drive to Everitt's house in Heathfield, remove the flywheel from the spare engine and deliver it to Brands. Martin Ingall, who was also in the paddock, said he had a spare gearbox casing at home and set off to bring back the part required. All was back together in time for the race, but the troubles were not over. On lap 7, one of the rear trailing arms broke and, although it was spotted by an alert marshal, he was not black-flagged. The loose suspension link soon cut through a brake pipe and Everitt did the last two laps without brakes. He still won the race and set fastest lap.

The following weekend, again at Brands, the car still had the flywheel that was not correctly balanced for the engine. However, he won the Otis Lifts MG All Comers Race at the Sun Free Race day, again setting the fastest lap. Not only did all the work carried out in the paddock illustrate Everitt's personal tenacity, but also the extent of his friends' loyalty.

Drivers using long-stroke crankshafts found they set up harmonics which would wreck the windings of starter motors. Everitt was one of many to experience this problem and, at one stage, was getting through a starter motor per meeting. He bought such parts from a chain of motor factors that had branches in many of the towns he visited in the course of his job. Tiring of regularly having to fork out for a new one, he started taking them back, under warranty, using a different branch each time. He would tell the assistant that he had only had it for a week or so, the paint was unmarked and, after all, it was from his old MG Midget that he only used at the weekends. He failed to point out that this particular Midget was a racing car capable of over 120mph.

In common with many competitors, Everitt used his company car as a tow barge. At one time he had a Morris Marina, which was due to be changed at about the time he was experiencing tappet adjustment problems with the Midget. This was traced to a worn rocker shaft, but the fault was only discovered on the Saturday afternoon before the next day's race – his usual pre-race preparation time. As all the garage parts departments shut at noon, there was nothing for it but to swap the shaft in the racer with the one in his road car. By then, the Marina was getting a bit long in the tooth and he was sure no one would notice if it ran a little unevenly. He also managed the operation without changing the head gasket on either engine.

His replacement company car was a 1600 Mark III Escort, its larger engine much more suitable for towing. It was soon fitted with Weller White Spoke wheels and a shirt button steering wheel, all contrary to company policy. The story goes that when this car found its way to auction, some two years later, minus the bolt-on goodies, the auctioneer was emphasizing that the car was the property of a well-known finance house and came with full service history. One motor trader turned to another and told him that it was Everitt's old car, adding that the last time he had seen it, it was doing 95mph up the M25 with a trailer and racing car on the back!

Although he undoubtedly enjoyed his racing, Everitt was always keen to ensure that car preparation caused the minimum disruption to his social life. When he lived in Sevenoaks and the car was stored in the barn, he would go to collect it the day before a race and park it on the trailer outside his parents' house in one of the town's smart residential roads. He would then work on it while it was still on the trailer, even manag-

The Garden Cottage team; left to right, Jenny Weightman (timing), Steve Everitt and Dave Woodgate (race engineer)

ing to change the diff without putting the car on the tarmac. The trailer was always parked in roughly the same place and, over the years, a large Hypoid oil stain appeared on the road. To the best of my knowledge, it is still there.

During his time racing, Everitt had three people who mechaniced for him at the circuits. The first of these was Paul Nicholson, a big lad who was in business as a mobile mechanic. In deference to his size, Everitt, who often holidayed in Greece, nicknamed him 'Scrofer', an endearing Greek term for 'ox', or so he told him. This explains why some of the entries in 1977 race programmes refer to Everitt driving a 'Scrofer Midget'. Later, he enlisted the help of Norman Lawrence, a tall fellow who became known as 'Big Norm'. Everitt would often light-heartedly refer to him as 'my minder'.

From 1978 to 1986, Everitt's right-hand man at the circuits was Dave Woodgate, his old friend from their days working together at Bluebird Motors. Woodgate towed the racer with his Triumph 2000 and latterly a Mark II Granada. He recalls Everitt as being unflappable. On the way to one Silverstone meeting, in the days before the M25, they got held up by a 'Right to Work' march in London. They arrived in the paddock just as the Midgets were going out to practise. Everitt ran to sign on, while Woodgate dragged the car off the trailer. They jumped the scrutineering queue, checking the oil and adjusting the tyre pressures while the car was given the once-over. Grabbing his helmet, Everitt got in the car just in time to do his three laps to qualify. He still got on the front row.

When Woodgate himself took up racing in his Jaguar S-Type saloon, in 1986, Steve gave him advice on how to drive all the circuits, taking him through the lines and braking points. His tips bore fruit. Woodgate won his class in 1990 and 1991 and was a member of the winning team in the Team Challenge three years running. In 1993, he was the Jaguar Standard Challenge Champion and was also awarded the Jaguar Car Club driver of the year trophy.

Everitt went racing strictly for fun and had no ambition to progress up the ladder into any other formula, although he was surely a good enough driver to have got into Formula 3 if he had wanted. His one departure from Midgets was when he was asked by motoring writer and PR man John Brigden to join the Charters of Aldershot/*Fast Lane* magazine Peugeot Diesel Team, for the 750 Motor Club Six-Hour Relay at Silverstone, on 18 October 1984.

The event marked the first-ever recorded race of a diesel-engined car in Britain. Brigden knew David Evans and Brian Llewelyn at Peugeot UK and managed to persuade them to come up with two diesel 309s. The third was loaned by Charters, the Aldershot dealers, who let the team have their demonstrator. The firm also prepared all three cars to RACMSA safety standards, fitted uprated brake pads and linings, and changed the wheels and tyres. The team comprised John Brigden, who usually raced a Mini 1000, Peter Dron, then editor of *Fast Lane*, which had been persuaded to co-sponsor the team, and Everitt, the most experienced and competitive driver of the three. Although he had never actually raced in a non-slick-tyred formula, Everitt quickly adapted. Brigden realized that, with their completely standard and non-tuned cars, they would stand no chance of overall honours, but considered that they would do well in the handicapped results. He felt sure that the handicapper would underestimate the cars' ability, which would give them a bit of a head start.

The cars ran well, but close to the bottom of the field, during the first three hours. At the start of the fourth hour, it started to rain. While other teams' lap times plummeted in the increasingly bad weather, the Peugeots only dropped about a second a lap and began to climb the field on handicap. As a result of the worsening weather, the race was stopped after five and a half hours and the team was classified 8th on handicap. Had the organizers not knocked six laps off the team's handicap allowance after practice, they would have been 5th.

John Brigden is convinced that, if the race had run its distance, this result would have been bettered. Everitt, whose Midget did not handle that well in the wet, was revelling in the adverse conditions in the Peugeot and was amazed how well it cornered, although he obviously noticed the difference in power. As a 'first', the endeavours of the Peugeot diesels received a great deal of coverage in the motoring press, and sponsors *Fast Lane* carried a feature on the team's efforts.

Unlike many drivers, Everitt always managed to attract sponsors, not only because of his successful driving, but also because of his great ability to talk to people. It was very hard not to like the man. During the latter part of 1977, he approached Dennis Gurr of Sevenoaks-based Bintcliffe Turner and the following season the car appeared in the aerospace engineers' silver livery. For 1979 the colour remained the same, but the car bore the name of Deltight Industries Group, the parent company. In 1980, Everitt persuaded Paul Lee-Kemp, the MD of Sevenoaks Hi-Fi, to back his efforts and the car changed colour to the firm's dark blue. It was, on occasions, towed to events on the back of one of their Transits, but contrary to the paddock jibes, the racer was not fitted with an in-car music system as part of the deal.

In 1982, Everitt met Crowborough businessman Chris Bunch and over the next six seasons the Midget appeared in cream, orange and day-glo red, successively bearing allegiance to Garden Cottage Foods, Martin Whale Engineering, and Moving Still Photography, before reverting to Garden Cottage Foods, with its now familiar thatched cottage logo. This period of Everitt's racing career was to be his most successful. He won the Midget Championship for four consecutive years.

From the start of the 1984 season, till his last outing at Snetterton on 25 October 1987, Everitt won thirty-nine out of the forty-four Modified Midget races he started, only failing to finish once, when he retired on the first lap at Mallory in April 1987. On the occasions when he did not take the laurels, he came 2nd five times and 3rd once. During the same period he set thirty fastest laps out of the forty-four starts. His main rival, Steve Watkins, took twelve of the remaining best laps of these forty-four races, and I took the other two. Watkins also took victory in all the races Everitt did not win.

Steve Watkins remembers one particular incident involving his old rival – something which happened in the paddock after they raced against each other at Mallory Park on 20 September 1987. Everitt led from lights to flag, with Watkins shadowing him every inch of the way. The two were so evenly matched that Watkins was unable to get by and was beaten by a scant 1.7 seconds. About five minutes after the race, he was sipping a drink in the paddock, having just removed his helmet, when Everitt came up to him. Wiping his finger across his rival's brow he said, 'I'm glad to see you're sweat-

Steve Everitt and Dennis Gurr of Bintcliffe Turner shake hands on sponsorship for the 1979 season

Steve Everitt

The splendid Steve Everitt Memorial Trophy

ing too, mate', as a great grin came over his face.

After Everitt's untimely death, his father Derek set up a fund to back the Steve Everitt Memorial Trophy. In 1989, Malvern-based sculptor Chris Davis was commissioned to cast a bronze of Everitt's car, aptly set on a chequered flag. This fine trophy is awarded each year to the winner of the Steve Everitt Memorial Race, at Brands Hatch, Everitt's home (and favourite) circuit. In addition, a prize fund makes awards to the placed drivers in each class.

Everitt's famous car, now minus its once-familiar Lenham front, owing to a change in the regulations, is still among the front-runners in the hands of its new owner, Ted Reeve. Reeve so nearly won the trophy at the 1993 race, and Steve's mother Doreen, who presented the prizes, urged him to try harder the next year. To date, the Memorial Trophy has been won by Graeme Adams (twice), Julian Cutler, Lawrence Cutler (twice), Mike Chalk and Chris Montague (twice).

During the last four years of his life, Everitt's driving record was phenomenal. His ability behind the wheel and his ever-cheerful banter in the paddock are sorely missed by all the drivers who knew and competed against him during his twelve years as a club racer.

Bibliography

The majority of the research for this book has been carried out by contacting the people involved. However, the following publications have been consulted in order to verify certain information.

Abbey, Staton, *The Pitman's All-In-One Book of the Morris 1000* (Pitman, 1977)

Allison, Mike, *The Magic Of The Marque* (Dalton Watson, 1989)

Browning, Peter and Needham, Les, *Healeys and Austin Healeys* (Foulis Sparkford, 1976)

Dymock, Eric, *The Sprites and Midgets* (Motor Racing Publications, 1981)

Garnier, Peter, with Healey, Brian, *Donald Healey, My World of Cars* (Patrick Stephens Ltd, 1989)

Garton, Mike, *Tuning BMC Sports Cars* (Speedsport Publications, 1969)

Harvey, Chris, *MG and Austin Healey Spridgets* (The Oxford Press, 1983)

Healey, Geoffrey, *More Healeys Frog-eyes, Sprites and Midgets* (Gentry Books, 1978)

Hill, Graham, *Life at the Limit* (William Kimber, 1969)

Haynes, J. H., *BMC 'A' Series Tuning Manual* (J. H. Haynes, 1965)

Jacobs, Dick, *An MG Experience* (Transport Bookman Publications, 1976)

Olyslager, Piet, MSIA MSAE, *BMC Light Sports Cars* (T. Nelson and Sons, 1967)

Price, Bill, *The BMC/BL Competitions Department* (Foulis, Haynes, 1989)

Sharratt, Barney, *Post War Baby Austins A30-A35-A40* (Osprey, 1988)

Sprinzel, John and Coulthard, Tom, *Spritely Years* (Patrick Stephens, Haynes, 1994)

Index

Aaltonen, Rauno 12, 19, 30, 32, 115
Adams, Graeme 125, 175, 176, 178, 181
Alford, Chris 128
Appleby, Arthur 16, 18, 28, 31, 32
Ashby, Keith 60–62, 89, 92, 98, 100, 138, 144, 170, 173, 192, 199

Bahamas Speed Week 34
Bailey, Andy 87, 97, 128, 140–142
Baker, Clive 11, 13, 19–22, 26, 29, 30, 32, 35, 36
Baker, Jim 33, 36

Banks, John 151, 163–166
Bax, Ian 146
Baxter, Raymond 55
Beer, Malcolm 82, 83, 97, 98
Beer, Syd 82
Bending, Tony 54–55, 60, 61
Bernal-Ryan, Paul 144
Bolster, John 86
Boness, John 157, 192
Bradley, Bill 19
Brigden, John 204
Britten, John 49, 88, 104, 105, 116–128, 156

Brooker-Carey, David 176, 179–180
Broom, Tony 133, 146
Browning, Peter 96, 110, 114
Butler, Paul 133, 146

Cairns, Tim 173, 178, 182
Cape Works 5, 18
Carlisle, Crystabel 14, 77
Cars & Car Conversions 100, 149, 152, 155, 174, 199
Chalk, Mike 49, 140, 155, 174–176, 206
Charman, Colin 143, 179, 182

207

Index

Cobban, Gordon 168
Colgate, John 10–12, 35
Cutler, Lawrence 91, 171, 176–179, 181, 192, 195, 199, 206
Cutting, Brian 132

Donovan, Mike 128, 139, 142, 148, 156
Dutton, Ivan 66

Ecurie Ecosse 15, 16
Elvers, John 87
Enever, Roger 28, 48, 65, 66, 85, 102–106, 108, 112, 118, 120, 122, 131, 151
Enever, Sydney 108, 109, 112
Everitt, Steve 93, 125, 138, 140, 152, 154, 169, 170, 173, 175, 176, 192, 193–204
Everson, Roger 151
Eyers, Roy 149, 150

Foster, Alan 72–79
Foster, Ernie 138

Gallagher, John 158, 172, 196, 197, 198
Gamble, Richard 96, 112
Garton, Mike 13–16, 21, 54, 86, 113, 114, 125
Gaston, Paddy 60, 63, 116, 117
Gibson, Rob 70
Goodwin, Alan 56–57, 152
Gott, John 59, 121
Greene, Keith 35, 77–79, 82
Groves, Richard 15, 16, 21, 29

Hales, Mark 99, 156
Hall, Ian 130, 134–136
Hamilton-Smith, Simon 146, 197
Hawkins, Paul 10, 13, 20, 47
Healey, Donald 9, 18, 20, 34, 115, 155
Healey, Geoffrey 8, 10, 14, 16, 19, 20, 27, 29, 30, 36, 37, 46
Hedges, Andrew 26, 36, 38, 52, 72–82
Hill, Graham 78, 85, 52, 115
Hopkirk, Paddy 13, 26, 29, 30, 42, 80, 81
Hopwood, Barry 86, 127
Howie, Gordon 90, 129–130

Ibrahim, Richard 159–160
Ingall, Martin 147, 177, 185, 195, 202
Ireland, Innes 11
Ivey, Charles 131

Ivey, Paul 46, 88, 90, 132, 184

Jacobs, Dick 14, 47, 71–83, 87
Jackson, Peter 40, 44, 45, 48
Jenvey, Richard 99–101, 157

Konig, Gabriel 39, 104, 105, 118–125, 137

Lane, Roy 15, 56
Lees-Smith, Bunny 155–156, 172
Lemmer, Richard and Mark 133
Lenham Motor Company 48, 118
Lewis, Mike 43
Livingstone, Sue and Ron 147–148
Longman, Richard 88, 93, 137
Lucas, Dudley 18, 30, 54

Mac, Roger 80
Maher, Eddie 46, 85, 103, 107
Makinen, Timo 13, 115
Mannion, Pat 149
Martyn, Chris 77–79
Matthews, Derek 151, 162, 165, 166
May, Peter 49, 93, 108, 110, 122, 125, 128, 178, 181, 182, 183, 188
McLaren, Bruce 10
McQueen, Steve 11, 35
Menadue, Roger 9, 11, 13, 18, 27, 28, 34
Milne, John 72, 79–80, 82
Minshaw, Alan 130
Montague, Chris 178, 181, 183, 184, 206
Moore, John 15, 21, 22, 29
Moss, Stirling 8, 10, 11, 34
Motoring News 96, 129, 169
Mowatt, Jon 93

Neale, Steve 22
Nettleton, Robert 70, 136, 183
Neville, Bob 25, 96, 106, 108, 110, 111, 112, 113, 128
Nigogosian, Garo 49, 64–66, 104–105, 121, 124–125

Paddy, Graham 88, 90
Palmer, Jonathan 141, 174, 195
Percy, Win 131–133
Poole, Alec 13, 21, 22, 25, 28, 106–110, 112, 137, 148, 189
Poole, Arnie 108, 109
Price, Geoff 16, 31, 36, 106

Quinn, Larry 97, 168, 169, 172, 174, 180, 182, 201

Ramus, Nick 113–114
Redsell, Roger 145
Reeve, Ted 96–98, 150, 176, 178, 195, 206
Rhodes, John 19, 20, 26
Richings, Peter 139, 141, 156
Richmond, Daniel and Bunty 88
Rodriguez, Pedro 11, 115
Rogers, Barry 154, 155, 157, 173, 174, 192

Sheppard, Dave 90, 94, 97, 125, 138, 153, 171, 173, 192, 196, 197
Slark, Brian 93, 200
Smith, Chris 63, 66, 68, 163–166
Sparling, Roger 138
Sprinzel, John 10, 28, 35, 38, 40, 42, 85, 131
Steering Wheel Club 170
Stokes, Lord 110, 114
Surtees, John 147
Sutherland, Richard 55, 162, 175

Thacker, James 139, 166, 188
Thorne, Lynden 55, 67–70, 99, 109
Thornley, John 71, 72, 82, 102, 106, 108, 115, 128
Tuckett, Willy 23, 24
Turner, Stuart 12, 102

Venner-Pack, Reg 63
Vickers, Peter 146

Ward, Richard 90, 129–130
Ward, Russ 98–99
Warwick Cinema (former) 18
Watkins, Steve 92, 155, 179, 182, 205
Watson, John 4, 54
Weekes, Geoff 49, 146, 183
Welch, Denis 23
Weslake, Harry 84, 114
West, Vivien 142–144, 179
Wheeler, Jack 46
Whitmore, Sir John 19
Widdows, Robin 52
Williams, Barry 100
Williams, Frank 72
Williams, Geoff 89, 175
Williams, Tony 89, 137–138, 142, 172
Wilmshurst, John 145–146
Wilson-Spratt, Douglas 39–46
Wisdom, Tommy 29, 30
Wood, Barry 63, 122, 136
Woode, Alan 57–60, 87, 94–96
Woodgate, Dave 194, 196, 201, 203